This book is dedicated to the individuals and couples
who have had the trust and courage to open their most intimate lives
to us as they sought to claim lifelong exceptional sex.
We have been honored, inspired, and delighted by you.

Lana Holstein
David Taylor

Your Long *Erotic* Weekend

Four Days of Passion for a Lifetime of Magnificent Sex

LANA HOLSTEIN, M.D.
AND DAVID TAYLOR, M.D.

A PLUME BOOK

PLUME
Published by the Penguin Group
Penguin Group (USA) Inc., 375 Hudson Street, New York, New York 10014, USA
Penguin Group (Canada), 10 Alcorn Avenue, Toronto, Ontario M4V 3B2, Canada (a division of Pearson Penguin Canada Inc.)
Penguin Books Ltd., 80 Strand, London WC2R 0RL, England
Penguin Ireland, 25 St. Stephen's Green, Dublin 2, Ireland (a division of Penguin Books Ltd.)
Penguin Group (Australia), 250 Camberwell Road, Camberwell, Victoria 3124, Australia (a division of Pearson Australia Group Pty. Ltd.)
Penguin Books India Pvt. Ltd., 11 Community Centre, Panchsheel Park, New Delhi – 110 017, India
Penguin Group (NZ), Cnr Airborne and Rosedale Roads, Albany, Auckland 1310, New Zealand (a division of Pearson New Zealand Ltd.)
Penguin Books (South Africa) (Pty.) Ltd., 24 Sturdee Avenue, Rosebank, Johannesburg 2196, South Africa

Penguin Books Ltd., Registered Offices: 80 Strand, London WC2R 0RL, England

Published by Plume, a member of Penguin Group (USA) Inc. This is an authorized reprint of a hardcover edition published by Fair Winds Press. For information address Fair Winds Press, 33 Commercial Street, Gloucester, Massachusetts 01930.

First Plume Printing, January 2005
10 9 8 7 6 5 4 3 2 1

Ⓟ REGISTERED TRADEMARK—MARCA REGISTRADA

CIP data is available.
ISBN 1-59233-061-4 (hc.)
ISBN 0-452-28626-3 (pbk.)

Printed in the United States of America

BOOKS ARE AVAILABLE AT QUANTITY DISCOUNTS WHEN USED TO PROMOTE PRODUCTS OR SERVICES. FOR INFORMATION PLEASE WRITE TO PREMIUM MARKETING DIVISION, PENGUIN GROUP (USA) INC., 375 HUDSON STREET, NEW YORK, NEW YORK 10014.

Your Long

Erotic

Weekend

Contents

Introduction

*Gourmet sex, golden sex, transporting, life-changing sex
is a real possibility for every loving, committed couple—
and you and your partner can learn how to get from
okay to ecstatic in just one long weekend!*

Is your sex life the way you want it? The answer for most people is, "No, not really." The longing for sex to be better, to be all it once was, to be all it could be, is there inside most of us. No matter how much we love and cherish our partners, we daydream about more fulfilling sex.

And why shouldn't we want better a better sexual connection? Sex is one of the supreme pleasures of life: There's nothing else like it. Great sex is thrilling and comforting and sustaining all at once. It's a way to express and strengthen love, and at the same time it connects us to our senses and creates an incomparable feeling of well being. (Orgasm has even been shown to strengthen the immune system!) Sex is fun—and a path to the furthest reaches of the spirit. Great sex, in short, makes people happy.

You *deserve* better sex, and this book—distilled from years of medical practice, lovemaking, and presenting sex workshops for couples—shows you exactly how to get it.

As physicians, we view a healthy sex life as an important element of our patients' health and well-being. We can testify that there's enormous, silent dissatisfaction out there. We ask all our patients about their sex lives as a matter of course, and we're here to tell you that most folks are not getting what they want. All this frustration and resignation and despair is a crying shame, and entirely unnecessary. Gourmet sex, golden sex, transporting, life-changing sex is a real possibility for every loving, committed couple—and you and your partner can learn how to get from okay to ecstatic in just one long weekend!

Throughout our more than twenty-five years of clinical practice—the last ten years focused on lecturing, counseling, and presenting sex-enhancement workshops at a world-class health resort—we've developed a weekend program that has helped hundreds of couples make ecstatic, blow-your-socks-off sex something they can dependably achieve.

1

With this book, we'll give you the same tools to discover what makes you and your partner tick, along with straightforward information and doable exercises that will help you tap into the great resources that you as a couple have accrued through years of intimacy. Most important, you'll finish your long erotic weekend with a liberating and joyful new way of thinking about sexuality.

We know that good sex makes for strong and happy relationships. Moreover, the natural, God-given pleasures of lovemaking are your birthright. So why wouldn't you want it to be as good as it can be? Why wouldn't you want to get back the pizzazz of your first months together, and recreate the very best times since? Why wouldn't you want to go even higher?

You probably remember what your early days were like, but those passionate encounters have given way to mostly mundane, mediocre sex. Even partners in the most loving and passionate relationships often feel too busy or too tired for sex as the years go by, a development that is often the beginning of the end for a happy relationship. Since both partners rarely lose their desire at exactly the same time, their once-vital connection becomes snarled in quarrels about sexual frequency, and things head downhill from there. Other couples drift quietly into predictable, boring routines that become even less satisfying as the sexual consequences of aging begin to show. But these are the minor problems, the easy ones.

Other relationships are undermined by deep-lying problems, which require more work to fix. Many couples' connections are flattened or broken by affairs, or undermined by memories of bitter divorces and sexual traumas, or simply wither under the toxic influence of negative teachings and attitudes about sex. Deeply embedded sorrow, trauma, and anger can block the flow of sexual energy almost completely. Our program identifies and addresses *whatever* short-circuits the flow of sexual energy between two individuals—no matter what the origin of the dysfunction may be.

Our program is also wonderful for sexually happy couples who'd like to reach a higher level. Few Westerners have any acquaintance with the easy, highly effective soul-sex practices developed long ago in the Orient. What most of us think we do know about Tantra—sex as an ecstatic spiritual experience—is wrong: This body of knowledge has often been cheapened or badly presented in English. Tantra is so much more than scented oils and feathers! We introduce you to the real thing.

If you feel that you inhabit a sexual wasteland, that you'll never find that oasis of sexual energy shimmering in the distance of your imagination, you are not alone. You're not at all unusual, either, if you feel sexually at sea, trapped in the doldrums, awaiting a fresh breeze to send you back to the steady current of a vital sexual relationship. Many, many people are stuck in the same place. But not one of you is doomed to stay there.

We believe that you deserve that oasis, that fresh breeze, and that you can find it. We can teach you how to find your way out of sexual disappointment in a surprisingly short period of time. We aren't offering a collection of the sort of tips you see in magazines. Rather, this book contains a comprehensive, flexible, concrete program for recharging your most important relationship by empowering you and your partner to heal each other, and yourselves. In our exclusive weekend workshops, we teach couples to recognize their physical, emotional, and spiritual barriers to sexual happiness. We introduce them, step by step, to invaluable skills, and through a series of carefully planned exercises, remind them of just how splendid sensual contact can be. We don't *tell* our program participants to communicate freely, or to cherish one another, or to just get out there and loosen up. Instead, we *teach* them how to be closer, and why they want to make the effort. And it's all right here in this book—at a fraction of the cost you'd pay at a resort!

Our program works. For nearly a decade, we have led many, many couples on this delightful voyage of discovery of their sexual potential, and it's an experience that has left them energized, reconnected to one another, and equipped to continue on together toward their sexual Shangri-La. We have typically presented our program as a four-day residential (and therefore expensive) workshop for small groups of couples in a health-resort setting. Hundreds of couples with every possible history, relationship pattern, and set of sexual issues have thoroughly tested and evaluated our program. At this point, positive results are quite predictable. We are confident in promising participants better sex, because we understand what prevents people from having it, and we know how to demolish the blockages. The information and concepts we present—reinforced by specific assignments and exercises—do change lives.

We thoroughly love giving these workshops because each renewed relationship feels like a miracle. Even though we've witnessed many, many transformations, there's still nothing that moves us more than watching the resurgence of sexual vitality between lovers. And we've increasingly felt that it's sad that so few couples can have this experience. This book evolved from our desire to make our program available to everyone who wants to have that energy in his or her life.

This is not, as we've said before, a compilation of clever sex tips, unusual sexual positions, kinky ideas, quick tricks, or vague exhortations. Rather, it is dedicated to the idea that sexual love is a *skill*, something you can learn, practice, and excel at; an activity you can always be better at—which means that there is no end to the rewards to be reaped from its pursuit.

Imagine how great it will be to be able to say to your partner, time after time, "Now *that* was the best ever!"

ABOUT US

You might ask what qualifies us to give you advice and instruction about this most private part of your life. The media and especially the Web swarm with come-ons making unbelievable promises of extreme sexual gratification. Unfortunately, trying to enlarge your breasts or your penis won't help. Effective, for-real sex therapy involves rooting out attitudes that sabotage sex, practicing not only touching but also talking, and realizing how easy it is to fix anything that's physically wrong. What we offer is what works.

We're physicians with special training and much experience in solving sexual problems. Our education and training—David at Harvard, Lana at Stanford, and then both at Yale Medical School—gave us a solid understanding of sexual function. Our cutting-edge freshman course in human sexuality at Yale inspired Lana to continue into the clinical arena and learn couples sexual therapy with our professor. She has continued to include sexual counseling of individuals and couples in her medical practice for well over 25 years. As partners in a general family practice that encompassed a great deal of obstetrics and gynecology, we both had extensive experience in diagnosing and dealing with the intimate issues of a large, diverse group of patients.

In response to her patients' needs, Lana began to develop sexual-enhancement workshops for women, and before long, we were looking for more powerful tools for change in all the people we counseled. We both became certified in clinical guided imagery, now widely recognized as an extremely effective technique for accessing the mind-body connection. (You'll find a number of guided imagery exercises in the book.) Lana co-founded an Institute for Midlife Enhancement and brought her expertise in sexuality to its programs. This, in turn, led to her position as Director of Women's Health at Canyon Ranch Resort in Tucson, Arizona, where she found ample opportunity to develop a wide range of offerings in sexuality from weekly lectures and workshops to individual and couples' counseling. In 1997, she and David began to present the four-day *Sex: Body and Soul* workshops that are the basis for this book. She now devotes her entire career to sexuality, and, along with David, is currently presenting numerous sexuality programs at Miraval Life in Balance Resort, also in Tucson.

Meanwhile, David has pursued an interest in body awareness and skill in movement through a four-year course of study in the Feldenkrais Method®. This training has also proved useful in workshops—we include a number of Feldenkrais lessons later in this book. His practice in Physical Medicine and Rehabilitation emphasized the reclamation of lost bodily skills and pleasures.

Although we are proud of our clinical training and skills, perhaps an even more important qualification for this work is our own development as a couple. We met and married in medical school, and went on to train in family medicine and practiced together. We've always been literally and emotionally very close, and we considered sex to be one of the many strengths of our relationship. While our lovemaking had fallen into a fairly predictable pattern by our tenth anniversary, it never would have occurred to us to seek to improve on it. As clinicians, we knew that we were free of "sexual dysfunction," but had no clue about the higher levels of sexual function that were possible—we were making precisely the same mistake many people make when they consider themselves healthy just because they have no diagnosed disease.

It took a trip to Hawaii and participation in a Tantric sexuality workshop to open our eyes. We will always be grateful to the friends who recommended this experience to us, which started us on the path to Magnificent Sex. Imagine our surprise in discovering an entirely new realm of profound sexual connection previously unknown to us both as lovers and as physicians!

Each of us experienced this tremendous renewal differently. For David, the transformation was about the energy of love, and the way it unites a couple sexually through both body and spirit. For Lana, it was a reconnection with the deep sexual Feminine, which she had lost touch with during long years of professional training and hard work. For both of us, Tantra—which now informs all of our teachings about sex—decisively restructured our understanding of sexuality. We came away from that memorable week on Maui with a new-found sense of sexual maturity.

We soon realized that we were in a unique position to guide others to this realm we had found for ourselves. We continued our Tantric studies over the ensuing years, and we continue to include its fundamental precepts, especially those concerning sexual energy, in our workshops. We also explored aspects of transpersonal psychology and masculine/feminine polarity that deepened our understanding of Tantra. All of this will be coming your way.

One final credential: As a married couple, we practice what we preach. Our sexual connection has been a healing force in our lives and has been vital as we have sought to maintain a strong and loving relationship despite demanding careers, two teenagers, and life-threatening illness. As we approach our thirtieth wedding anniversary, we are more convinced than ever that Magnificent Sex is the key to a deeply satisfying and enduring life of love.

It has been gratifying to receive recognition for our expertise in presenting this unique approach to sexuality. For years, Lana has been a sought-after speaker and talk-show guest. Her ability to discuss the "forbidden" topic of sex openly, comfortably, and with humor has inspired many large audiences, and led to a public television special, *Magnificent Lovemaking*, aired in 2001 in over two-thirds of the nation's urban markets. Her first book, *How to Have Magnificent Sex: The 7 Dimensions of a Vital Sexual Connection*, was published by Harmony Books in 2001. Our workshops have been featured in *Ladies Home Journal, Spa, Fortune,*

Travel and Leisure, and *USA Today,* and on CBS's *Early Show,* as well as in the British magazines *Cosmopolitan* and *Red.* (The journalists who wrote about the workshops attended them, with their spouses. They—and their partners—were typically a bit distant and doubtful when they arrived, but finished four days later as enthusiastic, committed participants. In fact, one writer even picked our program as his "year's best experience" in December of 2002.)

We continue to feel honored and privileged to have such a deep and positive impact on the lives of others. Our participants' expressions of gratitude never fail to touch us, and ensure our continued dedication to this work.

—Lana and David

PLANNING YOUR LONG EROTIC WEEKEND

What This Book Can Do For You

You and your partner have the opportunity to take advantage of this program, to make sex a wellspring of your relationship—seize it! You can create a core of sexual vitality that sustains your connection. When you become expert lovers—sexual artists, really—sex will energize you, your partnership, and your enjoyment of life.

Your Long Erotic Weekend has four principal parts—one part for each day. We devote Day One to *Tuning Into Your Sexual Energy*. First, we will methodically challenge your old beliefs about sex, and present you with a fresh perspective on the relation of love to sex. We will introduce important ideas about sexual energy from non-Western traditions, and explore the idea of masculine and feminine polarity in depth. This polarity is the key to building sexual charge. Perhaps even more useful will be the discussion of the Seven Dimensions, our original formulation of the energy structure of sexual relationships. We will ask you to evaluate yourselves for strength in each dimension, and help you identify specific actions that will help strengthen and enliven *your* sexual partnership. In other words, you'll learn how to tune into your lover's sexual energy on all channels as well as how to tap into all of your own. The experiential exercises we give you throughout the day will help you ground all of this in your body.

Day Two will be devoted to *Pleasuring Her*, followed by Day Three, *Pleasuring Him*. These two days are the heart of the program, where you experience the tremendous, transforming power of giving and receiving sexual pleasure. We will, of course provide you with a useful, up-to-date understanding of the essentials of human sexuality. You need to know about anatomical, physiological, and medical factors that affect sexuality, and learn some specific erotic techniques. Then, armed with this information, you'll plunge into exciting and challenging structured assignments to help you explore the new ideas from Day One. Old habits are persistent, and at first "doing your homework" may feel awkward, but it's only by doing that we develop new and useful skills. (And once you get over your initial shyness, you and your partner will enjoy the assignments. We promise.)

Day Four is the culmination of *Your Long Erotic Weekend: Putting It All Together—and Making It Last*. We will show you how to create a practical plan of action to extend the delightful learning and discovery of the previous three days into the rest of your life together. We believe that couples can, and should, make their sexual relationship an ongoing mutual project. By the time your weekend is over, you will have created a new "division" of your mutual "company." Its mission will be to produce an ongoing stream of positive sexual energy that will flow to your "bottom line!" Then in your final pleasuring assignment, you will bring everything you have learned in the first three days together into a full, joyous multidimensional experience. You will celebrate the end of your weekend, and the beginning of a lifetime of the sexual ecstasy you've always dreamed about.

Along the way, there will undoubtedly be obstacles. Sex is powerful stuff, and changing anything about it has a way of bringing us up against our deepest, most difficult issues. At the same time, though, sex offers us a powerful way of working with and through these issues, and of becoming happier and freer people in the process. We have come to actually welcome difficulties and crises in our workshops, because they show exactly where change needs to take place. Do not despair if you encounter resistance in either of you along the way.

YOUR FELLOW ADVENTURERS

The couples who go through our program learn a great deal from one another, and hearing one another's stories and sharing feelings as the weekend unfolds, is important. Since you won't get the benefit of going through the program with other couples, we decided to give you your own group of four fictional couples to help supply this part of the experience. As individuals and as couples, our characters embody extremely common patterns of belief and experience. You'll follow their progress through the program, and see how they react to the information, the exercises, and the assignments. You'll also share their joys and their frustrations in the process. You'll get to see a few of the ways couples can get stuck, and the kind of advice we give them to help them get unstuck. Let's meet them now, and see where they're starting from.

⌒

"You know, you look good without the stroller," Kate said to her old friend Nicole as they browsed the bookstore aisle. It was the last stop on a rare outing without Nicole's three little ones.

"You're telling me," Nicole answered. "Some days I think that if I don't get out of the house and away from the runny noses and Cheerios, I'll just lose it. Today has been great. Thanks."

Kate had basically forced Nicole's husband, Charlie, to take the kids for the afternoon so that she and Nicole could have lunch and go to the mall. Kate was crazy about Nicole's kids—she was their godmother, after all—but she worried about her friend. Nicole had been jumpy and irritable since she'd quit her job to stay at home after the second baby was born.

They stopped in the coffee shop, ordered their lattes, and sat at a table. Nicole turned to Kate and asked, "So how are you and Steve getting along? You've been living together almost six months, haven't you?"

"Yes, and it's beginning to feel like we're an old married couple. Oops, I didn't mean... well, it's just that... I don't know, it used to be exciting— sex, I mean."

Nicole was quiet for a moment, and then responded, "Yeah, well, that's pretty much what happens, isn't it?"

Kate said, "What do you mean? I thought you and Charlie had a great sex life! I'd hate to think that my marriage role models were having trouble in bed."

"It's just that Charlie wants it all the time, and I'm so tired. Sex is the only thing on his mind when he comes home, and by the end of the day I feel like if one more person touches me, I'll scream."

Kate looked up. "I always thought you guys were so hot. Back when we were in the house..." (they'd met in their sorority) "...and you guys were dating, you were *the* couple. Everyone wanted to be you. I mean, Charlie's such a cute, fun guy."

"I don't want fun anymore," Nicole said sourly. "I want sleep."

"Well, I guess I'm more like Charlie. I can't seem to get Steve interested. I hint, I touch him, I plan romantic evenings, I buy sexy lingerie, all that stuff you read in *Cosmo*... All he does is work, work, work. That law office is just sucking all the energy out of him. It makes me wonder about the long haul if we get married. I love him so much, but I just can't do without sex." Kate looked down as she stirred her coffee.

Nicole sensed her friend's sadness, but couldn't relate to it. "I can't even remember what it was like before. I know there was a time when I enjoyed sex with Charlie, but now it's just another chore. Things change with kids, business, careers...I guess it would be nice to have good sex, but I don't have a clue how to get it back."

☞

It was Sunday morning, and Martin and Linda had just finished having their standard Sunday Morning Sex, which was, as usual, quick, efficient, and more or less satisfactory. Then they'd relocated to the kitchen, where he sat at the table, dreamily watching her make coffee. He'd been enjoying Linda's graceful movements and the gentle swing of her long black hair across the back of her red robe.

"You know, I love the way you move," he said, almost without think-ing.

Then she surprised him by turning around suddenly, tears her eyes.

"Oh Martin!" she'd exclaimed, "It's gotten to be so *ordinary*. Remember how it used to be? Sex was our heaven, and now look at us: Once a week on Sunday morning while the kids are still asleep. You push my buttons, I push yours, and, ping!... time for waffles."

She sat down across from him. "What's happened to us? Where did we lose it?"

Martin understood exactly what she was saying, as he usually did. Instant, overwhelming attraction had brought them together, and the most incredible sex of both their lives—plus the sweet, easy compatibility they'd immediately discovered—had proved their instincts correct. The sheer deliciousness of their lovemaking had sustained them through the backwash of two recent divorces and their kids' bewilderment and resentments and squabbles. They'd made it work and were still deeply in love after all these years—and still tired, broke, and worried about the kids. Linda had become so anxious the year before that her doctor had started her on antidepressants.

And somehow, during the last few years, their glorious lovemaking had settled into a pleasant but completely predictable routine.

Martin took her hand. "I don't know, sweetie. I feel it too. I still love you, you know."

"Of course I know *that*. It's just kind of sad to think that this is what our sex life is going to be like from now on." The tears began to well again.

"Well, we're still us, aren't we?" Martin replied. "But you're right, we have gotten into a rut. How do we get out? Get divorced and find each other all over again?"

"Nah," she said, brightening. "Too much hassle. Let's just cash in the college fund, sell the house, fly to Tahiti and mess around until the money runs out."

Martin grinned back at her. One of the kids had come in looking for breakfast, and that had ended the conversation.

"Well, what did you think about what Jeannie and Len said about their trip to Tucson?" Paulette turned to Bob as she hung her coat in the front hall closet. He was making sure the door had locked.

"What do you mean?" he said, really sounding as if he had no idea. Paulette recognized his playing-dumb tone.

"You know what I mean! About that sex course they went to at that spa."

Bob continued to stonewall. "Oh, that. Well, it sounded like they had a pretty good time."

"A pretty good time?!" Paulette was rapidly losing her temper. "They said it totally changed their love life. You *were* in the room. And did you notice how they were with each other tonight?"

"Well, yeah, they did seem a lot more lovey-dovey than usual, now that you mention it."

"We could use 'a lot more lovey-dovey' around here, if you ask me." She paused. "Being around them tonight made me realize how much I miss our being together."

Bob studied his shoes.

"We could go to a program like that, Bob."

He looked up, startled. "I'm not going somewhere to sit around telling strangers about the trouble I'm having!"

This was the first word he'd said about his difficulties. Paulette, who for months had been thinking things like, "Does he think I didn't *notice* it didn't get hard last night?" felt a rush of sympathy.

"Besides, it's not like everything's so perfect with me, what with the hot flashes and worrying about whether or not to take estrogen."

"So we should both go sit around in a circle and talk about it?" Bob looked just as panicked as before. "No way, Paulette. Not going to happen. I don't care how wound up about it Jeannie and Len are. I won't do it." Bob's jaw was set as he turned away from her.

"You do love me, don't you, Bob?"

"Paulette, goddamn it, don't start in. You know I do. It's been thirty years and if you aren't sure by now...."

"Alright—that wasn't fair. Of course I know. And you know I love you. But you've been sort of quiet and sad for a while now—you know you have. You don't make any jokes, and of course that's what I fell in love with you for." Now she was trying to get him to smile. "If we could get some of that old spark back, wouldn't you want that?"

Here's some background information on our couples. As you get to know them, their blocks to ecstatic sex will reassure you that you are in no way alone, while their solutions will provide examples of the rewards of creative perseverance using the techniques we teach. We hope you find them as interesting and likable as we do.

Steve and Kate—Both 32

Kate has been seeing Steve for two years. They moved in together six months ago, and they're very close to making a lifelong commitment. But before they do, they want to make sure they can keep the fires burning long-term. They're a work-oriented pair. Kate is funny and forceful; Steve is more reserved and often seems a bit distracted. They're both highly verbal and approach every problem with exhaustive discussion—or argument. They tend to overanalyze things and beat subjects to death verbally, in part because both have a strong need to be right. She is passionate about her job as an assistant principal of a middle school; Steve works long hours trying to move up the ladder in his law firm. They currently rent but are saving for a house, and are hoping to marry and start a family in two to three years. Kate is sexually passionate, and an adventurer in the bedroom. So is Steve, or at least he used to be; now he is so consumed by his work that he brings work home many nights. He often works so late that Kate is asleep before he comes to bed.

She wants this weekend.

Charlie and Nicole—34 and 36

Nicole is an at-home mom now. She was a banker but quit after their second child was born (they now have three). Charlie is going great guns running the dry-cleaning business he took over from his dad—he's opening new locations in several surrounding communities. Charlie *never* gets enough sex, but Nicole, who used to find his appetite thrilling, has lost interest. She doesn't want one more person to touch her after spending all day with the kids—now two, five, and seven—and usually tries to avoid him. He has begun watching Internet porn, which infuriates and depresses her.

He wants this weekend.

Martin and Linda—Both 47

They have been married—both for the second time—for twelve years. Their blended family includes his 17-year-old daughter, her 15-year-old son, and their 11-year-old daughter. Linda works for the Health Department on programs for the elderly; Martin is an engineer for IBM. They worry about having money for college and they carry enough credit-card debt to make them nervous. Linda's son is acting out and recently got arrested for a curfew violation. Sex was what attracted them in the first place: Both love sex, but it was awful for both of them with their first spouses. As soon as they met they clicked, and tumbled into bed fast. They're still very much in love, but are both physically and emotionally exhausted.

They both know they need this weekend.

Bob and Paulette—53 and 58

Paulette volunteers several days a week at the hospital now that the kids are on their own. She delights in their first granddaughter and looks forward to the next grandchild, due in four months. The couple's only real concerns at this point are health-related. She's going through menopause and is in a quandary about whether to take hormones; Bob is on blood pressure meds and intends to retire soon from his position as an onsite manager of a large construction company. Lately, he has had some intermittent trouble getting a good erection, especially when he is tired. Paulette is having vaginal dryness and some difficulty being orgasmic.

They heard about this program from friends and hope it will help them reignite the sexual fire they enjoyed for years.

COMMITTING TO THE WEEKEND: MAKING THE RESERVATION

Participants in our resort workshops must sign-up ahead of time, which involves filling out some forms and making a deposit. In this way they make a definite commitment to the program; they also commit by clearing their schedules, buying tickets, making arrangements for things to be taken care while they're gone, packing, and so on. They've invested in the weekend before they ever show up for the first session, and having made that investment, they're intent on getting a return on it once we begin.

We believe strongly that if you, too, commit to your weekend, you'll get much, much more out of it than if you just read and casually try a little something here and there. You, too, need to "make a reservation." (The form is below.) We encourage you and your partner to fill it out completely, because writing down your plan will help you commit. The reservation also contains a contract: Each of you promises to do something substantial for the other if you fail to complete the program. This is your deposit—what you'll forfeit if you stop part way. Finally, the form contains a brief questionnaire about both of your hopes and fears for the weekend. Getting these issues out in the open is the true beginning of your journey.

The Couples Make Reservations

Now that you know a bit about your fellow "weekenders" and about making the reservation, let's find out how each of our pairs goes about it.

Steve and Kate

As usual, Kate and Steve negotiate at length. At first, Steve says "no" to the whole idea: "Hel-lo? Nothing's wrong! Besides, I don't have time to read the damn sports section, much less blow four days getting it on. And it'll get so boring. Sex, sex, sex."

Kate fusses back for a bit, then stops squabbling and announces that if he doesn't want to spend time with her, maybe she'll just drive over to a friend's beach house and spend a few days on her own. Steve realizes he needs to go along when a mental picture from last year's Christmas party flashes through his mind. Kate was standing talking to an old boyfriend, sipping punch and giving off a glow he remembered but hadn't seen in ages. Later, when he'd confronted her, she'd indignantly denied having any continued interest in the guy, but that snapshot still bothered him. He says "yes" to the weekend.

He and Kate are able to agree on Christmas break as the time, and their condo as the setting—neither wants to blow any savings on a getaway. Kate promises to give up her one regular splurge, a weekly manicure appointment, if she doesn't complete the course; Steve agrees to go shopping for a whole day with Kate and to do it cheerfully without complaint.

Charlie and Nicole

Charlie's ready to start tomorrow—or maybe tonight! His problem, of course, is how to introduce the subject to Nicole. He decides that doing something for her is his best bet. He picks a weekend when they don't have anything going and then gets his parents to agree to take the kids for four days. A few nights later, he takes her out to an upscale restaurant and, after dessert, hands her the gift-wrapped book. She's surprised and pleased by the gesture, but then sees what it is.

"Damn Kate, anyway," is her response. She recognizes *Your Long Erotic Weekend*, the book Kate bought that day they had coffee together; she's sure she had something to do with Charlie getting it.

It's Charlie's big moment. "Sweetheart," he says quietly, taking her hand. "I love you so much. I can't be happy if you aren't, and I can't really enjoy anything if we aren't good. You've been avoiding me, and I don't know what to do different. Maybe this weekend would help."

Nicole is touched by how hard he's trying, and is swamped with guilt.

"Besides," he continues, "I've already got the babysitting all lined up."

"Well, at least let me take a look at it first," she says with a sigh.

Two days later, they've made reservations at a resort they stayed at while she was pregnant with their first. It's not very expensive, but pretty and comfortable—and they had a *very* good time there before. Nicole agrees to watch one soft-porn video with him if she fails to complete the program, but Charlie insists that she throw in a foot-massage. She's absolutely resolved that she won't quit and have to pony up. Charlie's deposit is to give up great tickets to a ballgame, and to watch the kids that afternoon, instead. He is certain that he won't be the one who gives up.

Martin and Linda

Martin studies the kids' summer camp/activity schedules and finds a window when all three will be away. Enjoying himself already, he plans a South-Seas-at-home vacation. He presents the idea to Linda with a piña colada (complete with paper umbrella) while he sings "Bali Hai" and swivels his hips. He proposes that they unplug all electronic devices for those four days and let the message machine pick up all their calls. Linda is thoroughly charmed and begins to get into the planning. She agrees to a day-long marathon at the movies with Martin if she bails out in the middle of the program. Martin agrees to send $200 to Linda's favorite charity, Big Sisters, if he doesn't complete it.

Bob and Paulette

Bob surprises Paulette by going to the doctor, overcoming his shyness, and actually getting a prescription for Viagra. He's a little anxious about taking it: excited but apprehensive. They decide to do the weekend and try the med as part of it. Their thirtieth wedding anniversary is coming up, which seems like the perfect date. Bob had already arranged to take a few vacation days around their anniversary, so the time is no problem. Paulette does some investigating and then books airline seats and a suite at a famous resort. They're all set. Bob agrees to take another long weekend from work and spend it doing what Paulette wants if he doesn't finish the program. For her deposit, Paulette takes a deep breath and agrees to help him put in the koi pond he's been wanting for their back yard if she quits.

Here's the "reservation form" for you and your partner to fill out to set up your long weekend. You'll need four days, plus whatever you might need for travel if you decide to go away from home. In considering that decision, remember that home is free and you'll have all your stuff there; but potential distractions abound and could seriously undermine your focus on the program.

Date: _____

Place: _____

Deposits: _____

   His: _____

   Hers:_____

Things to clear away: _____

   Work: _____

   Family responsibilities: _____

   Other commitments: _____

Distractions (email, phone messages, visitors): _____

Your greatest intention or expectation for the weekend: _____

Your partner's greatest intention or expectation for the weekend: _____

Your greatest apprehension for this weekend:_____

Your partner's greatest apprehension for this weekend:_____

Why do we ask you on your reservation form to list your greatest intention and apprehension for the weekend? Because it is crucial that you clarify at the outset what you want to get out of this, and the fears that might limit your full engagement in the program. It is just as important to be aware of the intentions and apprehensions of your mate. Even after you have both made your reservation and cleared the time for a great sexual weekend, unseen hesitations and resistances can lurk like booby-traps between you and the realization of your ambitious plans. Bringing your hopes and worries out into the open right up front lessens the potential for self-sabotage.

THE COUPLES' HOPES AND FEARS

Kate writes on their form that her intention is to reawaken Steve's sexual desire and bring back the life of passion they had at the beginning. She is apprehensive about Steve's rejection of her sexual energy. Steve's highest intention is to regain the intensity of love that used to exist between them. His greatest fear is that he will not be able to match Kate sexually and still have enough energy and focus for his demanding career.

Nicole's main intention is to learn how to sexually satisfy this man she loves so much. Her fear is that he is insatiable and that nothing she does will be enough for him in this department. Charlie's intention is to get more sex on a consistent basis. His greatest fear is that nothing will change.

Martin's hope is to recover the terrific sexual energy that he used to share with Linda. His worry is that although they will have a good weekend, it will not carry through to their hectic everyday life. Linda wants to feel awed by sex again, to have it touch both their souls. Her apprehension is that sex will remain mundane.

Paulette is determined not to lose connection with sex at this point in her life. She is worried that Bob won't finish the weekend. Bob wants to please Paulette and to be a good lover. He fears that this program may be too "touchy-feely" for him.

It's very important that you be able to spend four FULL days together without interruption. You don't have to spend thousands of dollars on a resort getaway, but you do need time alone. If you can afford to leave home, you don't have to go far. Rent a cabin in the woods; book a seaside cottage; or simply check yourselves into a hotel downtown or a local bed and breakfast. If you must stay home, leave the kids at Grandma's, forget about yard work, laundry, and television, and concentrate on one room—your master bedroom and bath.

Whether you make your love nest at home or elsewhere, there are certain preparations that must be made. Each day of the workshop comes with specific instructions, which you should review ahead of time, along with the following checklist of sensual supplies you'll need for the weekend. You definitely don't want to be caught without the essentials!

SENSUAL SUPPLIES

Whether you're staying at a five-star hotel, a cabin in the woods, or your own bedroom at home, you'll need to set up a pleasing, sacred-feeling place to make love. Don't scrimp here: Indulge yourselves.

Basic Love Gear

- Fresh linens
- Plenty of large, soft towels
- Pillows
- Massage oils and personal lubricants
- Scented candles, all shapes and sizes (and matches!)
- Flowers
- CD player and mood music (see below)
- Whatever makes you feel sexy and in tune as a couple—pink light bulbs, beaded curtains, bear skin rugs, your wedding album, etc.

Food for Love

- Picnic basket filled with aphrodisiac finger foods: oysters, olives, brie and French bread, grapes, chocolate, anything you can feed each other with your fingers
- Bottled water
- Wine

Music for Love

Music to your own taste of course, but here are some suggestions:

- Enya
- Prince
- Marvin Gaye
- Diana Krall
- Sade
- Andrea Bocelli
- Norah Jones
- Gabrielle Roth

Other Things You'll Need:

- Pen and paper
- Rumi, Neruda, or other sexy poetry
- This book
- The companion CD to this book (see ordering info on page 229)

You'll be encountering this symbol later in the book, next to the title of each exercise with a corresponding track on the CD, where we've recorded the instructions to the exercise to make it easier to do, without having constantly to refer back to the text and lose the flow of the exercise.

So you've made your plans, cleared away your schedules, made a material commitment to your partner, and articulated your hopes and fears. You've reviewed the instructions for each day and collected everything you'll need for your long erotic weekend. It's time to get down to business. Get ready to learn about a whole new way of thinking about the energy of love and sex, and how you can get it to flow more smoothly and abundantly in your life.

Day One

Tuning into Your Sexual Energy

DAY ONE

Suggested Schedule

MORNING:

- Read and discuss *Love, Sex, and Energy* .
- Honor each other with *Namaste*.
- Tap into your sexual energy with the *Breathing Exercise*.
- Tune into each other with the *Soulgazing Exercise*.
- Breathe as one as you master the *Reciprocal Breath*.

NOON:

- Enjoy a leisurely lunch in.
- Consider indulging in a little nap together.

AFTERNOON:

- Take the *Seven Dimensions of Sex Inventory*.
- Share the results of the survey with each other.
- Read about the *Seven Dimensions of Sex*
- Explore the ways in which you might enhance your scores.

EVENING:

- Turn on the mood music, light the candles, pour the wine.
- Picnic by candlelight on your bed.
- Learn to kiss all over again with the *Kissing Lesson*.
- Open your hearts to each other with the *Open Heart Exercise*.

MORNING

LOVE, SEX, AND ENERGY

Sex takes energy, right? That seems obvious, especially when married people with kids and exhausting jobs and a million errands finally meet up at the end of the day. What's less obvious is that sex can *tap into* and *channel* vast energies that may be otherwise inaccessible as we sprint through our daily lives. As we have come to understand it—largely through our study of the Indian discipline of Tantra—sex is not an act of release, but rather an ecstatic ritual of creation, renewal, and perhaps even worship. To follow our program for renewing your sexual connection, you'll need to start cultivating a new understanding of how love, sex, and energy intertwine. We'll begin by defining how we'll be using all three of these terms, starting with energy.

ENERGY 101

We're not talking about the energy you learned about in physics class, or about what Exxon Mobil produces, but about the life force, an ancient and widespread oriental concept of energy. If you've taken many yoga classes you've heard the Sanskrit term for it, *prana*. In the Far Eastern tradition the same thing is called *chi*, as in Chi Gung, Tai Chi, etc. Balancing chi as it circulates through the body's energy channels, or meridians, is what acupuncture is all about. Chi (or prana) flows through the world, and it flows through us when we breathe, move, or love.

The most important thing to remember is that this energy we're talking about is experiential. It's not measurable by any instrument—or at least by any instrument so far invented—but it's there. It's *always* there, and learning how to work with it opens up new realms of sexual experience.

The great yogis not only perceived the flow of the life force, they mapped out the anatomy of "the energy body," how prana circulates and behaves inside human beings. The centerpiece of their work is the chakra system, which relates emotions and life functions to certain points, called energy centers, in the body (see illustration).

Each chakra—and there are seven, running from the base of the spine to the crown of the head—focuses attention on a different experience of energy in the body. Although we Westerners, unlike the yogis, may not have a fully developed, systematic understanding of these energy centers, nevertheless our everyday language is full of phrases that express our sense of the various energies. We have our

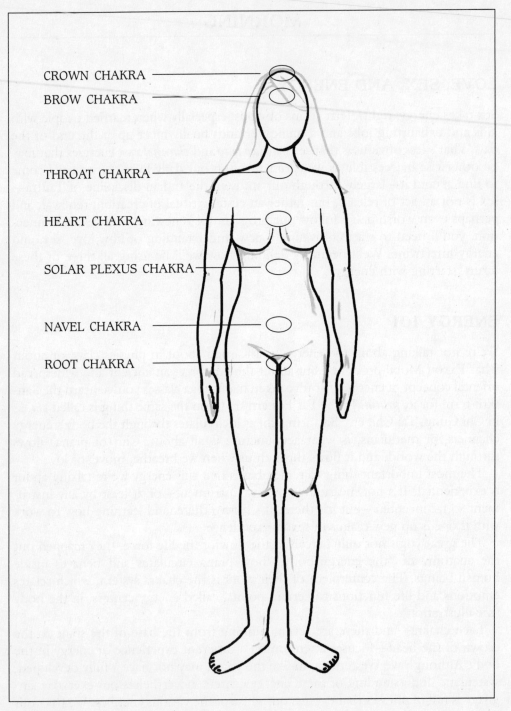

CROWN CHAKRA

BROW CHAKRA

THROAT CHAKRA

HEART CHAKRA

SOLAR PLEXUS CHAKRA

NAVEL CHAKRA

ROOT CHAKRA

The Chakras.

The Chakra System

In the traditional Indian system these perceptions are codified as the chakra system, which describes seven energy centers strung like pearls along the spine. The first or root chakra is situated at the base of the spine, and governs basic survival and physical functioning. It corresponds to the first or Biological dimension of sex. The second chakra is located in the lower part of the abdomen and has to do with the genitals and the Sensual dimension. The third chakra is located at the power center of the solar plexus and connects with lust and the Desire dimension; the fourth is the heart chakra, which is intelligible in any culture. The fifth, or throat chakra, governs communication and refined self-expression and it corresponds to the Intimacy dimension. The sixth chakra, also called the third eye, is situated in the skull at about brow-level. It's the seat of higher thought and correct perception and matches up to the Aesthetic dimension. The seventh, or crown chakra, is at the top of the head. It's where knowledge of the divine comes in, where the spiritual self resides. The crown chakra corresponds to the Ecstatic dimension of sex.

heads in the clouds, knots in our stomachs, broken hearts, hard heads, and lumps in our throats. We have gut-wrenching experiences, fires in the belly, know people who are pains in the rear, and pray for a light from above. On some level, we are aware of these energies and of their locations.

When we apply the chakra system of energy centers to sexuality, we begin to see that each of the seven domains of human experience is important to the full expression of sexual energy. As we move along, you will learn more about this, and even take a quiz to find out where you stand with the seven dimensions of sexuality. For now, just know that your body (and the body of your lover) has a very organized and sophisticated way of channeling the flow of life force.

LOVE AND ROMANCE

On to love. What is it?

Lots of people have taken a whack at that one. It's never having to say you're sorry, or it's a many-splendored thing, or it's all you need. And so on.

In fact there is one very simple definition we like—love is what happens when your heart is open. Maybe that sounds circular, but look again—it's an energetic

HeartMath

For many years, The Institute of HeartMath has investigated the human heart's generation of positive emotional experiences. Researchers there have focused on the sense of appreciation—that energetic quality of thankfulness—as having very definite effects on heart rhythm and on the powerful heart-brain interactions that affect physiology, cognition and emotion.

By analyzing heart rate variability, the beat-to-beat variation in heart rate that we all experience, they have found that emotions play a big role in the pattern of heart rhythm. Specifically, they have learned that anger, anxiety, and frustration disrupt the balance of the two branches of our autonomic nervous system (ANS)—the sympathetic and the parasympathetic. Love, appreciation, and compassion, on the other hand, enhance the order and coherence of these two divisions of the ANS.

The good news is that, potentially, we have a good bit of control over the balance between these two aspects of our nervous system. We can develop this control by learning to manage emotional responses (which recent research in neuroscience shows happen faster than thought, sometimes completely bypassing the mind's linear reasoning processes) by linking them to imagery that evokes good feelings.

The HeartMath folks have developed a technique called Freeze Frame that helps people alter their physiology by consciously shifting their attention during stressful situations. The technique involves learning to respond to stress by focusing on the area around the heart and summoning a feeling of appreciation. The idea is that when you have mastered this process, you will be able to call on it during stressful, disturbing times.

It is important to distinguish HeartMath training from more familiar relaxation exercises, which are designed simply to reduce arousal levels. These techniques increase parasympathetic activity—which is useful—but do not produce the much more effective system-wide resonance and synchronization of the nervous system and heart-brain dynamics. The use of the love and appreciation steps and the practice of these emotional states take the individual far beyond merely being calm or relaxed. Coherence has been shown to increase immune function, modulate hormones, lower blood pressure, produce better test scores in high school seniors and decrease anger in university students. It certainly has been fascinating for us to document that couples who Soul Gaze in our program enter into this wonderful state. For more information, visit www.heartmath.org.

definition. The heart is not some vague symbolic thing or a shape on a valentine; it's a center of a certain type of energy. When your heart is open, loving energy can flow through it and you can both give and receive this energy. We've all felt this embodied energy experience we call love. When love is strong, we feel it as a light, sweet sort of fullness behind our ribs.

Important conclusions follow from this energetic definition of love. Since love is an energy flow that you experience, you don't "have" it, and it doesn't have to be attached to just one other person, your "lover." When your heart opens towards your dog, or your mate, or your best friend, or your grandchild, or a work of art, or God, or nature, or towards everything that is, you experience love.

Love occupies an essential place in virtually every form of spiritual practice. It is the quintessential experience of energy. Teilhard de Chardin sums it up beautifully and powerfully, while underscoring the difficulty and enormity of the task: "Someday, after we have mastered the winds, the waves, the tides, and gravity, we shall harness for God the energies of love. Then for the second time in the history of the world, man will have discovered fire."

With such a powerful force occupying the very center of our bodies, why do we find love difficult, confusing—a challenge? Here's the point of confusion: we often tend to mix up love and romance, almost as if romance were the real thing and all other open-heartedness mundane. Actually, romance and love are distinct energetic species. Romance always involves a feeling of exclusiveness, a sense of rights and of obligations, a commitment to one particular person. Even if a romance is fleeting or mostly pretend, all these elements are there while it lasts. And since romantic passion seems to hold the answer to one of the essential problems of being human—aloneness—we put enormous effort into pursuing romance and idealizing our beloved. Everyone does it. We all yearn for the tremendous intoxication of infatuation.

The problem is that romance *never* lasts—that thrilling "falling in love" feeling *always* fades. And that's okay, because romance is not the same thing as love. If love is our home then romance is the doorway. You go through it to get in, but it's not a dwelling, not a space where you can live.

The really interesting and ironic thing about romance is that the person who initially seems to so exactly fit our pre-fab romantic daydream is inevitably the person who pushes all our buttons best—and whose buttons will also be uniquely accessible to us. The drug of romance helps enable us to hook up with someone whose strengths and weaknesses complement our own. We are seriously attracted to people who fit our deep psychic needs—needs about which we're likely to be completely and totally clueless at the beginning. There's nothing like a long relationship for helping us evolve as individuals. Some people go so far as to say that's what love relationships are really *for*.

So. Love feels good, does good, is good, and all we have to do is open our hearts to have it flood through us. Why, then, wouldn't we bask in this feeling every moment of our lives? Fear. And this fear is interesting. We shut love out because we're afraid of losing ourselves—one of the most profound terrors rattling around in our psyches. There is a part of our being that wants us to be separate and shies away from love's threat of fusion: The ego naturally resists anything that threatens to dissolve its edges. It must, because if it didn't, we'd never separate from our parents. Without resistance to love, we could never become ourselves. In addition to the basically resistant structure of our "I-part," we have all been through abandonments, betrayals, and disappointments. Those painful experiences just strengthen the ego's armor.

We need boundaries, of course, but we must also be able to drop the barriers if we want to be nourished by love. As we move through life, we become better judges of other people, of our safety with them, and we don't need our automatic defenses so much. But resistance to love tends to become a habit, and long after it's helpful, we continue to protect ourselves with the physical, mental, and emotional kinks we previously developed to block the flow of loving energy. We tense up to block the pain of remembered abandonment, a reaction that's as much physical as emotional. We restrict our breath, narrow our attention, and tense our muscles for fight or flight, and we do it so much that it becomes a knee-jerk (or should we say heart-jerk?) response.

Love, then, is an energy that is often initiated by romance but which has much deeper and more sustaining roots. It is the energy that bonds us to our lover. The full and free expression of the heart is the foundation of exquisite sex.

SEX: WHAT'S LOVE GOT TO DO WITH IT?

What is sex? A totally ridiculous question, right? You know, we know, everybody knows what *that* is.

Actually, from a scientific point of view, sex is anything that mixes DNA from different individuals, which is a pretty far cry from love. Most species don't need love to have sex and reproduce, and neither do we, really. We do, however, need one form of love—mother-love—for the survival of the species. Our young are helpless at birth and cannot manage on their own for many years, so a powerful attachment between mother and child is part of the package. Many other animals, most of them mammals, clearly experience mother-love; in particularly slow-growing *Homo sapiens*, love has expanded its range to the mating pair. Apparently, in the course of evolution, the energy of love has been co-opted by sex, yielding romance—the feeling of infatuation that leads to mating. The formation of a lasting emotional bond between a man and a woman confers an extra degree of success on their genes: The stronger the male's attachment to his mate, the more likely he is to zealously provide for and protect her and their offspring. In this way, evolution has inextricably intertwined love and sex in humans. Love in the form of romantic sexual attraction brings a couple together, and their continuing sexual attraction—a rare phenomenon in the endless range of reproductive strategies concocted by nature—has become a way for them to continue transmitting love. Looked at biologically as well as spiritually, sex is a medium of exchange, something like an arc of electrical current. Sex allows love to flow between two bodies in an intense, elemental form.

POLARITY

If sex is a conduit for energy, we need to ask where this energy comes from in the first place. This leads us to the concept of sexual polarity. The idea that the play of two opposite principles creates everything that exists is fundamental to the Eastern picture of reality. You've no doubt heard of yin and yang and seen the Chinese symbol that represents this idea. The basic idea is that masculine and feminine are universal opposites or poles. All sorts of paired qualities are associated with these poles: light/dark, dry/wet, hard/soft, plus more metaphysical pairings like heaven/earth, sun/moon, consciousness/energy, direction/vastness.

One of the things that makes this profoundly different from Western ideas about opposites is that neither pole is better or "higher" or more important than the other. Our habit of thought is to mix good and evil up in any duality, and to decide which side we're going to take. This way of thinking is totally foreign to the concept of yang and yin. Masculine and feminine *are*, and their eternal interaction sustains creation.

Yin Yang.

This is an energetic concept, and here your high-school physics *will* come in handy. Bring a positive charge (yang) and a negative charge (yin) close together and you get potential energy, a charged field created by the attraction between them. Positive and negative, male and female, want to come together, and that wanting makes energy happen. The stronger the charges at the poles, the more potential energy in between.

Think of a battery in a flashlight when you click the switch. You complete the circuit, the connection between positive and negative and—presto! you've got light. This is a trivial but pretty accurate image of how sexual polarity works. The essential principle of maleness (usually but not always embodied by a man) and the essential principle of femaleness (typically, but not necessarily, expressed by a woman) *want* to come together and release energy. The "more opposite" any two individuals are in their polarity the stronger the attraction, and the stronger the flow of life force when the two connect. (In other words, the better the sex!) For sex to be extraordinary, we need love, trust, mutual respect, etc., but we also need to discover and revel in the full eroticism of our sexual difference.

We'll be working on polarity a lot in this weekend, because the whole concept can be liberating. Our culture has really enormous trouble with the concept of masculine and feminine. One reason for this is that male and female are often assigned qualities of personality—strong/weak, aggressive/submissive, penetrative/receptive, active/passive, accomplishing/nurturing, and we rightly suspect any system that tries to paste expectations onto individuals just because of their gender. In our resistance to stereotyping and restriction, we have tended to deny that there is *any* real difference between masculine and feminine. (How many "There are no innate differences between boys and girls" parents have given up this belief by the second or third birthday of their second, differently-gendered child?)

Another huge problem is that our society strongly values masculine activity over feminine. Ironically, by trying to collapse difference to assure equality, we have made masculinity the norm. (Yes, our culture pretends to value the feminine—on Mother's Day, at least—but that's only a small token.) Career, compensation, goals, ambition, drive—these are all yang sorts of things, and they're what our daily lives demand. Feminine strengths tend to be undervalued, and viewed in a contemptuous, distorted way. Openheartedness is seen as weakness; joyful surrender is confused with submission; loving acceptance with sappy sentimentality.

There are quite different ways of looking at masculine/feminine difference. Tantra, the ancient erotic form of yoga mentioned at the beginning of this section, personifies the masculine and feminine poles as divine essences: Shiva and Shakti. Shiva is the prototypical male deity and Shakti is his consort, the archetypal goddess. Shiva is a great warrior, but compassionate and openhearted and humorous and an excellent husband. Shakti is a radiant, dancing, laughing goddess, but she's also powerful and fierce and uncompromising in her dedication to love. They

Energetic Symbols

Indian thought likes to personify forces and principles, and many Hindus worship Shiva and Shakti as divine persons; many others see them as useful symbols of vital energies. Don't worry—you do not have to accept a new religion to benefit from Tantra!

are very sexual gods—Tantra doesn't have our squeamishness about linking holiness and sex. Obviously, these ideals of male and female are rather different from the Western stereotypes we all know.

Shiva has a problem in our culture in that we're taught to be competitive and aggressive, but we don't see the Shiva traits of open-heartedness and generosity and humor as being particularly masculine. We don't even think these virtues are connected—if men aren't tigers, or rocks, they must be sensitive New-Age wimps, and who would want to be that? It can be quite a challenge to hold this complete masculine energy, especially when you're burdened and burned out.

What will help you balance your Shiva energy faster than anything is having a radiant source of Shakti energy nearby. We all hunger for radiance, for the heaven-on-earth that is Shakti, and when the real thing is missing, we turn to cheap, shiny substitutes like too much television, marathon web-surfing sessions, drinking, using drugs. Whether we're men or women, when we can't get that glow, we start prowling around, looking for anything that glitters, anything that provides escape.

Shakti has a corresponding set of problems. Women tend to spend their days in the masculine mode—scheduling, making things happen, getting things done—and usually don't get to spend much time in their dancing, openhearted, life-giving mode. This imbalance can be tremendously draining, especially for women who are with burned-out men—it's easy to feel unloved and disconnected from the wellsprings of life when nobody is wowed by your radiance. This extremely common chicken-and-egg-type situation saps the life out of millions of relationships—the guy's burned out because he doesn't have a radiant female in his life, and the gal's not radiant because her guy's burdened and discouraged and can't help her generate feminine energy. Result: no polarity to charge the sex batteries.

How do you restore polarity and balance—oh yes, and hot sex—to a burned-out relationship? The cure is to identify and nurture your own quality of energy, whether masculine or feminine, and to receive your partner's, and to know how to make that joyful fusion happen whenever you want.

Before we go any further, let's clarify an important truth about Shiva and Shakti—they are about masculine and feminine, but they're not always about gender. We've seen totally heterosexual couples where the male partner carries the yin energy and the female the yang: He's an artist, say, and she's a banker, and in their case, he carries the radiance, while she carries the direction and drive. (Same-sex couples can channel the two energies just as strongly as heterosexual partners.) The critical thing is that a couple recognizes and welcomes these opposite energies.

There's a lot of resistance to the idea of sexual polarity from the feminist perspective, because what we're asking is that women push to one side all the pressures about achieving parity in terms of wealth and power and recognition. Very retro. Actually, we're both staunch feminists and absolutely believe in equality, but what we're talking about in this book here is not the public, political self. We've become aware through personal experience, and through our patients, of the price competition and performance can exact on sexual relationships. Equality, freedom, fairness—those are great things and we're all for them. But none of them mean sameness, which is the extinction of the polarity that makes powerful sex happen.

So this is a vital fact about strong sexual energy—it can only arc between opposite poles. This means that if everyone's stuck in the masculine all the time, we might as well be neutered. Of course, you may *need* to be in a limited masculine or even neutral state to function all day at work, but if you're going to create a spectacular sexual connection, you've got to be able to put that aside in the bedroom. Learning about polarity is the first step toward tapping into the torrent of sexual energy that's all around, because polarity is what gets the juices flowing. Once you recognize what's there inside you, you and your partner can generate desire at will. All you have to do is perceive and serve the god or goddess in one another. This is probably not something you've had much experience with (to put it mildly), but we'll give you plenty of instruction and chances to practice.

> ## Me Shiva, You Shakti
>
> Share the ways in which you make each other feel "all woman" and "all man." Maybe he loves it when you wear high heels; maybe she loves it when you open the door for her. What other things can you do to bring out the radiance in your Shakti, and the warrior lover in your Shiva? Try some on this first day, just for fun—and feel the glow of sexual energy!

A NEW VISION OF SEX

So now you realize that sexual partners are manifestations of divine radiance and consciousness who exchange powerful, universal energies for their mutual benefit so that both partners grow more into love. Experience will make this clear. We promise.

These ideas about love and sex and the divine are very, very different from what we've all been taught. Most of us have been brought up, more or less explicitly, on the cyborg theory of sexual energy: Each of us is a bundle of drives and needs. There's energy inside us that causes tension so we have to discharge this energy before it messes up the system. If we're in love—a pure and vaporous state with no organic connection to sex—this discharge is safer and less complicated. Also, there's reproduction to contend with. Not exactly an exhilarating picture. And it probably doesn't capture much of your actual experience of sex.

Still, it's a very prevalent theory, and one that contributes to the commodification of sex in our culture. You know: sex is a kind of merchandise, something that you can barter. Think about how we talk: Did you get any? Did she put out? What a great piece of ass! This whole image of sex as commerce is brutal and ultimately destructive, and if we keep carrying it around, it keeps hurting us. Not anyone else—us. Deciding for ourselves that sex is a spiritual activity can completely change our experience of it.

So, if we enlarge our views enough to conceive of sex as a spiritually beneficial exchange of divine energy, then the ultimate sexual skill is being able to build and contain and circulate that energy through yourself and your partner. It is *not* about getting rid of sexual tension, a particular preoccupation of men in our culture: "Oh, I need to come so I can discharge all this tension and go to sleep so that when I get up I'll be rested and can hit the ground running." That sort of sex requires essentially no skill of any kind. But to become an ecstatic lover, you'll need to learn about the physics and physiology of how everything works, and you'll need to work at it. It's a rather nice course of study, as you can guess.

Good sex is an intentional practice. That's a concept we'll be throwing at you again, and if you're like most of our workshop participants, you'll resist it: "No, sex should be spontaneous and overwhelming and should just happen and everything should be naturally perfect!" It *will* be perfect if you're with the right person. Sex isn't something you practice! (or even intend) Sorry, but that's how you get mediocre sex—and get stuck with it for life. We believe very much in the idea of an intentional practice, a discipline, even, to develop your skills both individually and as a team in building, managing, and circulating sexual energy. It's totally the opposite of the Hollywood fantasy, where the hottest sex invariably happens spontaneously, magically, out of the blue, when both partners completely lose control.

How do you begin this practice? First, change your vocabulary. Words shape thoughts, and almost all Western terms for the sexual parts of us are hideous. Some are so clinical that when you hear them you can practically smell the examining room. Others are coarse and ugly and call to mind nothing more exalted than crude drawings on locker room walls. The Tantric vocabulary, on the other hand, has a nice, sacred feel to it and comes to us without any "sex-ed" or playground associations. We got our introduction to this with the Sanskrit words for the genitals:

lingam and *yoni*. The lingam is the male sex organ; the image associated with it is "wand of light." Yoni means vulva, and here the relevant image is "sacred space." Wand of light, sacred space—we're definitely entering a different sexual realm.

And speaking of sexual realms, you're going to want to create one before you go much further. Start thinking about making a beautiful, special place to make love. Get the laundry out of the corner and the stationary bike into the spare room and start making your bedroom a sacred, inviting space—one that satisfies your idea of beauty. This is easy to do and doesn't have to be an elaborate or expensive project: A few candles and scarves, a bowl of flowers and a well-selected CD can do magic. And magic is what you want.

Change takes place when you try on new beliefs within the context of action. We've just introduced you to quite a number of new concepts of love, sex, and energy. Now it is time to put these ideas into practice. Your homework assignments are designed to help you achieve the following experiential goals:

• To feel the energy between you and your lover.
• To build and circulate that energy rather than discharge it.
• To savor your awareness of your partner as a divine, radiant being.

We begin with the simplest of exercises: the Indian gesture of greeting and appreciation called *Namaste*, which we find useful and at times quite profound. Then we'll teach you an easy and fundamental breathing exercise that will help you learn to move energy around your body. Then we'll introduce you to an elegant and efficient way to connect your energy with that of your lover called *soulgazing*. In later sections, we'll build more complex exercises on these basics, and give you more explicitly sensual/sexual assignments. So go for it!

Your Own Sexual Realm

The environment you create for this long erotic weekend should not disappear on the fourth and final day. You need to transform your own bedroom into a permanent sexual realm—a special place for just you two. A place where two consenting adults can have a lifetime of great sex—no kids, no Monday night football, no ironing. You'll have a chance to work out the details on Day Four. Whether you decide to go all out—add that king-size bed, that fireplace, those sliding glass doors out to the hot tub—or do something more restrained but just as meaningful (like a simple love altar in the corner) you can, and should, create that sexual realm for eternity, right at home.

Namaste

The Sanskrit greeting, Namaste, has no unique equivalent in English, but it is usually translated as "reverent salutations," or "the light in me acknowledges the light in you." The sense of the greeting is to give recognition to the soul of the one greeted, and its connection to the divine, coming from one's own soul and one's own connection to the divine. Typically the word is accompanied by a gesture, which consists of placing the palms together in front of the heart (as in prayer) and bowing. This symbolizes the idea that God dwells in the heart of each individual self, and that respect and humility are called for in the presence of God.

We have our own rituals of greeting, parting, and appreciation in our culture, of course, and at least some of them have soulful origins. "Good-bye," for example, comes originally from "God be with ye," which is similar to the Spanish "adios" or French "adieu." But we generally don't have any handy way to express our heart-and-soul-felt appreciation for another person, nor to acknowledge their fundamentally divine nature.

We like this simple word and gesture, and use it often in our workshops as well as with one another. Try incorporating it into your greetings and thanks of one another, and see if it changes the quality of the feeling involved for you (see illustration).

Basic Breathing ☙2

If you've had any experience with yoga or meditation, you already know that working with the breath is the key to exploring and developing control over the mind-body connection. If this idea is new to you, let us explain.

Breathing is a unique physical function—it's the one vital body process that is both completely automatic *and* completely voluntary. You can't control your liver or your glands, but you do have considerable control over your diaphragm, the muscle that works the lungs. This is what makes the breath such a valuable tool in mind-body medicine and in spiritual practices. In fact, the word *spirit* comes from the Latin word for breath, *spiritus*, which is also the root of *respiration*, *inspiration*, and *expiration*.

In our program to enhance sexuality, we use breathing and imagery to develop awareness of energy flow in the body. Ultimately you will learn to breathe together with your partner in ways that will allow you exchange energy at will. For now, let's just learn to breathe while visualizing energy flowing through our bodies.

Begin by finding a comfortable place where you won't be interrupted, and sit down. You can sit in a chair, or cross-legged on the floor or on your bed—wherever you are most comfortable. If you decide to sit cross-legged—and it's a good

Namaste.

idea to practice doing this for the more advanced exercises—you may want to have a meditation cushion or a pillow or two under you.

Close your eyes, and just begin to notice your breathing and what it *feels* like to breathe. Notice when the air flows into you, when it flows out and what parts of you move or change shape as you breathe. Notice in particular the way your belly expands when you breathe in.

Now, imagine that each time you inhale, energy follows your breath in through your nose, down the front of your body, and into your belly. Concentrate on this image for a few breaths. Then see if you can imagine the energy sinking even deeper down your front and into your pelvis and genital region. There's no need to tense the muscles there in any way; rather, try to relax the entire area to allow even more breath, more imagined energy, to fill the pelvis.

Continue to breathe in this way, but now think about the outbreath as well. As you exhale, imagine sending the energy from the pelvis upward along the spine, and out through the top of the head. So each time you breathe in, you bring energy down along the front of your body into the pelvis and genitals, where you feel a fullness. Then, when you breathe out, you empty the pelvis and send the energy back up along the spine and out the crown of your head.

As you do this, you'll experience a circuit of flowing energy, and your attention will begin to move smoothly around your body, naturally and effortlessly coordinating with your breathing.

Continue this process for a couple of minutes, or as long as you like, enjoying a pleasant feeling of relaxation and calm. Observe as many of your internal sensations as you can without changing the way you're breathing or losing track of the image of the circuit of energy that is flowing down your front on the inbreath, up your spine on the outbreath. Then gradually let it go, and come back to ordinary breathing and perception.

Soulgazing ☉3

Soulgazing is a Tantric technique for gaining access to the spiritual dimensions of lovemaking. It serves to bring attention to the heart connection between you and your partner by using your eyes, touch, and breath, and it is the most important single tool we have garnered from our study of Tantra. Soulgazing is a fundamental ritual we teach all couples in our workshops, and we ask them to practice daily during the sexual training. It is potent, it is simple, and it is essential (see illustration).

First, sit across from your partner on the floor or the bed with your legs crossed in front of you. One or two pillows under your bum may make this easier. Now, take hold of your partner's hands in this way: Place your left hand palm up in your lap or on your knee, and your right hand, palm down, in your lover's left hand.

Soulgazing.

A Little Soulgazing a Day...

Your soulgazing ritual will be more powerful if you practice it every day. Consistent practice makes it easy to link your eyes and match your breaths, which means that you can concentrate on opening your hearts to each other with appreciative thoughts. What does he mean to you? What do you love about her? Why do you want to bring him into your body?

Your lover places his right hand on your left. The left hand represents receiving and the right hand giving. In a balanced and dynamic relationship, you have to be able to do both.

Now look into the eyes of your mate, steadily and calmly and *do not talk* (if you talk, you'll talk about money or the kids). Focus on each other. Looking without talking intensifies the connection—many couples say this is more intimate than even having sex! You might feel a bit exposed at first, and be distracted by thinking, "What is he looking at?" or "What is she thinking?" This is to be expected: The eyes are the only visible part of the brain. Because of the uncanny intensity of direct gaze, some societies believe that the soul can be stolen in this way, and protect against it. Quickly, though, this will begin to feel familiar and comforting. You are looking not into just anyone's eyes, but the eyes of your beloved.

The last, crucial step is to begin to breathe together. Maintaining your gaze, follow the movement of your partner's chest out of the corner of your eye, and gradually synchronize your breathing. Coordinating inhalation and exhalation is just the beginning: soon heart rhythm and other functions of the autonomic nervous system also become synchronized.

How do we know this? Because we have hooked up EKG leads to couples while they soulgaze and have found that their heart rate variabilities becomes entrained—tracings on the graphs we make of the gentle increase and decrease of heart rate for each partner show the same pattern. The classical Tantric practitioners knew long ago what we are just now documenting: Soulgazing's power to mesh the nervous systems of lovers.

Reciprocal Breath ⏾4

Once you have learned basic soulgazing, you will want to add *reciprocal breath* to your practice. This is merely timing the breath so that one of you inhales while the other exhales. The partner who initiated simultaneous breathing before can take the lead again: Switch to reciprocal breathing by squeezing the other's hand

and then holding the inbreath until your partner has exhaled and is ready to inhale. Now, the initiator breathes out as the beloved takes a breath in and you have established a new rhythm—a sweet swinging of the breath back and forth between you.

We so often come to bed out of synch with our lover; soulgazing is a swift and profound way to make the emotional and spiritual connection that is necessary for a wonderful sexual energy exchange. It reliably takes us deeper into the beauty of lovemaking.

THE COUPLES GET STARTED

Steve and Kate

Steve and Kate settle down on cushions on the floor of their candle-lit living room and look at each other a little awkwardly. Steve gives Kate a little bow with his palms together, and she giggles, but returns the gesture and says *Namaste*. They start the breathing exercise, following the instructions on the CD. Kate feels impatient—what does this have to do with sex? But Steve takes right to it. He interrupts the exercise to say, "You know, this really is kind of soothing. It'd be good to do at my desk."

Kate snaps at him to be quiet, then sighs, and starts the track over. She tries to get more into it this time (she wants to "do it better" than Steve), but finds her mind wandering again. She's never been that big on relaxation.

They begin soulgazing with good intentions, and Steve is struck by Kate's beauty. With his eyes open, though, it's hard for him to focus the way he did before, and his thoughts drift back to work. He starts making a mental list for Monday.

Gazing into Steve's eyes is a little difficult for Kate—she glances away several times—and so she concentrates on detecting energy flowing through their hands. She can't feel any, but she begins to feel very tender toward Steve for agreeing to the weekend and trying. Each senses that the exercise is uncomfortable for the other, but at the end they both lean in spontaneously and kiss.

Charlie and Nicole

After listening to the instructions for Namaste and breathing, Charlie asks, "Bowing to the *divine*? Breathing into your *pelvis*? This is just a bunch of yoga b.s. I thought it was supposed to be about screwing." He goes through the motions, though, distracting himself with fantasies about a girl he dated in college. But Charlie actually likes soulgazing. He enjoys studying Nicole's hair and face even though she won't look back at him. She can't turn away *this* time, he thinks.

Nicole, who sometimes takes a yoga class at their club to keep in shape, already knows how to do conscious breathing. However, she takes Charlie's remarks personally, becoming so irritated that she can't breathe steadily, or even look at him during soulgazing. She keeps her eyes shut and feels her heart pounding with fury throughout the exercise.

When they finish, Charlie pulls Nicole toward him, hoping to cuddle, but she pulls away and announces that she's going for a swim in the hotel pool. She carries her suit into the bathroom and shuts the door to change.

Martin and Linda

Sitting across from one another on their bed, Martin and Linda hold hands while doing the exercises. Namaste feels really good to Martin; he has no trouble sensing the light in his wife, and really tries to connect with it. Linda has been practicing stress-reduction exercises given to her by her doctor, so as soon as the voice on the CD begins she begins to follow her breath and feel her jitters subside. Martin has never done anything like this before, but catches on quickly. He's feeling a sense of internal space that's new to him.

Soulgazing makes Martin, then Linda, misty. Looking for long moments into one another's eyes is something they did a lot of when they first got together, and both feel a rush of vivid memories. Martin, especially, feels a flash of the carefree happiness of their earliest days as a couple.

Martin pulls Linda close and says, "Sometimes I forget just how much I love you." He proposes a bath and foot massage before lunch—take-out Polynesian delivered to the door—and she accepts.

Bob and Paulette

The day before they left for the resort, Bob felt the first signs of a head cold, and as he feared, the flight made it worse. As they settle down facing one another to do the first set of exercises, his congestion seems to grow more severe. Paulette is quite familiar with Namaste from her yoga practice, and gives Bob a graceful bow with the greeting to begin the session, but he is distracted by his dripping nose and only partly returns the gesture. After listening to the instructions for breathing, he begs off. Obviously, he can hardly breathe!

Paulette holds her tongue and skips to the next track on the CD, soul-gazing, and settles down again, determined to make Bob get with the program. As soon as they join hands, however, Bob has to get up to find the tissues, and then blows his nose repeatedly during the exercise. He doesn't really do it.

Paulette understands these diversionary tactics perfectly and is royally pissed. "Okay, it's safe to put the handkerchief away now," she says when the time is up. Bob looks hangdog but feels relieved it's over.

NOON

You've honored each other with Namaste, you've gazed into each other's eyes and beyond into your very souls, and you've breathed as one. Now order lunch in, a fun favorite like pizza or Thai food will do.

Lie in each other's arms, read Rumi aloud. Then take a nap together.

Once you've awakened from your leisurely snooze, grab your pen and paper and get ready to explore the Seven Dimensions of Sex.

AFTERNOON

THE SEVEN DIMENSIONS OF SEX

It is really not so hard to become an expert at sex, but no one ever gave us the map, the rules, the structure of sexual exchange. Certainly, no one ever gave us the tools! Sex is a skill. Understand, though, that we're talking about not just the physical side of things, but the emotional and sacred aspects, too. You and your partner can hone your abilities to open up, to provide comfort and support to one another, and to actively generate mutual desire. This section is about not just how to deepen your connection to your beloved, but about why you want to take the trouble. The rewards of letting go of your fears are incalculable—not just for your sexual connection, but for your whole life.

In coming to understand the seven key dimensions of sexual connection, you will discover a powerful tool to help you create the sensual intimacy you desire. We all know that knowledge is power. Powerful sex results when you and your lover learn to use the three positive aspects of each dimension—the outer, the inner, and the deep—and also learn to identify the negative features, the fears and inhibitions, that drain away sexual energy. Even more important, we will teach you how to avoid the traps in the energy dynamic of each dimension: those bleak, boring places where positive and negative cancel each other out and you and your mate get stuck, stuck, stuck. The great advantage of our systematic, analytic approach is that it helps you identify and applaud the innate strengths each of you brings to your sexual connection—lusty desire or romantic depth or exquisite sensuality—and to start discarding the useless cards from your sexual playing hand. It is just as important for you to root out resistance and negative patterns as to proclaim your strengths in order for the flow of sexual energy to sweep both of you into erotic bliss. It may seem counterintuitive, but being systematic about sex—as you must be about the basics of anything you want to be really good at— is actually the key to free-flowing, spontaneous loving. You can't come flying down a ski slope unless you've taken time to learn to turn and stop, and the sublime effortlessness of ballet dancers is grounded in absolute mastery of the first, simple steps. So dive into this analysis and thoroughly absorb the geography of each dimension, because expanding your positive potential in each area is the surest way to heighten your sexual experience. You will be so glad you did!

THE SEVEN DIMENSIONS INVENTORY

The following inventory is divided into seven sections that correspond to the seven different dimensions of sexuality. We'll explain each of the dimensions fully after you've completed the questionnaire. The inventory is designed to reveal what both you and your partner bring to your sexual connection. You'll not only get a score for your own answers; you'll also guess your partner's score in each dimension. Get ready to be surprised by some of your partner's responses—and by some of your lover's perceptions of you!

THE PHYSICAL DIMENSIONS

Biologic

- Do you easily lubricate (women) or get and maintain an erection (men) when you make love? Y=1, N=0
- Do you have an orgasm almost every time you make love? Y=1, N=0
- Men: Can you control your ejaculation? Women: Can you be multi-orgasmic? Y=1, N=0

- Does birth control or infertility interfere with your sexual response? Y=0, N=1
- Are you taking any medications that might affect your sexual response? Y=0, N=1
- Do you think that hormonal changes have affected your sexual performance as you've aged? Y=0, N=1
- Have you improved your skill as a lover over the past year? Y=1, N=0
- Do you feel confident of your sexual expertise as a lover? Y=1, N=0
- Have you been moved during sex with the awareness of possibly creating new life, perhaps even your own child? Y=1, N=0

Calculate your Biologic dimension score:
Guess your partner's:

Sensual

- Do you have favorite activities that you do mainly for sensual pleasure? (For example, long baths, massage, wine tasting, listening to music.) Y=1, N=0
- Do you often feel numb when it comes to sexual sensations? Y=0, N=1
- Do you regularly pleasure your partner outside the context of sex? Y=1, N=0
- Do you spend most of your time "in your head" rather than "in your body?" Y=0, N=1
- Are you often aware of sensual experiences throughout your day? Y=1, N=0
- Do you habitually use alcohol or drugs to become sensual? Y=0, N=1
- Do you habitually use books, magazines, the Internet, or videos to access your sensuality? Y=0, N=1
- Is it much easier for you to touch than to let yourself be touched? Y=0, N=1
- Do you easily become "lost" in sexual sensations (kissing, dancing with abandon, moving freely, touching)? Y=1, N=0

Calculate your Sensuality dimension score:
Guess your partner's:

Desire

- Do you allow your sexuality to be part of your image? Y=1, N=0
- Do you regularly initiate sex? Y=1, N=0

- Does your partner's sexual desire "turn you on"? Y=1, N=0
- Do you consciously build sexual charge between you and your partner? Y=1, N=0
- Are you comfortable with your own sexual power? Y=1, N=0
- Can you be spontaneous sexually? Y=1, N=0
- Do you sometimes withhold sex to get your way? Y=0, N=1
- Are you aware of the erotic in nature and everyday life? Y=1, N=0
- Do you consciously try to live a passionate life? Y=1, N=0

Calculate your Desire dimension score:
Guess your partner's:

THE EMOTIONAL DIMENSIONS

Heart

- Do you often give you partner gifts or tokens of love? Y=1, N=0
- Do you look forward to celebrations of your commitment to your partner (anniversaries, Valentine's Day, etc)? Y=1, N=0
- Are you easily able to receive romantic attention from your mate without immediately having to give back? Y=1, N=0
- Does past abandonment make you guard your heart? Y=0, N=1
- Is there a grudge you need to let go of in order to open your heart? Y=0, N=1
- Do you often experience your "stingy heart" interfering with your loving connection with your partner? Y=0, N=1
- Are you easily able to forgive your partner's mistakes? Y=1, N=0
- Do you "have sex" more often than you "make love?" Y=0, N=1
- Does sex make you love your partner more? Y=1, N=0

Calculate your Heart dimension score:
Guess your partner's:

Intimacy

- Are you comfortable making love with the lights on and your eyes open? Y=1, N=0

- Do you make time for intimate conversation with your mate? Y=1, N=0
- Do you keep secrets from your partner? Y=0, N=1
- Are their topics that can't be discussed with your partner? Y=0, N=1
- Is betrayal, past or present, a stumbling block to your relationship? Y=0, N=1
- Do you and your mate appreciate each other's humor? Y=1, N=0
- Are you good at accepting flaws in your partner? Y=1, N=0
- Do you sometimes find that you know what your mate is thinking or about to say before he/she speaks? Y=1, N=0
- Do you consciously try to help your partner accept and love himself (or herself)? Y=1, N=0

Calculate your Intimacy dimension score:
Guess your partner's:

THE SPIRITUAL DIMENSIONS

Aesthetic

- Have you created a beautiful space in your home to make love in? Y=1, N=0
- Do you consciously point out and share beauty with your partner? Y=1, N=0
- Do you know how to "light up" your partner? Y=1, N=0
- Are you in the habit of criticizing your mate, or of always having to be right? Y=0, N=1
- Are you aware of your partner's radiance when you make love? Y=1, N=0
- Do you sometimes find yourself watching and judging yourself and/or your partner during sex? Y=0, N=1
- Do you hear an inner voice criticizing you or insulting your body during sex? Y=0, N=1
- Do you feel beautiful when you make love? Y=1, N=0
- Does the beauty of your lover ever awe you during sex? Y=1, N=0

Calculate your Aesthetic dimension score:
Guess your partner's:

Ecstatic

- Do you regularly engage in a mindfulness practice like yoga, tai chi, prayer, meditation? Y=1, N=0

- Have you made an effort to bring a spiritual quality to your bedroom? Y=1, N=0

- Do you and/or your partner engage in any form of ritual to make sex more spiritual? Y=1, N=0

- Were you taught that sex is shameful or profane? Y=0, N=1

- Do you feel afraid of letting go or surrendering to the sexual experience? Y=0, N=1

- Have you ever used sex to heal emotional or spiritual wounds? Y=1, N=0

- Are you comfortable with the idea of embodying the divine during lovemaking? Y=1, N=0

- Do you believe that sex can be a path to the sacred? Y=1, N=0

- Have you ever experienced an ecstatic sexual connection, one in which you and your partner transcended ordinary experience and reality? Y=1, N=0

Calculate your Ecstatic dimension score:
Guess your partner's:

SCORING YOUR INVENTORIES

Add up your scores and guess your partner's. Together, these two sets of results are like an x-ray of your sexual connection. Here are some things to look for: Are there striking differences or similarities? Is one of you, say, typically lusty (strong in the Desire dimension) while the other is deeply romantic (high-scoring in the Heart dimension)? Dimensions where your scores are very different are often flashpoints, areas in which both of you may presently feel frustrated—but if you understand and accept where your loved one is coming from, these differences can become sources of discovery, balance, and strength.

Dimensions where you score about the same are probably easy, harmonious aspects of your union. It's possible, though, to be so comfortable together in some dimensions that you neglect others and end up in a pleasant but boring rut. Areas where both sets of scores are low are places where your relationship is likely to be "stuck." If both of you have high scores in intimacy and low ones in desire, for example, you may love and trust one another completely, but lack the spark for exciting sex.

Wherever you find real incongruity between what you think your partner's score will be and what it is, you've identified an opportunity to grow closer. Have you really been misreading your lover's true strengths and longings? Or is he or she simply deluded, and in denial? It may be that one of you has scored more optimistically, or you may really be on different wavelengths sexually. Straightening out these misunderstandings can quickly erase many mutual grudges. On the other hand, trying to discuss your divergent perceptions may be just the thing that presses all those hot buttons! Let's see how our four couples have handled this task.

THE COUPLES' INVENTORY RESULTS

Steve and Kate

Steve, who was doubtful about doing the inventory, is annoyed to find that he's weak in the Sensual, Desire, Heart, Intimacy, and Ecstatic dimensions—he only got three to five points in each—and embarrassed to have to record in the Biologic section the fact that he sometimes comes too quickly. This has not been a problem for them so far. He always makes sure Kate comes first by giving her oral sex, which she loves, and anyway, he can usually get hard again easily. Lately, though, it seems to be taking longer, and this worries him some.

Kate, who thought she'd do well in everything—she always does—turns out to be weak in the Heart, Intimacy, and Aesthetic dimensions (4, 4, and 3), which makes her irritable. Sitting across from each other at their kitchen table and looking over each other's answers, they slip into a familiar pattern, and start to argue. They've argued in every room in the apartment since they've been together, but the kitchen is where they usually have the knock-down, drag-outs.

"Well, no real surprises there," Kate says, looking over Steve's inventory. "You're pretty low in most of the dimensions. I didn't figure you for an eight in Aesthetic, though. Whatever that is."

"Yeah, appreciating beauty never was your strong suit. Get naked and get it on, that's your motto, and it definitely shows here: you're not so high in a lot of these dimensions yourself. And I think you're over-rating yourself in Heart," Steve replies, studying her sheet.

Kate looks at Steve's rating of her, and is outraged. "What?! You only gave me a *two*? What's that supposed to mean, Mr. Stuck-in-his-briefcase? At least I know *how* to get it on!"

Steve turns away, hurt. "Well, I can see where this is going. Just like every other 'discussion' we've ever had. This whole weekend was such a pathetic idea...."

Kate opens her mouth to make another biting reply, then stops herself. She doesn't want Steve to bail—this program was her idea, after all. She tries to think of something to say that will soothe him, but she is still in attack mode, and her mind is a blank. "We need help!" she thinks.

This is how we would counsel these two if we could magically appear in their kitchen at this point:

"Whoa! What you're doing is digging yourselves deeper into the same old rut instead of working on getting out of it. Let's look beneath your answers on the questionnaire and see what's really going on here," Lana says. "Kate, let's talk about what's going on with your Heart dimension. You know, it's unusual for a woman to have such a low score—Heart is generally our specialty. It makes me wonder if you've had some significant loss in the past that's making you guard your heart now."

Kate's voice is small. "My dad died when I was 15. He was my biggest supporter. We were so close..." She begins to tear up, her voice trembling. "I still miss him every day. Nothing was ever the same after the morning he collapsed."

"Closing your heart is a natural reaction to a loss that big. You instinctively protect yourself from the possibility of ever feeling that hurt again. It may be that you've never really let Steve into your deepest heart, even though you love him a lot. That might feel too vulnerable..." Lana paused, watching Kate carefully.

"I thought I'd feel less alone with Steve, but I don't, actually. I really love him, but..." She keeps her eyes on the table.

Lana nods. "But you haven't felt that you could trust in his love. Do you see what happened? Losing your dad hurt so much that right then you closed your heart, shut it tight, so you'd never be so vulnerable again. Your heart is still there, still tender, but it's been sheathed in armor all these years."

David turns to Steve. "Does that sound right to you?"

Steve, who's been listening closely while watching Kate, nods. "The sex was so fantastic at the beginning—she's so beautiful, and so hot. I still can't believe somebody so sexy and smart would want me, but we're not that close, you know? It's gotten to be sort of depressing, us having sex. I'm not really connecting with her when we hook up, and so it's like, why bother? I go ahead anyway sometimes, but there's something missing."

Kate looks up at last and meets Steve's longing gaze. She manages to look deep into his eyes at last, and bursts into sobs. This surprises Steve and takes him aback for a moment. Then he gets up, comes around the table and puts his arms around her while she cries.

"It's okay, sweetie. I do love you, and now I understand a lot better what's missing for us sexually. Let's keep going with this program and see where it can take us."

Charlie and Nicole

Charlie is inclined to dismiss the whole "inventory thing" as touch-feely nonsense. He comes out as weak in the Heart, Intimacy, and Ecstatic dimensions, (4, 3, 3).

"But look," he says, "I got a perfect score in Desire!"

Nicole's scores are abysmal in the Sensual, Desire, Intimacy, Aesthetic, and Ecstatic dimensions (2, 2, 3, 2, 3), which disturbs her. She hides her worry, though, and dryly answers, "What a shocker."

Charlie's answers in the Heart dimension are telling, and Nicole, who's strong in that dimension and knows her husband well, has a pretty clear idea what they mean. *Of course* Charlie looks forward to celebrations of commitment like anniversaries and Valentine's Day—they usually have sex on those occasions! He has admitted on the inventory to having a "stingy heart," and when she asks him why, he says frankly, "I get mad when you won't put out." He didn't understand the question about "having sex" versus "making love," and has written "What do you mean?" instead of answering. Finally, his response to the last query, "Does sex make you love your partner more?" is an enthusiastic "You bet!" Nicole's beginning to feel that she'd like to escape from their hotel room.

Martin and Linda

Martin and Linda evaluate their scores and guesses amiably. Martin is weak in the Desire and Aesthetic aspects (4, 4), but okay in the Ecstatic dimension (6), which intrigues Linda.

"I felt that sort of merging or blending way back when we were first together," she says. "Honestly, you still do?"

This makes Martin a bit shy. "Yeah. Sometimes."

Linda is a bit weak in the Biologic and Sensual (5, 5), and really weak in the Desire dimension (3). They're both a little concerned about the lack of physical enjoyment her answers reveal.

"I had no idea it was that bad," Martin says. "Maybe it's the damn Prozac."

"Could be, but you know that I can't function without it," Linda replies.

Bob and Paulette

Bob, who slowly and reluctantly fills out his form, is weak in the Biologic, Sensual, Desire, and Ecstatic dimensions (3, 2, 1, 4), (*oh great*, thinks Paulette) but good in the Heart and Intimacy dimensions (8, 8). There's never been any question about his devotion to the woman he married so long ago. Paulette has always felt his love, but is unexpectedly moved by this unequivocal "confession" of it. Bob is not much of a talker.

Paulette is weak in the Biologic, Heart, and Aesthetic dimensions (3, 4, 3), and great in the Sensual, Desire, and Ecstatic (7, 8, 8).

"And here I was thinking that this sexual wasteland was all him!" she thinks. She turns to Bob and says wryly, "Who would have thought we'd both score high in Intimacy? Well, I guess it's good we have *something* in common."

Bob goes back and compares their scores again. "You know, between the two of us we've got almost all the dimensions covered. They say that means we should be able to click somehow." He's not sure he quite believes that, since the quiz mostly makes it look like he and his wife come from different planets, but he also begins to feel a glimmer of hope.

Paulette, still strangely stirred by the realization of how deep his heart's strength goes, says, "We definitely need to find out more about these dimensions."

⌒

EXPLORE YOUR DIMENSIONS

Now it's time to take an up-close look at each dimension, identifying the ways in which you may be sabotaging your sex life, and the ways in which you can enhance it as well. Be sure to write down your ideas as you brainstorm each dimension—these are love notes that you'll need when we return to your questionnaires again on Day Four, and give you specific tools to help you in each dimension as you make plans to create your sexual future together.

THE BIOLOGIC DIMENSION

Like all the other dimensions, the biologic has a positive pole, a negative pole, and a stagnant place in between where lovers become trapped when their sexual energies cancel one another or where neither generates any energy.

The positive pole of the Biologic, as with all the dimensions, has a progression built into it: we start from the basic outward-directed aspect of good physical function and knowing what's what, then progress to the inward awareness of confidence in our sexual expertise as a lover, and finally mature into the deepest level of understanding that sex is how the species perpetuates itself. Sex also always contains the awe-inspiring potential for making babies.

The negative energy is physical dysfunction, whether due to hormonal decline, infertility issues, medications, surgeries, or aging. There is not much mystery about the negative pole of the biologic dimension.

The static zone in this dimension is ignorance, inattention, and silence. We know something is wrong but will avoid it at all costs.

How do you get all you can from this obviously basic dimension? How do you move from dysfunction, or from the trap of ignorance and inattention, to confident performance? First, you need to become aware of key information about your body or your lover's that you probably never had a chance to learn. You will learn about the stages of human sexual response, crucial facts of anatomy, and the hormonal pitfalls.

Second, practice! (This, of course, applies to the other six dimensions, as well.) We will give you a host of practice opportunities in your weekend, and you will definitely learn how to be a more skillful lover.

And third, talk with both your partner and with your doctor. An amazing number of problems with this dimension are easily solved once the communication is there.

The Golden Rule of Good Sex: Talk Rather Than Do Unto the Other

There is an important point about the nuts and bolts of sex that we need to clarify right now: assuming you know what your partner wants or needs sexually does not work. Talking to your partner is vital.

We emphasize the "golden rule of talking" throughout the book because it's not what most of us are inclined to do. Very few people just naturally feel comfortable talking to their partners about sexual technique. This begins when we're young, or newly involved. God forbid that we should come across as critical, or bossy, or unromantic! So most of us start out trying to guess what our partner likes and continue on as we began. Communicating your desires is bound to make you nervous at first unless you're a pretty unusual person. Think back: Where did you get your original information about how to please a lover, anyway? Probably from your highly informed junior-high friends, your own body, a parent who mortified you by revealing any awareness that sex even existed, or from a lover who was probably just as clueless as you, and just as terrified to say anything that might ruin the experience. Right? So why start talking about it at this late date?

Because you want good sex, and because this type of shyness results in some pretty silly stuff. Take for example this typical scenario: A couple has been dating for a while, and both partners are eager to get intimate sexually. Naturally, they really want to please each other. She, wanting to encourage something similar from him, is barely brushing him with light, teasing, feathery strokes. Unfortunately, this just makes him wonder, "Is this going to get started anytime soon?" So he, operating on the same principle of "I'll do to her what feels good to me," finds her clitoris and really goes to town on it, eliciting shrieks—not of pleasure— from her.

The moral of this story for all of you? You *must* talk. Even though male and female anatomy are analogous (as you'll see tomorrow), they're most definitely not the same, so unless you're psychic, you can't know precisely what your partner wants unless she (or he) tells you. After you've been together for years you still need to talk, because what your partner wants today may be different from what felt good yesterday, or even an hour ago. So the true Golden Rule of Good Sex is: Let your partner know what you want.

Biological Age and Sex

Another important myth about the Biological dimension is that sex necessarily disappears with advancing age. This is probably the most common and depressing misconception people have about sex. We are here to tell you that it is *wrong*. Whether couples have great sex, adequate sex, or no sex at all doesn't have a lot to do with their age. We've seen sexually dried-up couples in their twenties and ecstatic lovers in their seventies. So while it's perfectly true that our bodies change over time, those changes need not determine the quality or frequency of lovers' sexual connections.

Do aging hormonal levels affect sexuality? Yes, and hormone levels in our bodies change as we advance through life. While they're hardly the whole story, they are vital to biologic function. Not enough estrogen in women—a very common effect of aging —causes problems with lubrication and comfort. Dropping testosterone levels can also cause problems, for women as well as men. While we all know testosterone as the "male hormone," it occurs naturally in both men and women, and is crucial to libido—the Desire dimension. In addition, inadequate levels of testosterone can directly affect function in both sexes.

Many medications that we begin to need as we age also have an impact on desire and arousal and ability to be orgasmic—and sometimes the impact may be dramatic. Common drugs that may interfere with sex are things like blood pressure medications and some medications for controlling cholesterol. Some medications, such as most of the antidepressants, have an inhibitory effect no matter what the age of their users. And, of course, naturally occurring changes in things like blood flow and nerve function in the genitals can cause erection and lubrication problems.

As we tell our patients, though, the physical part is *easy*. It's incredibly sad that so many people resign themselves to "the normal effects of aging" when pharmacists have simple, elegant, dignified solutions sitting on the shelf. Hormone replacement, lubricants, Viagra, Venus Touch (with blood-flow stimulating L-arginine and L-ornithine), medication adjustments and other "fixes" can make an enormous difference. So there's the Golden Rule of Sex again: If you're having physical difficulties, talk to your doctor. If your doctor brushes you off, find one who'll listen.

THE SENSUAL DIMENSION

The sensual dimension is all about pleasure, which, if you think about it, is our usual motivation for having sex. We have evolved—or were created, if you prefer—with strong, innate sexual drives and bodies designed to get immense enjoyment from sex. Nature has concocted nearly as many schemes to propagate life as there are species. For us humans, pleasure does the trick. We're smart enough, of course, to outfox her plan when it suits us—which is most of the time—and to enjoy the sensations of sex while circumventing the baby-making part. So why not get all the pleasure from sex that we can?

One reason that the pleasure sex gives us is so intense is that it involves all five of the traditional senses—sight, hearing, smell, taste, and touch—plus the sixth sense, the kinesthetic. What happens to most of us most of the time is that we damp our senses down. Our culture strongly encourages us to overuse sight and hearing,

Sex Advice to All Creation

For an enlightening and very funny glimpse into the strange sex lives of many other species, we enthusiastically recommend *Dr. Tatiana's Sex Advice to All Creation*, by Olivia Judson. Sympathize with the virgin fig wasp who has noticed that males wasps are biting the females in half, worry along with a green spoon worm who's inhaled her husband, and feel the pain of the motherly male stickleback whose eggs have been filched. And you thought human sexuality was odd!

and to lose track of touch and the kinesthetic sense. It's easy to stay out of our bodies and in our brains, particularly our left brains. We tend to emphasize abstract, left-brain functions over the more intuitive, immediate concerns of the right brain, so we end up automatically preferring language to image, argument to gut feeling, analysis to intuition.

So, the positive pole of the sensual continuum is pleasure. The *outer* aspect of pleasure then is just what we have been talking about—being awake sensually. This requires a pleasure alert multiple times a day. Stop to enjoy the deep color of that flower, smell your lover's hair, taste your beloved's salty neck, paste your bodies together in a mega-hug. Exercising your senses is fun, and enriches every hour. Besides, it's an enjoyment that's free for the taking in a world where most entertainment costs a fortune.

The inner aspect of positive sensuality is the exciting and stimulating appreciation of physical sensations both outside and inside the bedroom. It is one thing to give the kiss, listen to the wind in the trees, or smell the salt air, but when we consciously appreciate our sensual involvement with the world, and most especially with our lover, we begin to automatically seek opportunities to increase sensuality. What a nice addiction! We get hooked on the infinite variety of experiences two people can have together.

But there is more—a deep level of sensuality where we merge with the experience itself. At this sensual level we become lost in our lover's soft, sweet, warm lips; or we dance with abandon—let-'er-rip, shake-your-bootie, jump-and-shout movement; or we allow music to swirl our lovemaking into higher more powerful ranges. Any sensual experience can be entered into in this way, so that we feel no difference between our selves and our perceptions. All it requires is letting go fully into our wonderful, sensitized, sensual bodies, and becoming pleasure itself.

Our Kinesthetic Sense

The kinesthetic sense is our experience of the body in space. We tend not to notice its input unless we're dancing or swimming or going for the basket, but it's active all the time. Right now, notice your left elbow—is it bent, or straight? Is it moving or still? Is it resting on something? Is it comfortable? You know all about what that elbow is up to already on some level, but you rarely need to pull it into consciousness. When we become more attentive to our kinesthetic sense, we feel more alive, more "embodied," which is exactly what we want when we make love.

The negative pole is, as you might expect, pain, either physical or emotional. Pain can ruin sex. It may be simple, temporary, or avoidable—you've just had a baby and sex is the last thing you want, or you have a urinary or prostate infection, or you've got some arthritis and certain positions hurt. But pain can also be emotional, and that kind of pain can be hard to get around.

Why would somebody have emotional pain during sex? For people who've been sexually traumatized, the most loving touch can trigger memories of an experience like rape or forced sex or something else frightening associated with sex. A woman who's had a really bad experience may love and want her partner, but if he happens to touch her neck, say, in just the way her attacker did long ago, she may not feel that touch as something wonderful but flash back to fear, humiliation, and pain. And it is not only women who have been seared by sexual abuse—it happens to men as well. The good news is that these wounds can be healed. Professional help is often necessary, but healing can also occur through sensual awakening with a completely trustworthy partner.

What's the stagnant no man's land? Numbness. This may also be the result of frightening sexual encounters—it is just easier to shut down rather than confront fear—but often the cause is more ordinary: we are just busy elsewhere in our minds. Oh, true, we are having intercourse, pumping away, but where are we really? Thinking about picking up the dry cleaning! Or still at the office, going over details of deals in our head. We're not really even there.

The way out of numbness is simply to start attending to our senses. They're the channels of physical awareness. If you know any artists, you may have noticed that they're more sensual than most of us. That's because these are folks who have always paid close attention to sight, sound, texture, movement. We can learn a lot from their perceptual habits. You can awaken to the world, too, by indulging your creative impulses. Is there some expressive activity you enjoyed in the past but you've given up? Or one you're always wanted to take a whack at? It can be anything from learning to tango to throwing pots—what matters is that you physically express the way you see and hear and feel the world. We have some homework later that will awaken your sensuality because this dimension is critical to full-on, joyous sex.

THE DESIRE DIMENSION

The next dimension, the last of the three physical dimensions, is Desire. This dimension is what we may think of as sex itself—lust, excitement, irresistible attraction. It's the oomph, the spark, the va-va-voom that gets relationships going and keeps them hot. It's what sex looks like in the movies. Desire is the crackling charge created when male and female energies come close.

The positive aspect of this dimension is attraction—outwardly presenting an attractive, "I'm vital and sexual" persona to the world. It also involves allowing yourself to be attracted by others, to recognize another's sexual life force. This attraction is basic, and fundamental—it's the powerful energy inherent in the mating drive. Utilizing this energy can be tricky business, because we would like to tap into the vitality of desire without seeming cheap or sleazy or like a tease. In fact, the blatant use of sexual come-ons often is a hoax—people can act sexy but not actually feel that way at all. Their allure is superficial and bound to disappoint if posturing ever does turn into to action. Still, most of us want to feel desirable, so we take some trouble to dress, act, talk, and look attractive.

Internally, awareness of desire is also powerful; the current of sexuality flowing between our lover and us energizes daily life. However, when we take a look at our internal sexual self, we often find more confusion. We want to be wanted sexually by our partner but we don't feel sexually magnetic; or we have the lust running but are clumsy in our approach to our mate; or we might be afraid to allow our lust free rein—who knows if there is a nymphomaniac lurking just under our skin? However, a healthy sense of desire and comfort with lustful feelings is a terrific source of energy. In fact, coming to grips and finally to peace with this healthy-animal aspect of sex in all of us helps us create safe boundaries. You know that you are sexy, you are comfortable that you are sexy, and *you* decide who gets to experience all the delights of your sexy self.

There is, however, an even deeper level to the positive pole of the Desire dimension—erotic passion. Here desire and lustful urges weave durable fibers into the fabric of life itself. As we explained earlier, the Eastern idea of the power of sexual polarity—yin and yang, feminine and masculine, all-encompassing energy and directional force—describe essential, universal life patterns. It is the "oppositeness" of the male and female essences (which, as we have explained, do not necessarily correspond to actual gender) that attracts two people and sustains their sexual bond. Further, the stronger the polarity of the two partners, the stronger the connection in this dimension. The partner with the feminine core has access to the stream of energy that flows through all things; the partner with the masculine core draws that energy forth into the world, which is thereby enriched and celebrated.

Desire, then, is ultimately all about dancing with erotic sexual power, summoning the life energy. It's the alpha male and alpha female joining up to create the next generation—and it's the most natural thing in the world.

Mutual desire is the nuclear fuel of marriage. Without that essential fuel, the most caring, committed, loving couple in the world is not going to have great sex, or much sex, or maybe any sex at all. Loving couples who have lost their desire and don't revive it may not even be able to stay together.

Desire does have many everyday enemies. Negative energy in this dimension shows up as rejection, the flip-side of personal power (the third chakra) that says

NO to sex and mating. For women, this negative energy is usually generated by one of the *three F's*: fatigue, fury, and fear. In men, on the other hand, sexual or work-world humiliation or financial losses commonly squelch sexual energy. Rejection comes in a variety of strengths, from the occasional "Not tonight, honey, I have a headache," to "Stop bugging me, you're such an animal!" to deeply wounding verbal and non-verbal expressions of personal loathing: "I hate servicing you!"

More common, however, is the stagnant no-man's land of the Desire dimension: indifference. Sometimes this takes the benign form of two partners who are low in the biologic substrate of desire—low testosterone is a common culprit. Their relationship may be one of deep mutual respect, trust, loyalty, and cooperation, but neither partner brings any sexual power to the table. There is no spark to start the engine.

Another common situation is the one in which one partner feels no desire, but chooses to accommodate the other by "providing" sex rather than making love. This partner—often but not necessarily the woman—is participating in the sex act, but isn't really there. She wants to make her partner feel better, but she's exhausted and wants him to go to sleep so she can wander into dreamland herself; it's his birthday but she feels too worried about the bills (or a child, or work) to get into it. Sex happens, but energy is not flowing in this dimension—one partner is generating it, but the other isn't receptive, and the encounter ends up feeling dead for both.

And then there is the ultimate dead zone of the Desire dimension, the celibate relationship. The sexless (or nearly sexless) state develops as couples become increasingly awkward and distanced by the daily wear and tear of living, "no time," deep-seated worries, or simmering anger. They avoid confronting the three F's by sidestepping fury, fear, and fatigue and withdrawing their sexual energy. They effectively protect themselves from further humiliation and disappointment by denying desire. The typical process goes like this: one partner refuses to respond to the advances of the other, and the other, tired of the humiliation of being rejected, gradually gives up. The situation deteriorates into a profound and chronic power struggle in which the partner who wants sex *least* is the one with control in the bedroom, and once-loving partners silently vie for the coveted title of Least Interested. When the sexual charge of the Desire dimension is diverted into power games like this, its creative potential energy is wasted as friction and heat. And the longer it's trapped this way, the greater the inertia to be overcome in order for things to start up again.

For many of us, then, re-energizing desire means recognizing and deconstructing old beliefs about sex and about ourselves that block its natural flow. Some half-forgotten wound, perhaps from as far back as early childhood, may have been constricting your free enjoyment of sex all these years. You may have beliefs acquired from your mother about the danger of male desire, or insecurities about your sexual competence. Anything that reduces our confidence in our sexual power short-circuits lust. If the beliefs that sap desire go very deep, people with trouble in this dimension may want to talk to a skillful counselor. But for many couples, seeing the nature of the problem clearly is half the battle. The most desire-sapping belief of all is that lust always grows cold. It doesn't, and we'll show you exactly how to reunite with that life-affirming, erotic life force.

THE HEART DIMENSION

It's no accident that the heart comes right in the middle of the seven dimensions. Just as the physical heart is the center of the body, the middle chakra, and the mainspring of life, the heart dimension is the warm, vital core of glorious sex. It's critical for any intimate relationship—without a strong heart dimension, a relationship that may have many other strengths will inevitably wither away. But for a relationship that still has heart, there's always hope.

It's a pleasure to be around open-hearted couples, partners who have an easy love. You've met them. They're the people who always seem happy in one another's company, who take it easy on one another, who openly admire and enjoy one another. At the other end of the heart dimension are partners who are sour and unkind, who snipe or complain about "all women" or "what men are like." It's excruciating to spend time with such couples.

The heart dimension is all about love, and love is essential to any long-lasting sexual connection. So is it important that the heart be connected to the genitals? It's crucial! Take a solid grounding in the first three dimensions of sex—the physical ones—and unite them with generosity and openness of heart, and sex becomes something much bigger than a simple physical act. Remember: Love is what *is* when your heart is open.

Our everyday language reflects our shared conviction that feeling somehow resides within that pump. Heartless, coldhearted, hardhearted, warmhearted, lighthearted, all heart—we can hardly avoid mentioning the heart when we talk about emotion. As we discussed previously, there is in fact a strong and measurable connection between the actual, physical organ and our emotional state. The heart is constantly exchanging electrical and chemical signals with the brain and nervous systems, so that we can learn to reduce stress reactions simply by focusing attention on the heart while remembering states of great well-being. (Yogis, the great technicians of body and mind, have known this for centuries.) And the heart really does radiate energy—its electromagnetic field has been measured from ten feet away—and two hearts actually can beat as one. Experiments have shown that the heartbeats of lovers tend to become synchronized when couples are close to one another. When we speak of the heart, we mean both the poetic symbol and the actual organ. They cannot really be separated.

What does the heart dimension look like? At the positive pole are the exquisite romantic experiences of falling in love and commitment. If all goes well, one follows the other, which is what all the ritual of a wedding is about. The rings, the bouquet, the veil, the vows—it's all about promising to sustain the easy, openhearted good will of courtship after real life has set in. Tokens and symbols, valentines and flowers and little gifts, are the natural currency of the heart, because love truly is about joyful giving and receiving. These are all part of the outer aspect of the Heart dimension. Of course, the giddiness of new love is bound to fade, but here is where the inner strength shines—that unbounded give and take can expand throughout life if we give it the sustenance it needs. As with the other dimensions of sex, when we *pay attention* to the heart dimension, it becomes stronger and deeper.

Finally, the deepest level of Heart connection manifests sexually when you experience the beauty of complete emotional dedication to your partner, the joy of witnessing your partner's love for you, and the exquisite luxury of wide-open love flowing between you during sex. As so many couples solidly acknowledge, this is the foundation of commitment, the place where their physical joining of bodies is infused with potent heart energy. This is *making love* rather than having sex. When your heart is open, when you have dealt with the negative fears and traps, this expansive sex will be yours.

The negative pole of the heart dimension is abandonment. Every one us has felt abandoned and unloved at some time or other, and we've got the scars to show for it. Our mother favored a sibling. The kid next door found a new best friend. Our greatest high school love dropped us. The first wife loaded up the furniture, cleaned out the accounts, and left.

This, too, is embedded in language, and in every classic country-western song—broken-hearted, disheartened, living in heartbreak hotel. If we allow old scars and new hurts to pull the heart closed, the open heart that easy love requires is lost.

The trap here, the place where the positive energy of love and commitment is neutralized by the negative energy of abandonment fears, is stinginess of heart. The stingy heart devotes all its energy not to giving and receiving love but to building walls and guarding gates, and one sure sign of it is counting. "We haven't been out to dinner for six-and-a-half-weeks and he watched basketball for four hours last night and hasn't bought me flowers for Valentine's Day for three years;" "She's turned me down the last five times I tried to get her into bed, *and* put $500 on the credit card last month without even mentioning it. Plus, she made that nasty remark about my brother and never apologized." This kind of stagnant, dank thinking—which can become a habit before we know it—doesn't accomplish a single thing. We may succeed in punishing our partner by holding grudges and keeping score, but it's ourselves we really damage. Conversely, an open heart gives and forgives, sympathizes and admires and enjoys, not because we want to be declared saints, but because we want to be happy and secure in our love. Only by giving will we receive. If we want to live, now and forever, in that warm, safe, comfortable space that two openhearted people can create between them, there is no other way but to open our hearts.

THE INTIMACY DIMENSION

The positive pole of the Intimacy dimension is trust. At first glance, distinguishing Intimacy from the Heart dimension, trust from commitment, may seem odd. How can we love without intimacy? How can we be intimate without love? Easily, and we do it all the time. We may love our parents or grandparents dearly without knowing very much about what goes on deep inside them. We can trust and confide in a therapist, a financial advisor, or a colleague without investing any emotion in the connection. Love and intimacy are different animals.

We tend to confuse them, in part, because these two dimensions must fuse if our most important relationship is to be joyful, free, and strong. When we trust as well as love, the emotional core of the relationship is solid. Without trust—when lovers have stopped talking to one another, or have wandered off into lying and cheating—love is on shaky ground, and the quality of our sexual connection erodes.

Trust is fundamental to great sexual connection because we make ourselves exquisitely vulnerable when we make love. Consequently, we can only really let go with someone we know isn't lying to us. Giving one's body, like revealing one's inner self, both requires and creates the trust needed for passionate, full-on lovemaking.

A trusting relationship is founded on truth at three levels. First of all, there are the day-to-day operations of house, kids, friends, foes, and finances. We trust our partner to offer honest opinions and genuine feelings about our outward life. We count on our partner's truthfulness, on promises being kept, and on certain information we share as a couple being strictly private. There is a familiarity to this level of intimacy—a certain exclusiveness—as with a very good friend who in this case happens to be our lover. Some couples do not even share this degree of honesty—they keep secrets from one another and only reveal the truth to close, same-sex friends. This is the beginning of the end of trust. It's not that we are advising that you schedule a mutual confessional session each week, but watch out for that secretive tendency. It can really undermine intimacy.

A trusting relationship also functions on a more profound level of truth. Think about when you first fell in love. You talked endlessly, fascinated by everything about your beloved and eager to share in return every deep secret and silly little detail about yourself. You could not know or reveal enough—there always had to be another meeting, another phone call, another long, delicious session of getting to know one another. Lovers often reveal things to each other that they've never told anyone else, and every time one partner accepts and understands an aspect of the other's inner reality, the couple's pool of mutual trust grows deeper. This is what it means to become intimate. It is this second, inner aspect of the authentic self that takes us further into the positive rewards of this emotional dimension.

Many lovers lose that openness as time passes. What happens to the giddy intimacy of the early days? For some couples, it was never really there, as one partner or the other has always concealed part of him or herself, usually for reasons that may reach back to babyhood. Most men and many women who protect their inner selves learned to do so as a way of hiding from scary, unpredictable people in their early lives. In addition, innumerable women have been taught to change themselves to please others—especially men. These women may lose track of their authentic selves. They may really not have much sense of who's in there.

In many relationships, the partners start out telling each other everything, but have clammed up because they fear that the truth will be disregarded or lead to an argument. Or they may become so overwhelmed by the demands of daily life that they've gradually stopped talking about anything other than what needs to get done.

In truly intimate relationships, the deepest well of intimacy stays full without words, perhaps because we have shared so much over so many years with deep conversations. Now, we do not even need to talk. We sense our lover's mood. Distraction, contentment, irritation or pleasure all show up on our exquisitely sensitive radar. We may often know what our partner is about to say. We say, "You know, I was just thinking about…," only to have our partner exclaim, "That's exactly what I was thinking!" It seems magical, this blending of minds, and perhaps it is, since there is sweet satisfaction in being so emotionally close, so validated in this Intimate dimension.

You can imagine the flip side of unrestricted truth, self-revelation, and deep understanding—betrayal. For some couples, an affair has ripped the fabric of trust in a terribly painful way. One partner feels betrayed and bewildered and unable to believe anything the other says; the other feels permanently guilty, defensive, and beaten up. We have learned, though, to look deeper than *who wronged whom*. Often an affair is as much the product of silence as the source of it. Most people who stray are, at some level, looking for intimacy their marriage doesn't provide—more than sex, they want *to be known*. This is the truth lurking behind that awful old cliché, "My wife doesn't understand me."

Affairs are never okay, of course, but often they do break through the hard, dry surface of relationships that are quietly dying from lack of communication. For couples whose love is still there, the shock of betrayal may be an opportunity for renewal. We believe that marriages can survive the revelation of an affair if the Heart dimension remains strong. However, betrayal causes such deep wounds that couples who want to heal must seek help from an objective, compassionate third party. The feelings that an affair brings to the surface are too intense to work though independently. Whether a couple wants to rebuild or call it quits after the revelation of an affair, *both* partners need counseling.

If the positive pole of the intimacy dimension is trust, and the negative end is betrayal, then the static zone is withholding. Not speaking to one another is the extreme form of withholding, and there are a few fantastically miserable couples who only communicate through the children. But many more maintain a civil façade while giving nothing away. This type of withholding is an insidious relationship-wrecker. If we don't keep watch, it can easily develop from one angry episode into a habit, or even a competition: "You want to shut me out, huh? I'll show you what shutting out really means!" This is how two people, who once felt that they knew one another, completely transform themselves into unhappily married strangers. To avoid this pitfall, you both have to be committed not only to telling the whole truth and nothing but the truth, but also to finding the time for sharing this truth.

The most inspiring truths are our hopes, dreams, and visions for the most passionate life possible, and exchanging this is what we need to make time for—our ultimate, profound potential, because this is what we find erotic in one another; this is the turn-on, this is vitality and purpose. We want to make love to this potent person, to the genuine being, and we deepen our knowledge with the sexual exchange—discovering ever more of their unveiled self through pillow talk and love whispers.

THE AESTHETIC DIMENSION

With the last two dimensions, the Aesthetic and the Ecstatic, we're approaching the ultimate payoff—sexual nirvana. All the work of throwing out the misconceptions and destructive patterns and inhibitions that limit the first five dimensions is necessary to get here, but it's not enough to reach the heights of transformative sex. You can have great sex without anything going on in these, the spiritual dimensions, but you're not going to be able to reliably achieve magnificent, soul-shaking sex. Most of us have had sexual experiences that touched every nerve and emotion, that left us feeling like we'd discovered a new erotic continent, but we usually don't know exactly how it happened, or *why* those particular times were so fantastic. Most of us don't have a clue about how to make that lovely thing happen again, so we're stuck with the memory of what it was like, and the hope that at some time lightning will strike again.

The spiritual dimensions are the key to making that kind of sex a dependable part of life. Great sex requires that the first five dimensions are energized, but really spectacular lovemaking involves body, heart, *and* soul.

"Soul" is a word that we Westerners often find a bit embarrassing, and when someone brings it up in the context of sex... well... there's no need to stick with "soul" if it makes you nervous—what we're talking about is spirit, essence, inner radiance, the continuity of being that carries us intact, and growing through life. The soul is the pattern expressed in our lives; it's what lives in the minds of our loved ones after we die. It's the part that makes us feel our oneness with all that exists. If you are a religious person, you may think of the soul as that which longs for God.

When you and your partner are giving and receiving the energy of the first five dimensions, sex is good, satisfying, even great. But when you learn to bring that inner radiance to making love, sex is more than just great. It's magnificent.

The Aesthetic dimension is all about beauty, and, at its deepest level, the positive pole is awe in the presence of radiance. The awe we feel standing silently in nature at dawn, listening to transcendent music, touching the face of a child— that is the soul responding to beauty.

But, let's start with the first, outer level of the positive Aesthetic dimension, which is attentiveness to beauty—something that surrounds us every day. You might call your lover's attention to a crystalline blue sky as you both walk out the door, you may devote loving effort to making your bedroom beautiful, or you might share an evening at the ballet. Such human grace and powerful movement is beautiful—and erotic. Being aware of beauty is a turn-on because it heightens our connection to our world and ultimately to our lover.

Next, you need to include your self and your partner in your inner experience of beauty. The skill here is awakening the radiance and beauty in our beloved. It's easy and just plain fun to beam a giant smile at your honey and watch him (or her) light up—as if we had just charged the batteries! It is infectious, fun, and beautiful. A bigger challenge is to claim your own beauty. Being looked at during sex, even by our trusted lover, can be quite intimidating. Allowing your partner to bask in the radiance of your sexual arousal is an enormous gift.

Finally, the most potent positive feature of the Aesthetic is the transformation that takes place when meaning cleaves to gratitude—when your soul thanks this beautiful being for making love to you. At the same time, of course, you are probably aware that your beloved is filled with gratitude for your existence. At this point, both have entered rarefied space where the Aesthetic becomes powerfully sexual. When partners perceive the radiance in one another, their relationship soars to extraordinary heights. In short, when we put away distractions and see through the surface and into the unchanging beauty of the soul, we can begin to feel the sacredness of sex.

All this sounds very ethereal, no doubt. But just as with the more mundane aspects of sexual plenitude, you don't have to sit around *wishing* that this dimension were available to you. You can take clear, definite steps to strengthen the Aesthetic in your life, and we'll show you what they are.

The negative pole of the Aesthetic is shame. Shame is the dark side of seeing and being seen, and it's an unending source of human unhappiness. It begins to develop as soon as we realize that we are observed, judged, and found wanting. As little children we cannot hide from the judgments of our parents, so we take them into ourselves. If our elders often seem disappointed in us, we begin to save them the trouble of telling us so by becoming our own most vigilant critics. We work hard at intercepting anything that could expose us to humiliation, and put a lot of effort into concealing big chunks of our selves. Our sexual selves, of course, are often what we are most anxious to keep from view.

Everyone is susceptible to shame, but cultural and religious attitudes about sex, the body and desire usually have greater impact on women than men. Girls start getting the message very young—don't touch yourself, genitals must be sanitized, don't ever let someone kiss you there. There's nothing really sinister in this—the structure of society has always rested on women's willingness to follow the rules, and acculturation begins at birth.

In addition, our culture is crazily fixated on the image of a certain type of young woman, an obsession that gives another twist to women's anxieties. *My looks aren't perfect and I'm getting older every day. That's obviously unattractive and certainly not sexually appealing. Must hide everything!* Among the most precious gifts deadened by shame are radiance and freedom of sexual expression.

This whole business of personal, physical shame is foreign to most men—that's why they sometimes hurt women's feelings with quite innocent remarks. "You're right. You don't look as fat in that dress as in the red one." (It's usually young men who make this classic mistake, and they quickly grow cautious about such conversations.)

The reason they put their foot in it is that their ideas about beauty and sex are quite different from women's. Take a guy who's stopped working out and developed a belly in the last couple years. He may want to lose the weight—he may even be quite self-conscious and unhappy about the bulge. But does he think that he doesn't *deserve* to enjoy sex because he's gained ten pounds? No.

We have encountered the occasional man who requires his woman to be physically perfect, and threatens her with abandonment if she fails to meet his exacting standards. This shallow position betrays a narcissistic disregard for the value of the radiant aesthetic connection; both partners lose. The criticizer is never satisfied, and the one being judged is wounded, and hides her inner beauty.

But the typical man, in our experience, does not look at the woman he loves with the eye of a judge at a beauty contest—although she may be convinced that he does. We cannot estimate the number of times we've witnessed the following exchange in counseling sessions:

Him: (tenderly) I think you're beautiful. I love the way you look.
Her: (indignant) No you don't!

Many women are so critical of their appearance that they refuse to consider the possibility that their lovers see them as alluring sexual goddesses. And yet it's when lovers experience each other—and themselves—as vessels of erotic radiance that sex unleashes all its power to heal and bring delight to living. Even a glimpse of the divine can inspire us to identify the origins of shame and begin to root them out.

The burnt-out zone of the Aesthetic dimension is blindness. Blindness can develop from a number of sources. Usually, it stems from the habit of inattention to beauty; there is so much to *do* each day. We are not necessarily hypercritical or judgmental of our partner or our self—we just have the blindfolds of everyday business on. We have our lists, our family obligations, and even our usual sex. You know the kind: same bed, same person, same positions, and definitely the same uninspiring experience. We forget to really look at our partner when we kiss them, we underestimate the power we have to awaken their glow, we ignore chances to amp up the smile, and then we wonder why we are bored. The trap of this dimension is so universal many couples feel strange or even a bit suspicious when their mate notices their deep attractiveness. Their first reaction is likely to be suspicion: "What does he (or she) want now?"

The way to a radiant sensual connection lies through the doorway of self-acceptance of our grace and beauty as part of the human race. When we accept ourselves and our lover in all our imperfection *and* in all our essential beauty, we create a secret garden for two, a place where shame falls away and beauty reigns. This is the place where ecstatic sex happens.

THE ECSTATIC DIMENSION

Ecstatic, transcendent, gone-to-heaven sex is the realm of the final dimension. Here we venture beyond the merely human and connect with universal divine energy. This is not as rare or as impossible as it sounds. In fact, most lovers have experienced sexual ecstasy sometime in their lives. The tremendous surge of energy we feel is so unexpected, it seems like magic, a stroke of grace: "Where did *that* come from? Did you feel it too?!" We tend to attribute it to circumstance: the romantic setting, the wine, the stars in perfect alignment, whatever. But the truth is that you can create Ecstatic sexual experiences: repeatedly, reliably, and as part of an otherwise prosaic, everyday life.

Once you and your partner have established an open exchange of energy in the first six dimensions, you need just two things to make your sexual connection sacred and transformative. One is the simple belief that such a connection is possible and worth creating. The second is an advanced technology of sex. Fortunately, this technology has existed for at least three thousand years. The discipline known as Tantra developed in classical India as one of the eight traditional yogic paths to enlightenment. All the practices of yoga, which literally means *union*, promote the spiritual evolution and integration of the individual. Tantra is the branch of yoga that includes sexual ritual, considered sacred physical practice, and its aim is to unite and balance the energies of male and female through perfected sex. The basic text of Tantra is the *Kama Sutra,* which you've probably heard mentioned as a sort of exotic sex manual. Interestingly, it was developed specifically as a practice for the common man and woman—people who didn't choose to retire from daily life to seek enlightenment. It is the most egalitarian branch of yoga, and an explicitly feminist one—in Tantra, the woman is the eternal source of life energy, and her partner must appreciate her as such.

Tantra is not about feats of sexual prowess, but rather about the generation and release of sacred energy for the good of the universe. And what's good for all living things is bound to be good for us. In the fullness of transcendent sex, we awaken the Divine within our lover, sense that radiance within ourselves, and gratefully exchange our energies. Sexual connection becomes profoundly healing as we bathe in the stream of loving energy that flows through the world. Happily, having incredible sex is how you make all these good things happen.

As we consider the three levels of the positive domain of Ecstatic sex, we need to outwardly accept the sacred nature of sexual connection and be willing to participate in activities that not only allow but enhance spiritual fusion. We have already taught you soulgazing, our favorite way to enter the spiritual zone, and invite you to consider other daily habits and rituals that make Ecstatic sex accessible. The inner work, on the other hand, is not about structure, but about release. Letting go of boundaries, being willing to merge, and turning a deaf ear to the warnings of the ego, which wants to maintain separateness above all, are all tasks to be accomplished before we can enter the sweet space of Ecstatic sex. We may know, believe, and even cry out for this sexual bliss, but unless we are ready to surrender the safety of being two, we will not enjoy the exhilarating expansion of becoming one.

Yet, there is an even deeper level to sex in this dimension: it is the conscious decision to make love to the sacred being who resides in your partner. Here, you see God in your mate, that part of the Divine that exists in each one of us, and you honor your beloved with a wide-open being—heart, soul, skin, pelvis. In this beautiful connection the vagina really is the Sanskrit yoni or sacred space, and the penis truly is a lingam, or wand of light. And it isn't only Eastern religions that teach that sex is sacred. The lyrical Songs of Solomon eloquently express it:

"Kiss me—full on the mouth!
Yes! For your love is better than wine,
Headier than your aromatic oils"
Song 1:2-3

And the Sufi poet Rumi:

"Gamble everything for love,
If you're a true human being.
If not, leave this gathering.
Half-heartedness doesn't reach into majesty.
You set out to find God,
But then you keep stopping for long periods
At mean-spirited roadhouses.
Don't wait any longer,
Dive in the ocean."
The Illuminated Rumi, p 58-9

So the positive pole of the Ecstatic dimension is the sacred. The negative pole is the profane—the belief that sex is, at best, worldly rather than heavenly, and at worst, the work of the devil. The Puritanical tradition in our culture is that sex is shameful, sinful, a temptation that leads us astray from the good and righteous life. While few people nowadays subscribe to such a negative view of sexuality, it remains a heavy undercurrent, coexisting uneasily and ambiguously with the overtly sexual imagery that saturates popular culture. Sadly, neither of these currents evokes the sacred feeling so crucial to energizing this dimension.

In fact, most of us are stuck in the middle space, between heaven and hell, if you will, in a purgatory where disbelief in the sacred power of sex allows no sexual energy to flow to the crown chakra, or where the conflict between sacred and profane, soul and ego, chokes off this energy. We need to discard these limiting beliefs and embrace a higher view of sexuality if we are to tap into the vast power of the Ecstatic dimension. This may sound like an overwhelmingly difficult or implausible task. Yet we have found that it is easily within reach of most of the ordinary couples we have taught. It is easy because the soul yearns for it. A few simple exercises, which we will soon share with you, will give you a glimpse of this realm and whet your appetite for further exploration. Ultimately, there is no limit to the flow of energy that is possible in the Ecstatic dimension of sex.

LOVE IN SEVEN DIMENSIONS

This morning we introduced you to a new and exhilarating view of sex—as a source of energy and a living connection to the divine. Just understanding that can change your life. Sex as a sacred act is a powerfully liberating idea.

This afternoon, you've learned to assess your sexual strengths and understand the likely roots of your weaknesses. We have introduced the paradigm that we, as doctors and therapists, have used successfully for years.

You now have the means to begin exploring the limitless realms of pleasure and joy, so here's your first homework assignment. We strongly advise you to do every exercise we assign—they've helped hundreds of "stuck" couples rediscover the power that once made their relationships so exciting. Remember, nothing's more about *doing* than sex.

EVENING

You've taken inventory of your sex life, identified all the ways in which you may be sabotaging your sexual energy, and explored all the ways in which you may enhance it. Pause now to freshen up—take a shower together, wash each other's hair, relax in the hot tub.

When you're refreshed and ready, slip into something that brings out the Shiva and the Shakti in you. Spread a blanket on the bed or the floor, light the candles, and put on some mood music. Get out that picnic basket and feed each other with your fingers. Have fun, play, and tune into each other's sexual energy. With Shiva and Shakti in the house, this could be one of the most sensual meals of your life. When you start licking each other's fingers, stop—and learn to kiss like you've never kissed before.

KISSING: A FELDENKRAIS® LESSON ☺5

This exercise is not meant to teach you how to kiss. You already *know* how to do that. But actually, our long experience with our bodies is part of the problem—not just with kissing, but with almost everything we do. When we already know how to do something, it's hard to learn how to do it better.

This lesson is designed to help you sense yourself better, and to develop sensitivity that will lead to a different kind of experience when you kiss. This new awareness will awaken you to new possibilities that can become part of your repertoire—or not, as you choose.

Begin by kissing your partner in your usual way, whatever that is. Take your time. What do you notice about it? What kinds of sensations come to your attention? Are you aware of your own lips, or is it more your partner's lips that you notice? Do you sense only your lips/mouth/tongue, or are there other parts of you (or your partner) that enter your awareness? Observe the quality of the sensations (softness vs. firmness, warmth vs. coolness, wetness vs. dryness, etc.). Then separate, so each of you can do the next part on your own.

Close your eyes and take a moment to sense the area of your mouth and lips. How big does your mouth feel? How full are your lips? How much space do they take up? Do they feel relaxed, or a little tight? Do they turn in or out? Don't try to change them, just notice what they're like right now.

Then begin to push your lips forward a little in a puckering-up movement, and allow them to come back to the resting position, repeating a number of times. Make this pushing movement very soft and slow, and make the return movement just as gentle. Don't make the movement as big as you can make it; rather, do a lot less than you're capable of. Keeping the motion small and slow will help you sense what you're doing a lot better. You may be surprised to find that it's not so easy to make a small, slow movement of your lips like this—they may tend to quiver and twitch a bit instead of moving smoothly and evenly. That's okay—just reduce your effort even more, make it smaller and slower, and be patient. The quality will improve naturally as we proceed.

Take a rest for a moment, and do nothing special.

Now gently take hold of your lower lip with the thumb and index finger of each hand. Use as little grip pressure as you can while still keeping hold of the lower lip. Then begin gently to pull the lip forward, turning it slightly inside out, and then let it return to its resting position, still keeping the same light hold. Repeat this many times, not *stretching* the lower lip but gently *coaxing* it forward, using as little force as possible. Notice the elasticity of the tissue as it returns to its resting position. You might slightly change the position of your grasp and see how that affects how the movement feels.

Eventually, let go of the lower lip, and grasp the upper lip in the same way, and repeat: Gently coax it forward, turning it a little inside out, the way you might move it for kissing, but using the muscles in your fingers, hands, and arms to supply the slight force needed, rather than the muscles of the lips and mouth and face. Let your face relax completely—this will help make the movement as soft as possible.

Now let go of the upper lip, and rest for a bit. Then, when you're ready, go back to pushing the lips forward in a gentle kissing movement again. Do you notice that it feels different now? Is the movement smoother and more even? Do the lips go farther forward with less effort?

Stop making the kissing movement, and just sense the feeling around the mouth and lips again. What's changed? Do the lips feel softer and fuller? Does your mouth feel bigger?

Now turn to your partner and kiss him or her again. How is this different from the beginning? Have your lips changed, or have your partner's, or both? *What* changed? Was it the lips themselves, or was it your ability to sense with your lips, or both?

This simple exercise demonstrates how much tension we unconsciously hold in our lips and mouth, and how to let go of that habitual tension quickly, using a procedure that improves body awareness. The type of process we just went through can be usefully extended to virtually every other area of movement and function: We are all governed by habits that we've acquired over time, habits that keep us from discovering new things. We'll return to this kind of learning for another lesson or two later in the course. For now, just enjoy the new feeling in your mouth and lips, and put it to good use!

Time now to open your hearts to one another, in an exercise that can deepen your lovemaking literally overnight.

OPEN HEART EXERCISE ⊙6

The electromagnetic energy of the heart—the strongest created within the human body—can be measured from ten feet away. This means that we are very often within the "heart field" of other people, and certainly within that of our lover. In fact, researchers have documented the pattern of one individual's EKG or heart electrical activity in another person's EEG or brain waves when they are sitting near each other!

The purpose of this exercise is to access the energetic state of the heart when it is in the calm—parasympathetic—condition. In this state, there is a gradual, rhythmical increase and decrease of the heart rate that is healthy for all body systems and organs, including the brain. In addition, when we have developed the ability to be in the calm, parasympathetic state, we are better thinkers, problem solvers, lovers, and we are not flooding our bodies with the stress chemicals adrenaline and cortisol, the messengers of the sympathetic nervous system. Most of us unconsciously abuse these incredibly powerful substances, which were actually meant for emergency use only, for fighting or running for one's very life. Learning to produce the heart's parsympathetic condition of relaxation, open-heartedness, and appreciation is necessary for achieving magnificent sex... and is a wonderful tool for life.

Sit down in a comfortable chair, or on the floor with some back support. Close your eyes. Now begin to think of a person and situation that upsets you, that makes you mad or scared, or that makes your blood boil with fury. Picture the scene in detail. See the person's face, the room, the position of the people or objects in the space—really be there. Then notice where in your body—right now, sitting there—you feel the anger, frustration, or fear. Is it in your stomach, your chest, your jaw, your arms or legs? Does it feel tight, or heavy, or burning? Let yourself fully *experience* unpleasant sensations that may actually be quite familiar to you.

Okay, now let that go, take a few deep breaths, and switch the image to something you deeply appreciate: Your dog, your grandmother's front porch, your grandchild, your garden, the image of a beautiful sunset. It can be anything you love in an uncomplicated way. Again, experience this mental image fully, with all the details. Go inside the scene. How does the sky look? Are there any smells? Notice the light in the room or outside. Do you hear any sounds? Now focus your attention on the sensations in your body, and especially in your chest. Can you feel the physical shift between the angry and appreciative images? Notice how your heart feels to you now. Is it larger, softer, beating more calmly, more vividly colored?

Now find your partner, face each other (sitting or standing), and hold hands. One of you will go first being the sender. That person is going to call up the image of the angry, fearful, or deeply irritating situation. Can you *feel* the emotion in your lover's body? What do you notice about your partner's face, torso, arms and/or body in general? What about your connection through the palms of your hands—can you feel anything there? Now ask your honey to recall the appreciative, loving image. After a few seconds, can you tell the difference? How?

Practice Makes Perfect

When it comes to an open heart, practice makes perfect. Practice every day, in ordinary situations, being in your open heart space. You could, for example, decide to have lunch, talk to a co-worker, or check out at the supermarket with an open heart. You will notice that other people, especially those in your electromagnetic field, will react to you differently—with much more openness of their own. Notice that the world feels like a warmer, more serene place when your heart is open. It does not hurt to get in a few practice sessions for the times when you really are angry and do not want to have your body swept into the biologically expensive fight-or-flight state. Also, it is important to cultivate the open heart if you want to reap the harvest of making love with a wide-open, freely giving, and receiving body.

Next, it is time to switch, and your turn to remember the angry or loving image in all its detail—but do not tell your partner which image you are going to do first. Do not try to fool your lover or pretend that you are taking a lie detector test. Just let the image you choose fill your mind and body. Can your partner guess which image you are thinking of? Find out what they noticed about your body and the signals you were sending. Now switch and see if that helps them key into the energy radiating from you.

Now it's your partner's turn to do the imagining, and your turn to try to feel the kind of energy that's coming at you. See if your guess about their energy—their state of sympathetic or parasympathetic nervous system dominance—is accurate. Share any observations. Communicating nonverbal states of being may be a bit awkward at first, but it is key to understanding each other and ultimately to being able to change our emotional states and physiology at will.

The reason we have you practice both states of being at first is so that you begin to recognize the difference in your body. Now, you can begin to choose the calmer state by opening your heart using loving images. As we said earlier, when we discussed HeartMath, there is a tremendous amount of research behind these practices and their value for the individual. Now we want to begin using this heart energy to forge a bond between you and your lover. Coupling the open-heart skill with soulgazing is a potent combination and one that can take you deeper into lovemaking almost instantaneously.

It's not too early to start thinking about your Celebration Gift. At the end of the weekend, you will give your partner a token of your love and a pledge to stay committed to the adventure you've begun, but do not start planning a run to the florist. Your gifts must conform to three rules:

1. **They cannot be bought. You each must create or find your offering.**
2. **They must express or symbolize your feelings.**
3. **There must be words involved.**

⌒

THE COUPLES' PROGRESS

Steve and Kate

Steve *loves* the kissing lesson. It becomes very intense for him as he connects strongly to his body and remembers the wonderful times he and

Kate had "making out" before they got to the point of sleeping together. He really notices Kate's lips at the end. How has he not been taking every opportunity to kiss her beautiful mouth?

Kate likes the kissing, too. She's always adored the way Steve feels, and tastes, and smells, and it's fun to just kiss.

She's been thinking a lot about what the doctors said about her closed-up heart, and during the heart imagery exercise she feels it begin to open. It's a long-forgotten sensation, and suddenly she recognizes that down deep she *has* kept it walled it off since her father's death. She shares this realization with Steve afterwards.

Both are intrigued by the gift announcement, and like the challenge of coming up with just the right thing without spending money—especially since they are both committed to saving for their dream-house.

"The best things in life are free, right hon? But I wonder if you'll come up with something as cool as what I'm going to do for you?" Steve's teasing a bit—they've both been feeling pretty bouncy since the kissing lesson.

Charlie and Nicole

Predictably, Charlie is enthusiastic about the kissing lesson—finally they start getting to the good part! He tries—illicitly—to touch Nicole's breasts while they kiss. She slaps his hand away, but does it playfully.

Nicole, on the other hand, thinks the kissing lesson is funny—she laughs but goes through with it and loosens up a little in the process.

When it comes to the Heart Imagery/Heart Opening exercise, Charlie is uncomfortable and starts to fidget.

"This stuff makes me feel ridiculous," he tells Nicole.

"It's part of the deal and you've got to do it," she insists. "Besides, nobody's going to know but me."

"Okay, but only if I get a reward," he says, nuzzling her neck until she irritably shrugs him off. Still, she agrees, and they go back to the Heart Opening exercise. Charlie tries to get it this time.

They have sex right after the exercises. It's mostly their standard routine, but there are some subtle changes: She's less frazzled and more aroused than usual, and she's not as repulsed by Charlie's urgency. He, in turn, is a bit more relaxed and less pushy.

Nicole's first reaction to the gift assignment is that she'd *like* to have Charlie spend some money on her, but then, mulling it over, she decides that she'll be okay with whatever he comes up with. It amuses her to try to imagine what he'll do. As for his gift, she starts mentally going through her luggage, trying to figure out what she can give him.

Charlie is unsure what this gift thing is all about, and begins to worry that he won't do it right. They talk about it while they're lying around after making love.

"Am I supposed to cut out little hearts and make you a Valentine or something?" he asks. "What's the point of that? Anyway, you said you liked that tennis bracelet down in the gift shop."

"Gotta play by the rules this time, big guy," she tells him lightly.

Martin and Linda

Both like the kissing lesson, and both feel their hearts open during the exercise. Martin especially likes the imagery. Afterwards, they compare notes:

"I'm just thinking about how much time I've spent lately not feeling much of anything," Linda says. "Work, the kids, Jacob's arrest... It's been so exhausting for so long."

Martin is still flying high on the flow of good feeling they've just created between them. "It's too much, sweetie. You've been carrying most of it. We've got to fix that—and we've *got* to find time to do this more often."

They go on to talk about the gift assignment. Both think that finding the perfect present around the house sounds like fun, and fun is something they both realize they need.

Bob and Paulette

Bob is clumsy and embarrassed in the kissing lesson—Paulette is so much more graceful than he is, he thinks. He can tell his awkwardness irritates her. Thankfully, he remembered to take some decongestants for his cold and he can breathe again.

Paulette, in turn, recognizes that he's trying, though it's hard for her to be patient with his clumsy kissing. Later, she's surprised by Bob's reaction to the heart imagery—he lets himself go with it much more than either of them would have expected.

"You know what I saw?" he says, still with a faraway look on his face. "I saw little Gracie grinning and waving from the other end of a see-saw, and I had the new baby in my lap and we were all going up and down. I could even smell the little guy's hair—that nice baby smell. So that's what an open heart means, huh?"

Paulette, still acutely aware of the warmth and openness in her chest, stares at him for a moment when he shares this with her—she saw their granddaughter too.

"You know, that's our Intimacy dimension. We do share thoughts," she says. "Sometimes I forget just how close we really are. Right now, it feels like magic to me. Do you feel that way?" Bob, returns her smile and nods as he continues to hold her gaze.

The gift assignment makes Bob feel anxious again. Will he be able to come up with something for Paulette that will satisfy her? Paulette, on the other hand, is sure she'll come up with something grand, but then lets the assignment slip from her mind.

☞

You may have had some of the same reactions as our couples to these assignments—a bit of embarrassment, some awkwardness with kissing or the Heart Opening imagery. And you may be wondering as well what you are going to get for your lover as a gift. At this point, all of those reactions are perfectly normal. Just remember that anything new is by definition different from the way you have been in the past. A completely aware kiss is distinct from your habitual one, practicing the open heart is an activity we rarely consider, and allowing the perfect gift to appear requires patience and trust in your own creativity. However, these exercises are building blocks in the new sexual structure you are creating. Staying with the project will result in a lovely dwelling for you both.

NIGHT

You're in your beautiful private space together. The candles are burning, and the music is playing. You've feasted on finger food, you've kissed like you've never kissed before, you've opened your hearts to one another. Time to retire to your bedchamber, with the blessing of Shakti and Shiva. What you do now is up to you, as long as you do it with open hearts.

Day Two

Pleasuring Her

DAY TWO

SPECIAL INSTRUCTIONS

Men, this is your day to spoil, indulge, and worship your goddess. Make your bedroom an altar to her erotic beauty, and fill it with the things she loves. Think only of her pleasure and strive to please her as you never have before; her body has erotic secrets waiting to be discovered. Take your time and she'll reveal her radiance to you. Remember, what comes around will go around tomorrow, when it's her time to pleasure you.

Women—let your lover cater to your every whim. This is your day, think only of yourself and your own pleasure. Let your man discover the eternal source of his radiance—you!

Suggested Schedule

MORNING:

- Goddesses, sleep in if you like.
- Men, make your preparations to honor your Shakti Goddess.
- Greet each other with Namaste.
- Connect with soulgazing.
- Read *Becoming a Sexual Goddess*, and *Blocking the Radiance: The Three F's* (following).

NOON:

- Enjoy a leisurely lunch.
- Take the *Emotional Sabotage of Your/Her Sexual Energy Quiz* (women's or men's version as appropriate).
- Compare notes and results of the Emotional Sabotage quiz. Explore ways in which you can eliminate the Three F's from your life and enhance the fourth F: *Fusion*.
- Learn to connect with your lover simply and quickly with the *Yab Yum Exercise*.
- Increase the power and intimacy of your connection with the imagery of the *Heart Lingam, Heart Yoni Exercise*.
- Goddess: take a bath while your lover prepares the room for the assignment.

AFTERNOON:

- Do *Awakening the Goddess*: a structured sexual assignment.
- Rest.

EVENING:

- Cuddle up comfortably and talk about the assignment. Practice listening and being vulnerable.
- If it feels right, go for "extra credit" and revisit the assignment—but it's okay just to cuddle if that feels better.

MORNING

- Namaste on awakening
- Soulgazing
- Then dive into the following:

BECOMING A SEXUAL GODDESS

Becoming a sexual goddess, an avatar of Shakti, is not about transcending the physical aspects of life, but about exploring them to their limits. Shakti is not a wispy or ethereal sort of goddess—she's no sparkly lady in a bubble. She *is* gloriously divine and eternal, but above all, she is sexual. The feminine is fully realized only through the body, and it celebrates the material world and its life at every moment. The better you understand the body, the more you will appreciate its design—and the more wonderful things you can do with yours.

VERY BEGINNING ANATOMY: SAMENESS AND DIFFERENCE

Sexual anatomy—like everything about sex—is intriguing. For example, it's a fact of embryology that everybody starts out life looking female. Strange but true. Every embryo looks female before testosterone gets to work in males-to-be and starts transforming the original female structures into male ones. In males, the ovaries become testicles and drop down through the inguinal canal and into the scrotal sac. Sometimes, if that passage stays open, males can end up with hernias. That's why inguinal hernias are common in men and rare in women. Ovaries never go anywhere.

The testicles reside in the scrotum, which, if you've ever gotten up really close to check it, has a seam down the middle. Ever wonder why? It's because the scrotal sac forms from the labia majora, the thick outer "lips" of the vagina, which fuse together in the male fetus.

There are many more interesting male-female genital analogies: The shaft of the penis forms from the labia minora; the thin, smooth inner lips that become plump and dusky as they fill with blood during arousal. This is something like what happens to the penis when it becomes erect, although the penis has evolved some very specialized spongy tissue that expands and firms up when blood is trapped in it. (But we're getting ahead of ourselves. More on erections tomorrow.)

It may be fairly obvious that the clitoris and the tip of the penis are analogous structures that develop from the same tissue. What may not be so obvious is that although the clitoris has just as many nerve endings as the tip of the penis, and is therefore exquisitely sensitive (these nerve endings are packed into a much smaller area), it often doesn't get the attention it deserves. If you think about the mechanics of plain old intercourse, you'll understand why men tend to be more enthusiastic about it than women. Just in and out, in and out, gives the tip of the penis plenty of stimulation. In the meantime, though, the clitoris is off above all of the action saying, "Uh...hello?" Most women—although this depends on individual anatomy, which varies greatly—do not get much clitoral stimulation during intercourse. They certainly don't get to enjoy the intense, direct stimulation their partner's penis gets. So you can see why sixty-five to eighty-five percent of all women need direct clitoral stimulation to be orgasmic. It's simple anatomy.

Then there's the G-spot. Though it's not a clear-cut, anatomically dissectable organ, it is not, as some skeptical medical men have claimed, a myth. This erotically sensitive area on the roof of the vagina, about an inch and a half inside, has long been identified in the Tantric tradition, and called the *Sacred Spot*. It responds to stroking by swelling and developing a ruffled texture that's different from that of the rest of the vagina. There is good reason to think that the G-spot corresponds

---

This Bears Repeating

Sixty-five to eighty-five percent of all women need direct clitoral stimulation to be orgasmic.

The Secret to Sacred Spot Stimulation

Gentle, patient stimulation of the Sacred Spot produces a very different sort of erotic sensation than clitoral stimulation. It's often more deeply satisfying and diffuse, rather than exciting and focused—more yin than yang. It is definitely worth exploring manually during lovemaking because of the distinctive quality of energy it evokes. However, intense stimulation of the Sacred Spot may be uncomfortable at first, especially for women who haven't been touched there before. For couples who want to explore G-spot stimulation, we recommend that the man use his non-dominant hand, a very gentle touch, and a curious, exploratory approach. It is also helpful to remember that many women require some clitoral stimulation first, to increase their level of arousal before Sacred Spot massage will feel good.

to the prostate in the male. The G-spot, like the prostate, sits at the base of the bladder around the urethra, just where the "legs" of the clitoris (and the erectile bodies of the penis) end. And in the female, there is vestigial glandular tissue around the urethra that is embryologically the same as the prostate.

We have found that many couples neglect the art of manual stimulation of the yoni, thinking of it as an immature way to relate sexually, something teenagers have to settle for before they can really "do it." These mature lovers unwittingly give up stimulation of an important erogenous zone that many women find deeply satisfying.

For some women, Sacred Spot stimulation, if it's continued long enough, leads to female ejaculation, the pleasurable release of a special fluid from the urethra called "amrita," or honey, in Tantra—and it's not urine!

⤳

"I'll be damned! Paulette, listen to this." Bob read her the passage about female ejaculation. "You know that time you thought you lost control of your bladder when you were really, you know... excited? I bet that was this... what do they call it?... 'amrita'."

Paulette blushed. She remembered the episode well. They had been making love in a position unusual for them, with her on top and leaning back a little. This was back before Bob had started having any problems with his erections, and she recalled how totally aroused and … *powerful* she had felt at the time. And then all this watery fluid had come out of her and all over Bob and the bed. She'd been mortified, and quickly lost all of her excitement. Bob had taken it really well. In fact, rather than showing disgust, he had seemed…well, more *awed* by it than anything, which still didn't make any sense to her. However, she never tried that position again for fear of "peeing."

Paulette felt her old shame turn to curiosity. "Maybe I really ejaculated," she thought. "That certainly puts another light on that episode."

Women who have ejaculated but are unaware of the phenomenon are likely to think that they've somehow urinated. Naturally they might feel embarrassed and inhibited about such a loss of control. But just because female ejaculate comes out of the urethra, this does not necessarily imply that it is urine, any more than semen is. It's been shown that the fluid that females ejaculate contains acid phosphatase, an enzyme that's absent from urine and has been thought to be produced exclusively in the male prostate. The conclusion is that amrita is produced by those periurethral glands that are the female counterpart to the prostate.

Think of ejaculation as something quite special, and certainly not as something to worry about. Women who are concerned about this liquid messing up their partner or the bed can just put a beach towel down before starting to make love, which is a good idea anyway. Stains and wet spots from massage oils, lubricants, whatever, tend to be really distracting for women: "Oh, lord, now I have to get up and change the sheets," or "The housekeeping staff will know what we were doing!" We suggest buying a stack of cheap towels and having them in your nightstand or closet and always spreading one out before you begin. No more fretting about the linens as you engage in erotic play.

The Amrita Blessing

In the East, the spurt of amrita is welcomed as a great blessing, as it indicates a particularly intense release of pure feminine Shakti. Often there's also a feeling of bearing down with it, as if you're trying to turn the vagina inside out. It's almost like a re-creation in miniature of childbirth, complete with the water breaking: a very powerful feminine experience!

THE FOUR STAGES OF THE FEMALE SEXUAL RESPONSE CYCLE

Only in the last fifty years have scientists identified stages of female arousal that correspond to the much more obvious stages men experience. William Masters and Virginia Johnson were the researchers who contributed the most to our scientific understanding of sexual physiology. They identified four stages in the sexual response cycle, for both men and women: arousal, plateau, orgasm, and resolution. (Later, others pointed out the importance of adding another stage at the beginning: desire, which obviously needs to be there in at least one partner for the sexual connection to progress.)

Arousal

The first stage beyond desire is arousal. In men this is marked by erection, which is about as obvious as you can get. But in women, the hallmark of arousal is lubrication of the vagina, which is a good bit subtler than erection; so much so that women are often not adequately aware of their own state of arousal, and correspondingly, their readiness for intercourse. In our culture at least, it tends to take women longer to lubricate than it does for males to get an erection. It's fairly common for the guy to have an erection even before actual physical contact has begun; maybe he's been walking around the bedroom showing it off, while his gal is just beginning to be mentally ready to connect sexually and isn't even really lubricated. This common discrepancy in arousal curves creates many possibilities for mutual misunderstanding (and, of course is the basis for lots of jokes about foreplay). But, it's not that she wants sex less; it just takes her longer to be ready for it. Instead of fighting this phenomenon, it is best to avoid judgment and consider that men are like microwaves, women are crockpot cookers. In any case, one of the major complaints we hear from women is, "It takes me a long time and he's already there...boom...and so I begin to worry that he wants to come inside me before I'm ready." She knows that she is not yet adequately aroused: there's not enough fluid secreting through the walls of the vagina, and penetration will be unpleasant—and maybe even unhealthy—for her because of excessive friction.

Is this a cultural or an innate difference? Probably, it's primarily cultural. Women actually are physically quite capable of becoming lubricated as quickly as, or even more quickly than, their partners can become erect. Just ask a woman who's into reading steamy romance novels what happens when she gets to "the good parts!" But, it may be a very different thing for a woman in the context of sexual interaction with a man, given all the societal prohibitions about sex and about their own bodies that burden women growing up in our culture. Whatever the cause of the discrepancy in arousal times, it's important to understand that the female partner needs to be at more or less the same place physiologically as the male before progressing further with intercourse. More kissing, more breast stimulation, more clitoral stimulation, more wonderful erotic whisperings: whatever it takes to make the physical response occur. That is what's essential for synchronization of the arousal stage.

Plateau

The plateau stage is that highly pleasurable time between becoming aroused and reaching orgasm. The labia are swollen and darker because the tissues have become engorged. Heartbeat and respiratory rate are faster, lubrication is sustained by all the blood that has come flooding down into the pelvis, and basically, you're at a very high level of arousal. We feel that it is a shame that couples tend to hurry through the plateau stage: It is delightful to linger here. Both sexes can ride this stage for a long time if stimulation continues and urgency to reach the goal (orgasm) can take a back seat to just relaxing into, and hanging out in this steady state of intense arousal. (The skill of male ejaculatory control, and the lack of it—known as premature ejaculation—are certainly relevant here.) For the woman, the plateau period allows her yoni to elongate and balloon at the upper end: she really has an inverse erection that can then accommodate the lingam without discomfort. In fact, the ligaments that support the entire uterus shorten and lift the cervical tip of the uterus up and out of the way so that it does not get rammed by the lingam during intercourse. Clever Mother Nature has made intercourse easier by these pelvic changes, so do not hurry through the plateau stage.

Orgasm

When Masters and Johnson published their scientific results back in the late sixties, the female orgasm really "came out of the closet." They wanted to make the study of sex scientifically respectable, and focused on collecting hard data that no one had dared to get before. They took sex into the laboratory, where they rigged up all kinds of measurement devices, including plastic penises with internal cameras and pressure transducers. Orgasm became a phenomenon defined in terms of things they could measure: vaginal blood flow, volume, and rate of lubrication; number, strength, and location of contractions. What they found was that orgasm in a female was consistently characterized by contractions of the top third of the vagina and the uterus every 0.8 seconds. Although they were certainly aware of subjective differences in the orgasmic experience of women, Masters and Johnson were struck by how similar all orgasms are physically, and this is what they emphasized in their reports—to the point of establishing it as dogma:

Orgasm *is* this pattern of contractions, no matter what the person having it says is happening to her.

Now, there are plenty of women who are aware of this contraction pattern and identify it with orgasm. But women's experience of orgasm varies *a lot*. Many women, offered the Masters and Johnson definition, will look puzzled and say, "When *I* have an orgasm, I am somewhere else...my mind leaves my body." They are not aware that these contractions take place; but it's likely that they do register at an unconscious level. Some women who've had a hysterectomy miss feeling the uterine contractions because the womb is simply not there anymore. Others, however, say that their pelvis felt so heavy and painful before the surgery that sex is much more enjoyable afterwards, and of course they are still capable of orgasm even without a uterus. It is not uncommon for women to feel uterine contractions that are pleasurable during nursing, although most women do not classify these as "having an orgasm."

Along with the pelvic contractions comes that very pleasurable mental state of release followed by a sense of satisfaction. The brain is certainly involved in orgasm; many pleasure chemicals such as endorphins, enkephalins, and oxytocin are released, which makes orgasm a whole body experience. (Some of Lana's patients have reported being orgasmic at the moment of childbirth, which actually makes sense from this neuroendocrine perspective: all those hormones are flowing very strongly at that moment.) The pleasure chemicals are thought to play a very important role in emotional bonding, both between mother and child and between mates.

⌒

Nicole laughed out loud as she read this last part.

"What's so funny?" asked Charlie, taking off the headphones he was using to listen to the sports reports on the radio.

"They say some women actually have an orgasm at the time of delivery!"

"Well, pizza *is* pretty good, but I wouldn't say really *orgasmic*..."

She laughed again, and Charlie realized he hadn't seen her laugh much lately. He missed it.

"No, silly," she said. "Delivering a baby! I guess I was about as far from orgasm as you can get when I had our babies. Not that I would really know..."

Charlie's smile suddenly disappeared. "What do you mean, you wouldn't know?"

Nicole suddenly realized that she was in deeper than she had intended. "Well Sweetie, it is hard for me to come, you know that."

"Yeah, but when we were first going out, you used to, didn't you?" he persisted.

"I think maybe I did once or twice, but sometimes I was so embarrassed that it was taking me so long and you were so eager for me to come, that I just kind-of... sort-of... well, I just pretended." *There*, Nicole thought, *I said it*; something that I have kept from him for so many years.

Charlie was quiet. "Honey," he said after a while, "we have to fix that. No wonder you aren't all that hot to jump into bed. I thought that at least *some* of the time you were getting off." He reached for the book. "I bet there are things in here for me to do for you."

Nicole cringed. She knew Charlie loved a challenge, but she wasn't at all sure she wanted her orgasms to be his goal. On the other hand, she did want to have them, and she had been very close many times. That much she knew.

❧

At the other end of the spectrum from Nicole are women who have been orgasmic since early childhood, when both their hormone levels and interest in sex were just as submerged as those of other children. For example, it's not unusual to hear from women that they discovered playground orgasms in grade school, sliding up and down the fireman's pole. Some females' stimulation-orgasm "circuits" seem to work more easily and freely than most. If we could figure out what the difference is, we might be able to help less responsive women.

Then there are the women who will tell you they do not know for certain whether they have orgasms. To men, and many easily orgasmic women, this may seem incredible. "How could she *not* know?" But, some women really are not familiar with the sensation, or they haven't identified what they've felt as being an orgasm. They may need to actually *learn* to be orgasmic. And just about all women, if you ask them, will say that they have experienced big ones and little ones. So the whole thing is not nearly as clear as male orgasm, which happens—or doesn't—in a way that's obvious to just about everyone. (Although, as you will see, there is a good bit more to learn about the male orgasm that will make this distinction between men and women a lot less obvious.)

There's also a whole tangle about women faking orgasms and how can they ever stop doing that since that would *really* hurt his feelings? Most women who'd like to have better sex and be more open feel that this is a unique fix they're in. Let us tell you—it is anything but. There's probably not a woman who's never faked orgasm. And why? Not for herself—you can bet on that. She faked it for her partner. What her partner really wants, though, is not a wonderful theatrical performance, but her genuine pleasure. He wants the satisfaction and joy and security of knowing that he has done for her what she does for him. One of the best things this book can do for you is to free you both up to ask, "Okay, that worked in the past, but what do you really enjoy right now?" Asking is one of the best things you can do for your relationship. Honest communication flows both ways, and it will begin to open up other important areas of life that you may not have even realized you've kept closed to discussion.

Resolution

The last phase of female arousal, which really just means the time period when everything returns physiologically to baseline, is called resolution. Breathing, heartbeat, blood flow to the pelvis all slow. The nipples soften, and the sexual flush on the chest fades. Of course, the resolution stages in men and women are different in one important way: In women, resolution doesn't lead to a refractory period as it does in men. Women simply do not have an "in-between time" when they are not physically able to have intercourse. In fact, after an orgasm, a woman remains physically responsive, able to return to plateau phase, and then, if stimulation continues, have another orgasm... and another... and another....

≈

Kate broke off in the middle of reading this section to Steve. "You wouldn't believe all the discussions we used to have at the sorority house about orgasms: clitoral orgasms, vaginal orgasms, multiple orgasms... you name it. I wonder—are there really two different kinds of muscular/vascular events, or does the same thing feel different at different times, or for different people? And what about multiple orgasm? That sounds interesting!"

≈

There's no simple answer to Kate's questions. As we said above, Masters and Johnson asserted that all orgasms are identical. In terms of contractions of the vagina and uterus, we suspect that this is probably true. However, there is no question that the subjective experience of orgasm can vary tremendously for any given woman, and much of the variation seems to be due to the predominant type of stimulation that leads to it. We talked earlier about the different qualities of sensation between clitoral versus Sacred Spot stimulation: yang versus yin. The same sort of distinction holds for clitoral versus vaginal orgasm. When women describe clitoral orgasm, it's usually as a very intense, piercing, focused event that is very much centered in the genitals. The orgasm that comes with stimulation of the Sacred Spot (which is what is really happening with a "vaginal" orgasm) is, by contrast, a more total-body experience, and feels more melting—like letting go of, or even leaving the body. A lot of people cleverly and skillfully blend these two kinds of orgasm by having intercourse in positions that permit both kinds of stimulation to happen at once. For example, the guy is coming in from behind, so the head of the lingam is right on the Sacred Spot, while she touches her clitoris.

As for multiple orgasm, it's true that women are physically capable of having orgasm after orgasm—until they "beg for mercy." But some women don't want to do that. Their genitals are so sensitive right after an orgasm that they can't stand to have them touched, and instead of resting, they simply stop. Resting for a bit is an alternative, though. If you have in your mind that your clitoris or your G spot is too sensitive to be touched right after an orgasm, and you think you might want to be a bit more multi-orgasmic, you might want to consider that everything is not over—that you are merely *resting* without stopping. Your partner can touch your thighs, or breasts, or feet, or stroke your hair, or kiss you so that you're still stimulated while your pelvis recovers a little. Then, you can try starting more direct stimulation again. It's worth experimenting with prolonging your sexual experience. Of course, all this presumes that your partner is still involved; if he's already ejaculated, chances are he's already sawing logs. So part of *her* exploring her potential for multi-orgasm may involve *his* exploring his potential for ejaculatory control.

☙

Linda couldn't help feeling sad as she read about multiple orgasms. She had experienced them with Martin in their early days and wanted them back. In fact, just last month she'd seen a women's magazine piece on Viagra for women that had mentioned that it might be particularly helpful to those on antidepressants. What about that?

☙

The Viagra phenomenon has brought a great deal of attention to the sexual effects of genital blood flow in women as well as in men. Researchers have theorized that deficits in blood flow might well be at the root of many women' difficulties with arousal and orgasm, and this thinking has led some doctors to try Viagra in some of these women. Many of these studies are still ongoing, but we already have good, solid data supporting the use of Viagra to counteract the adverse effects of the SSRI antidepressants (Prozac, Zoloft, Paxil, Celexa, Lexapro) in women as well as in men. There are also a number of non-pharmaceutical approaches to the blood flow issue.

Jumpstarting the Clitoris

Several non-prescription creams are now on the market for use on the clitoris. Venus Touch (www.venustouch.com) is one of our favorites, since a controlled study in over 1200 women has documented its effectiveness in improving sexual responsiveness. There is even an FDA-approved device (Eros by Urometrics) that applies suction to the clitoris to improve blood flow!

Clearly, not all the questions are answered yet about female sexual stages and the effects of mind, matter, and meds. We do know that there is incredible variation in women's orgasmic response. Masters and Johnson found that some women were orgasmic with fantasy alone—"Look, guys, no hands!"—while others were orgasmic with only breast stimulation. Others are orgasmic with many different types of clitoral stimulation. Lately, a hot area for research has been the whole topic of blood flow and stimulation and how to increase blood flow into the clitoris and G-spot so that women could enjoy effects like those men get from Viagra. The idea is that not enough blood flow into the whole clitoral body is one reason women have trouble being orgasmic.

And then, of course, there is the issue of sufficient stimulation, which is where vibrators come into the bedroom. Vibrators can deliver really intense stimulation—much more intense than someone's hand or mouth. You can try all different kinds, if you're interested. There are fake-penis types, curved ones specifically for the G-spot, dual clitoral/G-spot models, and wearable ones—you name it. And, they can be really great, because many women simply are not getting enough stimulation—for them—for orgasm. Of course some men may be really offended by the idea that you might want to use one, as if this implies that they are inadequate or superfluous. You can avoid this message if you incorporate your vibrator into lovemaking and use it on both of you—as a sensual toy, like Sacred Spot wands, fur mitts, and feathers.

FEMALE HORMONES

Hormonal effects of course are also crucial to optimal sexual function for women. As we have discussed, the vaginal tissue and labia need enough estrogen to maintain their elasticity, fullness, and ability to lubricate. Now there are local applications of estrogen for women who do not want to take estrogen systemically—vaginal tablets, which are less messy than the creams, and a silastic ring that releases estrogen slowly

---

Sex Toys and Tools

Try whatever strikes your fancy—vibrators, clitoral stimulation creams, Sacred Spot wands, fur mitts, feathers, lubricants like KY liquid, and more. And they're not all just for the ladies. Take turns.

---

for ninety days before it has to be replaced. The amount of estrogen that enters the blood stream with these treatments is miniscule—they can even be used by women who have had breast cancer.

Of course, it isn't necessary to use estrogen to improve vaginal lubrication. We are fans of the many lubricants now on the market—KY and Astroglide are the ones we most often recommend. Those that have been FDA-approved are called "personal lubricants." Not only are they safe for the vagina (in contrast to some silicone-based products), they have also been tested with condoms to ensure that they do not weaken latex. Lubricants are fun and sensual—on him, on her—and you definitely do not have to be estrogen-deficient to enjoy them. The average buyer of KY is just 33—hardly menopausal!

There are also some important facts to know about testosterone in women. First of all, the ovaries produce half of the testosterone in a woman's body; the adrenal gland makes the rest. When a woman goes through menopause, not only does her estrogen drop precipitously, so does her testosterone. In fact, when doctors prescribe systemic estrogen, it causes the reflex production of a protein that preferentially binds what little active or "free" testosterone there is. Because of this, taking estrogen can actually further depress a woman's libido. Presently, there is tremendous interest in replacing testosterone in women suffering from lack of desire and diminished sexual response. The hope is that this could work in much the same way that gels and patches used for men do. Unfortunately, we do not have large, long term studies about testosterone replacement in women, but for many years Lana has used small doses in women with significantly low morning levels of total and free testosterone. Sometimes this is all it takes to restore a woman's flagging libido.

If you think that low testosterone could be a factor for you—because you have had your ovaries removed, have gone through menopause, or have had other pelvic surgery that could interfere with the blood flow to your ovaries—have your doctor check your blood levels. A little testosterone might just be the ticket to reclaiming sexual desire and pleasure. In our experience, however, a simple pill or patch is rarely the complete solution to problems of sexual desire in women. We need to look further.

BLOCKING THE RADIANCE: THE THREE F'S

Now we move on to the much trickier subject of psychological blocks that can hinder a woman's quest for radiance. Most women aren't connecting with their full sexual energy because of the Three F's: Fatigue, Fear, and Fury. These are fundamental frustrations of most women's lives that stand in the way.

When Lana questions women about their sexual energy—"Where is it going? What's going on?"—this is the answer she gets most often: "I'm tired, I'm so tired, I'm exhausted. There is always so much to do, so much more to do, that I can't even *imagine* having the energy for sex. Fatigue is what's really holding me back."

Another common answer is Fear. That usually gets expressed as something like, "I'm not sure I want to get into it, I feel kind of afraid of becoming involved, at least right now. So that's why I'm kind of holding back."

The third common block is Fury: "I am mad. I am angry and upset. I am not happy and when I'm not happy, there isn't going to be any sex." Naturally, the three F's aren't mutually exclusive—we often encounter women who answer with a long, complicated tangle of all three reasons.

Fatigue

We've all been there. Resisting, telling ourselves we're just too tired, and then, afterwards saying, "That was great! Why don't we do this more often, all the time? Wow, I really needed that!" And then that next time comes around and there you are, too tired, and resisting your partner all over again.

The proof that sex soothes and energizes isn't just the experience of millions of people; researchers have shown that orgasm triggers the release of endorphins and other brain chemicals that make us feel good. That expansive, everything's okay feeling that enwraps you after a really satisfying love-making session is at least partly due to this energetic chemical soup flooding into your bloodstream.

The habit of putting sex last on our list of clamoring demands on our attention—kids' homework, holiday obligations, paying bills, creating nutritious meals, getting adequate exercise, having a beautiful home, planning vacations, arranging household help, attending to our aging parents' needs, and, of course, maintaining a gorgeous and serene appearance—reveals our ignorance of the power sex has to contribute to our fund of energy. We allow this idea—that we have some other, more important use for the precious little energy we have at the end of the day—to obscure our inner knowledge that making love replenishes us.

Fatigue is a reality of our over-busy, demanding lives. But sex does not have to be that last item on the list that you never get to. Rather it can be the *antidote* to mind-numbing exhaustion, one that can remind you of the juicy enjoyment of life, the energy of your pelvis, and the sweet surrender of connection with your lover.

FUSION

Last night I didn't want to.
Too tired,
Things on my mind,
Worries,
So much to do.

You said we had a date.
True enough.
Guilt...
You didn't look turned on.
And I, already in my PJs,
Night cream applied.

But...
Well...
We should...
Oh, okay, I'll just take my
bottoms off.

Then it happened,
Again.
How could I have forgotten?
You captured my eyes first.
I reached out for your body.

My top flew off because it had to,
I let go because there was
nothing else to do,

I invited you in because you
belonged there.
We swirled into that familiar
vortex.

Later, I lay in your delicious aura,
Musing once again
At my impossible,
inexplicable inability
To remember

The joy,
The heat,
The satisfaction,
The peace,
Of fusion.

"Remind me,"
I demanded,
"To never forget this again."

"Okay,"
You answered indulgently,
Knowing that I would.

Fear

We talked about fear a bit already: Fear in all its many guises—some of them fairly subtle—commonly short-circuits sex in several different dimensions.

Danger messages that begin in childhood really can create profound sexual caution, which can continue to block many women's free expression of their sexuality even when it's perfectly safe to let go. Girls are taught very early to watch out for any sexual messages directed towards them—and that's both appropriate and necessary. Parents need to keep them safe from predators. Boys can of course also be victims of sexual predation, but it's girls we worry most about, and it's girls who get the strongest messages about the dangers of all things sexual.

That teaching starts out as protection, but the idea that sex is dangerous, bad, scary, or nasty, often lasts and becomes an elaborate system of defense against the whole realm of the erotic. Women's early training is the basis for phrases like, "Why buy the cow when you can get the milk for free?" These sayings, which girls pass around like gruesome horror stories, reflect a view of men and of sex that can be seriously chilling to young women. The best way to keep from "getting a reputation" is simply not to be sexual. Respect and sex are at opposite ends of the spectrum—and boys are taught that, too. We all know that a woman who has sex too soon, or with too many partners, or with the wrong partner, is a slut. Right? All this works to divorce women from their sense of themselves as sexual beings, and keeps them from thinking of sex as a good and happy thing.

There's a sort of victimology at work here, too. Girls are warned that they may get pregnant, or get a disease, or get a bad reputation if they are sexually active. Sex is something that, if it "happens" to them, could make them pathetic and helpless. But in addition to the danger messages, you've also got messages about loss of control and even self-hood. Let this person into your body to "use you" and you give up control! You're somehow under his power, especially if he realizes that you actually *want* sex!

These scare tactics often create profound, unacknowledged fears about what might happen if a woman were ever to let her sexuality come forth. These anxieties, and the excessive control over sexuality that women typically learn as a way of dealing with them, can emotionally hobble them even in loving, safe, committed relationships—even when they desperately long for more closeness and better sex.

Lana once had a woman come to her who expressed with great clarity the dilemma of women who equate loss of self with the full expression of their sexuality. The woman was disappointed by the physical side of her marriage, which baffled her because she'd had great sex in the past. "I had this one guy, and you know, we had *fantastic* sex."

When Lana asked her why it had been so fantastic, she answered, "With him I could let myself go completely. I'd yell and make noise and just do anything. It didn't matter."

So Lana went on to ask about what had happened to that relationship, and the woman said, "Oh, I didn't love him. I just had great sex with him."

Then Lana wanted to know how the woman felt about her husband, and she said, "Oh, I love him with all my heart." And so of course, Lana asked what was going on with the sex in the marriage, and the woman said, "Well, I don't know. I think I'd be sort of afraid to have that kind of sex with my husband." Why?

She thought for a moment and then said, "Because then he would have all of me."

He would have all of her—that was her fear. She had been able to let go sexually, be her real sexual self, with a man she didn't love. He didn't have her heart and she knew it. But her husband, to whom she'd given her heart and soul, couldn't have her sexual energy, because somehow in her mind that would make her completely vulnerable to him. She did not want him to have all of her.

This story illustrates how deep you sometimes have to dig to find the beliefs that hold you back. For some people, the fear of becoming vulnerable goes right down to dread of losing themselves entirely in the heavy surf of really passionate sex: It is so strong, so big, that they feel as if they were ever to stop resisting, they might not come back.

Past trauma, as we mentioned previously, also leaves a residue of emotional apprehension. For women who've been molested as children, or date-raped, or assaulted in some other way, fear is a significant factor in their perception of sex. Can they ever get over that? Yes, absolutely! We have worked with many, many women with emotional trauma from such experiences—in our culture, sexual assault is unfortunately a pretty common occurrence. And, we've seen them acknowledge and mourn their bad experiences and actually allow their partners to heal them—sometimes a man can be the healer of the wounds another man has made. This becomes a particularly profound experience of bonding for a couple that really deepens their intimacy and commitment.

There's another whole realm of fear that's associated with the body. It has to do with shame and fear of exposure, and its roots are in perfectionism. To be worth anything, we must have the perfect kids, the perfect house, the perfect abs, no cellulite, no scars. Everything must be ideal for us to be totally happy. Well, who is that perfect person? Have you ever met her?

It's silly, of course, but women in this society measure their looks against impossible standards and feel terrible. We spend our time trying to hide all of our shameful imperfections, instead of connecting with our inner sexual radiance. We worry that not only will our partner not be attracted to us, he might actually be turned off. Which brings us to body shame specifically focused on the genitals. Women who feel this way try to keep their partners away. They'll say, "Oh, I don't want him down there because I don't look right or smell right." These women probably got some very negative messages about their "down there" when they were young; messages that have never stopped echoing in their heads. It's all about fear of exposure and the reluctance to let your lover enjoy the body, the genitals, that you have spent a lifetime feeling anxious about.

All this shame results in not being able to let go when you make love. You're too busy watching and judging to really get into what's happening. Habitual judgment splits you into an observer on the ceiling watching two participants on the bed, grading yourself on how you look and how you're doing.

The body is like an earth. It is a land unto itself. It is as vulnerable to over-building, being carved into parcels, cut off, overmined, and shorn of its power as any landscape. The wilder woman will not be easily swayed by redevelopment schemes. For her, the questions are not how to form, but how to feel. The breast in all its shapes has the function of feeling and feeding. Does it feed? Does it feel? It is a good breast.

The hips, they are wide for a reason, inside them is a satiny ivory cradle for new life. A woman's hips are outriggers for the body above and below; they are portals, they are a lush cushion, the handholds for love, a place for children to hide behind. The legs, they are meant to take us, sometimes to propel us; they are the pulleys that help us lift, they are the anillo, the ring for encircling a lover. They cannot be too this or too that. They are what they are.

There is no "supposed to be" in bodies. The question is not size or shape or years of age, or even having two of everything, for some do not. But the wild issue is, does this body feel, does it have right connection to pleasure, to heart, to soul, to the wild? Does it have happiness, joy? Can it in its own way move, dance, jiggle, sway, thrust? Nothing else matters.

—Clarissa Pinkola Estés, *Women Who Run With the Wolves*, Random House

Fury

Anger: it is common, it is frequently convenient, and it is certain to kill good sex. This is where a lot of women end up sexually. Anger has many forms, from mild irritation to extreme bitterness. Often the source of anger is outside the bedroom, but the rage doesn't stay there. All couples get mad at each other, but healthy, loving partners learn how to let the anger go, so old fights don't come creeping into bed with them.

Anger can be about small injuries or large injustices, but one thing is consistent—people have a tendency to cherish their bitter treasures, no matter how much this prolongs their own suffering.

One woman we met had harbored a fierce grudge against her husband for years because he failed to show up for her mother's funeral. Genuine circumstances had prevented his attending, and she knew this. But, she was still as mad as she'd been the day of the service. His inability to be there, no matter the reason, signaled for her his lack of caring, and since he "always" wanted sex, she could demonstrate her lack of caring about *his* needs by denying him sexual access.

For another woman who came to us, it was about a miscarriage she'd had early in her marriage. She'd called her husband at work, but he'd really felt he couldn't

TRUE NATURE

Eyes narrowed and
heart constricted,
I look about to see
how to blame you.

It must be your fault
that I am not happy
today.

Where are my flowers?
Why is there not enough
money
for me to be
expansive,
extravagant,
my true nature?

Stuck on the thorns of
anger,
I wait for you to become
the silken pillow amid
opulent gardens.

I resist the lesson of
self creation,
preferring to sit,
wide-bottomed,
on the stoic cushion
of disappointment—
my fingers wrapped
around the mug
of steaming circumstance.

I sip its poison of
powerless broth,
and continue to die,
inside out.

leave his job because he'd just started there, he didn't know his coworkers well, and the couple was financially strapped. A girlfriend had to take the young wife to the doctor's office and then to the hospital. She never forgave him for not being there. Years and years later, her anger about that afternoon was still coming into play in their intimacy.

Sometimes fury is not about any particular thing; it's just long-stewed general bitterness about everything. Often women admit that they have ended up feeling very bitter about their marriage, about life, and one way they get back at their partner is to deny sexual access. They say, "Well, you didn't do this, or you *did* do that, so guess what...you're not getting any, pal." Couples use sex as a battleground in the ongoing war that is their marriage. Clearly, our prescription to have more sex to energize the relationship is not likely to transform a marriage like this. But professional counseling may be able to uncover underlying strengths in the relationship that can ultimately lead to a more constructive relationship—one that includes sex.

Sometimes the anger *is* about what occurs in the bedroom. Plenty of women have told us, "He doesn't know what he's doing! I tell him over and over again, 'Don't do it like that, do it like this,' but does he listen? He doesn't care enough about how I feel to bother!" And she is ready to *kill* him if he does X one more time. Now we don't know whether he really wasn't paying attention, or he thinks maybe X will work this time or that he believes he's now doing X the way she likes, but we do know that these technical issues can make women furious. Sometimes, though, it's her fault—she hasn't really told him clearly, even though she thinks she did.

Sorry, ladies, but different pitches of "mmmm" may fail to get the information across. So if some technical glitch is distracting you when you make love—let's say it once again: Talk to your partner!

Another sexual issue that infuriates some women is their sense that their partner's lovemaking is very mechanical—not really personal at all. They feel that they're just servicing him—he needs an oil change and perhaps a lube job and she is the nearest garage. The sense that you're not connecting, that your partner approaches sex in a mechanical way, is deeply alienating, for men and especially for women.

It can also be the man's irritability that obstructs the flow of his partner's Shakti energy. For example, we once had a woman come in with her husband; a guy who was always blowing up. Not at her or the kids, but he was always angry about something, and he was very explosive and sarcastic, yelling, screaming, stomping out. (Naturally none of this was his fault: He couldn't help it that all he ran into wherever he went were morons and incompetents.) Her role was to trail around after him apologizing, explaining, and generally picking up the pieces after his tantrums. And he wondered why she didn't want to have sex with him. What was wrong with her, anyway?!

Lana's assignment for him? No anger for 24 hours. What? He could not imagine it! He was stunned that this should be asked of him. How could he avoid the imbeciles that were everywhere?

But he finally accepted the assignment as a challenge. When they showed up 24 hours later in Lana's office, the wife was so relaxed that she looked years younger. He hadn't actually made it the full 24 hours without becoming enraged, but he'd been much, much calmer. She was absolutely thrilled, and feeling *much* more like having sex with her husband. Though still a long way from sexual Nirvana, this couple had definitely made a significant step in the right direction.

Another source of frustration for Shakti is her lover's failure to pay her the sort of attention she needs to let go. Men can be too wrapped up in themselves, in what they're doing and striving for, to provide the kind of solid presence their women need if they are to access their full sexual power. In order for a woman to let go, to allow the Goddess full rein, she needs to know she can trust her man to *stand in*, to not go running off emotionally or physically when she opens her heart and lets that primordial Shakti energy flow.

So, having examined Fatigue, Fear, and Fury in detail, what comes next? How do we deal with all the long-standing habits and dysfunctions that keep us mired in these energy-depleting traps? We recommend a fourth F: Fusion.

Fusion

For women especially, awareness of your partner's ability and desire to honor your heart is a crucial piece of setting the goddess free. When you begin to trust him to stand in for you, you can surrender to him sexually and to his skill and desire to please you. (Remember: Surrender is not submission; it is a choice.) You also have to make a decision not to use sex to win out-of-the-bedroom battles. And you have to believe in the power and desirability of this Shakti goddess, or queen, or however you prefer to think about her. You have to say, "I'm going to claim the piece of me that I've gotten out of touch with. Now I recognize that I've ignored her because I was taught that enjoying sex was slutty, or because I got hurt once, or because I've been locked in a power battle with my partner, or because I've been so tired that I've forgotten how sex can energize me." There are a multitude of reasons for locking Shakti away, but now it's time to let her out. Not to please anyone else, or because you *should,* but because you want to have her energy sparking your life. Because you want to be happy. To set her free, you have to say, "I'm going to believe in the power and desirability of my sexual energy." And then you have to act on that belief.

NOON

Take the quizzes below. There's one for each of you. You'll get to see how your four companion couples respond too.

Then we'll introduce you to the Yab Yum position for exchanging the energy of love, and to a powerful imagery to do in this position that will really amp up the energy flow: the Heart Lingam, Heart Yoni Exercise.

What Holds You Back?

The following quiz will help you define more precisely the role of the three F's in your own sex life, and will help you see how to take more responsibility for handling them.

Emotional Sabotage of Your Sexual Energy (women's questions)

1. Do you often feel too tired to have sex?

_____ Yes, because _____

_____ Yes, especially if it's in the:

morning_____ afternoon _____evening _____

_____ Sometimes; if we go ahead anyway, then I feel _____

_____ No, it usually energizes me.

2. Do you feel anxious or fearful about sex?

_____ Yes, when I remember _____

_____ Yes, when my partner _____

_____ Sometimes, but only if _____

_____ No, I feel comfortable with sex.

3. Are you irritable or angry when it comes to sex?

_____ Yes, when I think about_____

_____ Yes, when he _____

_____ Sometimes, when I have to _____

_____ No, sex makes me happy.

4. Do you feel embarrassed or ashamed during sex?

_____ Yes, when I'm aware of_____

_____ Yes, when I sense my partner _____

_____ Sometimes, when I can't _____

_____ No, I feel secure and confident during sex.

5. Do you find sex boring or tedious?

_____ Yes, especially since _____

_____ Yes, when he _____

_____ Sometimes, if we forget _____

_____ No, sex is still interesting.

6. Do you feel as if you are "trying too hard" during sex?

_____ Yes, and I get frustrated by _____

_____ Yes, unless I can relax by _____

_____ Sometimes, especially when he _____

_____ No, I can usually relax and let go.

THE WOMEN RESPOND

Kate

In answering the questionnaire, Kate recognizes that her irritation when Steve turns her down covers a sort of despair. She feels terribly anxious when he won't make love to her, and this, as the doctors have suggested, is a feeling she associates with her father's sudden death. She considers the possibility that a powerful fear of abandonment that really has nothing to do with Steve or with sex, is feeding into her reactions.

Question 4 also goes deep. She feels embarrassed over how much weight she's gained since they first met, and the suspicion that Steve is disgusted by her body has been robbing sexual contact of much of its pleasure—she thinks of times when he's seemed to be really into making love while she's felt stuck in her head, monitoring whether her thighs are jiggling. (Steve's answers to the questionnaire reveals his total ignorance of her worries. He thinks she's gorgeous, and it's never occurred to him that she might not like her body.)

Nicole

Nicole's answers show her how tightly closeted her goddess must be: She's tired, fearful, angry, embarrassed, *and* bored. Mostly, she just wants him to hurry and finish so she can sleep. Most of her answers revolve around her exhaustion, which is what she expected. But now that she thinks about it, she recognizes that she's been angry for a long time about how Charlie "pesters" her. She interprets his persistence as insensitivity to her feelings. (Reviewing both their responses, Charlie begins to recognize that his constant sexual nagging may be making her *more* tired and *more* angry.)

Linda

Linda's questionnaire brings up for her how tired and stressed she is, and how that contributes to her dissatisfaction with their recent lovemaking. When they don't connect, sex is boring and just makes her sad. (Martin looks through her responses and recognizes that he hasn't been putting enough time and energy into "lighting her up." Martin is especially intrigued by the discussion of energy and sex. He's read that part twice—and is eager to get to work on bringing the god and goddess together.)

Paulette

Paulette's questionnaire responses reflect her enjoyment of sex, her feelings about Bob's dysfunction, and his refusal to do anything about it. She's not just concerned about the issue; she's mad at him about it, and she feels bored when he fails, and feels burdened by having to bring all the energy to their connection. When he reads over her answers, Bob is surprised and a little hurt.

"Well you haven't gone rushing out to solve this lubrication problem you talk about embarrassing you. Maybe you can understand how I felt about going to the doctor for my thing," he remarks.

His sharpness takes her aback—Paulette is the one who points out mistakes and inconsistencies, not Bob. Her first impulse is to snap back, but she stops herself. After a moment, she says, "You're right. I hadn't looked at it that way. But," she can't help adding, "you've got to admit that your 'problem' is more of an issue than mine."

What Holds Her Back?

Emotional Sabotage of Her Sexual Energy (men's questions)

1. Does your woman often feel too tired to have sex?

_____ Yes, she says it's because _____

_____ Yes, especially if it's in the:

morning _____ afternoon _____ evening _____

_____ No, it usually energizes her.

_____ When she's too tired, I respond by_____

2. Does she feel anxious or fearful about sex?

_____ Yes, I can tell because she_____

_____ Yes, especially if I _____

_____ No, she feels comfortable with sex

_____ When she seems anxious, I respond by _____

3. Is she irritable or angry when it comes to sex?

_____ Yes, I can tell because _____

_____ Yes, especially when I _____

_____ No, sex makes her happy

_____ When she gets irritable, I respond by _____

4. Does she feel embarrassed or ashamed during sex?

_____ Yes, I can tell because she_____

_____ Yes, especially if I _____

_____ No, she seems to feel secure and confident during sex

_____ When she seems embarrassed, I respond by _____

5. Does she find sex boring or tedious?

_____ Yes, especially since _____

_____ Yes, when I forget _____

_____ No, sex is still interesting for her

_____ When she seems bored during sex, I respond by _____

6. Does she seem to be "trying too hard" during sex?

_____ Yes, she gets frustrated by _____

_____ Yes, especially when I _____

_____ No, she can usually relax and let go

_____ When she's trying too hard, I respond by _____

For each question with a "yes" answer, identify ways in which you contribute to the problem.

THE MEN RESPOND

Steve

When Steve fills out his questionnaire he sees immediately where they are having problems—he keeps trying to discount Kate's irritation at not having enough sex (question 3) by reminding her that he is focused on their shared financial goals. But he's completely missed the obvious: they have intimacy goals too, and they need to be just as high a priority. He can see that he has to take some responsibility for making sex as important a goal as making money, but question 6 gives him some insight into another reason why he has been holding back from sex with Kate. He feels that she doesn't really open up to him when they have sex, that her approach is mechanical, and that sometimes she's so focused on having orgasms that he feels "like a human vibrator" and spaces out. He concludes that not only does he needs to do a better job in setting priorities outside work, but that he wants to learn how he can help her open up to him emotionally when they make love.

Charlie

Charlie admits when filling out the quiz that he is guilty of "bugging" Nicole for sex even when she is exhausted (question 1). His sense is that she enjoys sex once they get into it, but that it's hard for her to let go of her resistance because she thinks that she's doing it "just for him." Of course, when she refuses him, he gets a beer and watches cable or Internet porn for a while, and he knows she hates that. Charlie tells himself, "I would much rather have sex with her, but I don't know how to make her like it more. I do try new positions and other stuff (question 5), but that doesn't help. All I know is that I need a lot more sex than I'm getting!" In thinking about ways he's possibly contributing to the problem, Charlie has trouble coming up with much. He admits that helping her more with the kids might make her less tired, but otherwise he can't see what he can do differently. This questionnaire is frustrating because he wants so much make things better and it doesn't give him a clue as to how to do it.

Martin

For Martin this exercise puts down on paper what he already knows. He has been pretty negligent in activating Linda's goddess energy. He writes that he just "lets sex go" if she is tired (question 1), that he does the "same old things" when she is bored (question 5), and admits his own complicity in letting their sex life together become dull and predictable. Question 7 makes him realize that his masculine responsibility is to introduce more innovation and energy into their cooling connection, but that he needs some ideas about how to get things going again. In fact, as he keeps going over the questions in his mind, he gets more uncomfortable about the passive position he has adopted in their relationship. "I've really been expecting Linda to find and show me her light—her goddess self—all on her own. It's so important to me," he thinks, "but I've been pretty lazy about nourishing that part of her. I really have to wake up and step up."

Bob

Bob thinks that Paulette is fairly healthy sexually and answers almost all the questions with "No, sex energizes her, sex is comfortable, she is secure and confident, it is interesting, and she can relax and let go." But Bob's quiz reveals that he's troubled by Paulette's irritation over his "ineptitude" and his erectile difficulties, and that in the past, he's dealt with her sarcasm by simply leaving the room (question 3). More clearly than ever he sees that his almost childish embarrassment about his erection problem has almost destroyed their sexual relationship. "I don't know why I was so sensitive about asking the doc about Viagra—he didn't even blink an eye and started writing the prescription immediately. Well, she's a great, sexy woman; I don't blame her for being upset with me over this."

⌒

So far today, we've explored the far reaches of women's anatomy and physiology—plus a fair amount of psychology, including your own. Now it's time for something practical, easy, and comforting—Yab Yum, one of the best Tantric practices we know for bringing two people closer. It's done sitting down, clothed or naked, and need only take a few moments. Yab Yum is so simple and relaxing that it's perfect for low-energy times; like first thing in the morning, or when you both get home from work.

Yab Yum, which translates as "Open Lotus," also works as an advanced sexual position. Images of Shiva and Shakti usually show them making ecstatic love in Yab Yum (see illustration).

Yab Yum Exercise ⊙ 7

This classic exercise will help you get back into your body and connect with your partner simply and quickly. In our couples course, this is a favorite method of being close to the Beloved. It incorporates breathing to circulate energy, awareness of your energy centers, and connection of your energy to that of your partner in a way that emphasizes the male-female, yang-yin, Shiva-Shakti polarity. We think it's fantastic, and that you should practice it a lot!

First, men: you are to sit on the floor with a cushion, or on a bed with your legs crossed in front of you. Ladies, lower yourself into his lap, so that your legs circle around your partner's back as you face him. For both of you, your arms are hugging your lover, and your energy centers—pelvic, belly, heart, and perhaps brow chakras (if you touch foreheads)—are physically connected.

Just experience the wonderful intimacy of this position for a few moments before you continue. Feel the warm touch of breasts, bellies, and encircling legs, and make minor adjustments for maximum comfort. And for those of you that cannot sit in this manner, you can do Yab Yum in a chair with the man seated and the woman sitting on or between his thighs, facing him.

You may notice that you just naturally begin the breathing that you learned with Soulgazing—easy breaths, in and out together. Some couples like to rock gently, some occasionally pull their heads back to look into each other's eyes, while others like to rest their heads on their partner's shoulders. It is such a luxury to relax into the body of your lover this way.

Next, you can begin the reciprocal or exchanging breath—one of you inhales while the other exhales. Now it feels as if, when you exhale, you are energizing each of your mate's chakras in turn, filling first one and then the next with light, breath, and love. If you are good at sending energy, that's fine, but don't forget to take the loving energy back into your own centers with each inbreath.

After you have mastered the basic position, you can use this connection for actual or "imagined" intercourse. The actual intercourse is easy to envision—lingam in yoni while you are sitting, facing one another. It is a very close and connected position for lovemaking, in which very subtle movements can be extremely exciting.

Yab Yum.

Heart Lingam, Heart Yoni Exercise ⦂8

When you do not have enough time for the real thing, try doing a lovely variation that we call Heart Lingam/Heart Yoni. Imagine, women, that while sitting in Yab Yum, you have a "heart lingam," a projection from your heart that can penetrate your lover's "heart yoni" with loving, potent energy. Envision the heart yoni as a soft, imaginary opening in the middle of his chest. You are entering him and giving him your powerful, sexual force where he needs it the most—in his heart. With your outbreath, imagine this flow of love first illuminating his heart, then spreading through his torso, and finally reaching his genitals and actual lingam. From there it moves into your pelvis with your inbreath, through your yoni and up into your heart—and out into him once again on your outbreath.

Men, as she imagines entering your being through your heart center as she exhales, feel yourself being lovingly penetrated there as you inhale. You absorb her feminine heart energy on the inbreath, send it down to your pelvis, and on the outbreath you send it back to her, transformed into masculine energy that enters her yoni from your lingam.

This circle of love, this mutual cycle of penetration and being penetrated, is a very powerful image, especially when linked to the breath. Each exchange deepens the energetic connection and stokes the Shakti/Shiva furnace. Tantric sex is conscious and controlled, and it is hot!

AFTERNOON

You've learned a lot about Shakti's body and emotions today, and had a chance to explore and process some of your own reactions to this information. Earlier this afternoon you've had a chance to reconnect and re-energize, and perhaps take a rest as well. Now it's time for the most challenging and interesting exercise yet.

SHIVA'S ROLE: AWAKENING THE GODDESS

Now that we've made the case for Shakti, and explored some of the ways in which most women hold themselves back from fully embodying her, it's time to take a closer look at Shiva's role in all this. Tantra teaches what men already know intuitively: that the woman is the channel he must tune in to in order to access the deep current of infinite, life-affirming energy. It also asserts that a man's sexual energy is more fragile and easily depleted than that of a woman who is fully connected to this current. However, to be able to make this connection and release this vast energy, she needs to surrender, and for this, she needs her man. Surrender requires a trustable and solid masculine presence in which she can feel totally safe to really let go. When she does, both the goddess and her lover exult in the flow of energy.

If this sounds counterintuitive, or too ethereal and theoretical, think about it this way: what really turns a guy on? Isn't it the sight/sound/feel of a woman who is offering her sexual passion to him with complete abandon? The vast and lucrative pornography industry exploits men's desperate need to experience Shakti this way, even in fantasy. But what really turns her on? It's not at all the same thing. Rather, it's much more the image of strength, steadfastness, and devotion. That's why pornography doesn't sell so well with women, but romance novels do.

So, men—If you want to enhance the depth of your sexual connection with your goddess, you need to learn how to help her tap into this energy. Your job is not just to know which buttons to push, but also how to "stand in" sexually, to embody the image of the warrior lover, so that she can surrender her heart and soul. Your quest is to light her up in all Seven Dimensions. Your dedication to acquiring the knowledge and skill to do this will be repaid many times over.

So here is your chance to practice Sexual Presence: your first—and most crucial—homework assignment. It will give you the opportunity to try out the ideas and concepts in the preceding sections, and actually experience a new kind of sexual connection. New experiences, not interesting theories, are the things that will change your sex life for the better.

The Warrior Lover in You

Often the way we, as men, respond to our woman's energy has a way of making things worse, and doesn't get her—or us—to where we need to be to optimize lovemaking. Rather than seeing her negative mood as a kink in the flow of love in *her* life, we tend to see it as an obstacle to our own goals. We make the mistake of trying to analyze it and fix it through a rational process. Or we think it's about us personally (often she's informed us of this quite explicitly!), so we feel attacked and have to defend ourselves. What works a lot better is to realize that what she wants most of all is to feel the flow of love in her heart, and that it's you as her warrior lover—warm, open, trustable, humorously present, and lovingly devoted to her—that allows her to feel it.

Of course, both of you are likely to have some resistance to the idea of a structured sex exercise. After all, you've never done it before, and neither has anyone you know. It's bound to feel at least a little awkward. And then there's that belief that sex has to be spontaneous and unpremeditated to be really good (Erica Jong's infamous "zipless fuck"). But trust us—it's worth working through the awkwardness and the uneasiness that is guaranteed to accompany anything unfamiliar.

The assignment is basically this: you will pleasure your woman, without intercourse, and without her reciprocating.

~

Charlie interrupts his reading at this point to moan, *"When* are these people going to let me do what I came here to do?!"

~

Intercourse is not allowed so that all your attention can be directed to enhancing her pleasure, and all her attention can be directed to letting go. You have a goal in this exercise, but it isn't the usual goal of having an orgasm. The goal in this assignment is to become Shiva by helping her connect with her Shakti, so that she can let go and surrender herself to love. You will do this most effectively by bringing each of the Seven Dimensions into play. We'll give you specific instructions and suggestions on ways to do this for each dimension:

- Biologic: specifically stimulate the clitoris and sacred ("G") spot.
- Sensual: create pleasure through all the senses—touch, smell, sound, sight, taste, movement.
- Desire: put forth masculine sexual polarity—your desire for her, your confident presence, and your loving humor.
- Heart: transmit heart energy so she can feel your generosity and loving connection.
- Intimacy: communicate openly, honestly, reveal your vulnerability.
- Aesthetic: enhance awareness of radiance (hers and your own) and gratitude.
- Ecstatic: cultivate a sacred quality to your connection.

Remember the opening of the old *Mission: Impossible* television show? A tape recorder starts to play and an ultra-serious male voice begins, "Your mission, should you decide to accept it..." It's the quintessential masculine paradigm—growth through challenge. So here it is, men—your mission is to find the elusive Shakti, awaken her, and restore her to her rightful place as ruler of your realm! Be assured: this mission is *not* impossible and this tape will not self-destruct. Your assignment is, in fact, highly structured, with instructions and suggestions for every stage of your encounter.

⌒

"Thank God," sighs Bob. "If anybody needs expert help, it's me."

⌒

YOUR ASSIGNMENT, STEP BY STEP

As Shiva, you are the orchestrator of the entire experience. This is a sacred ritual. Give every aspect your awareness, but don't let yourself worry too much about doing things "right." It will distract you from being present in the moment. The following script is meant to help. If you treat it like instructions for changing a timing belt, you'll miss out on what could have been an extraordinary experience. Communicating your full, adoring presence is the essence of this exercise.

Preparation

You'll need to set aside a full hour for this exercise. Be sure that there will be no interruptions: phone off, *Do Not Disturb* sign on the door, whatever it takes.

Next, well ahead of time, prepare the room. Create a sacred space in which to bring forth your goddess's energy. Try to arrange this space with care and attention to detail—the setting should appeal to every sense. Think about lighting, music, scent, arrangement of pillows and bedclothes, availability of refreshment. The room should be as serene, clean, and orderly as possible. Don't just turn the television off—cover it! Goddesses respond to all this. It makes your love visible and palpable to her.

Now you assist your woman in preparing herself to receive pleasure, and prepare yourself just as carefully. Send her off to bathe (ask if you may run the bath for her) while you ready yourself to encounter a goddess. You should be freshly shaved and showered, and your nails should be clipped. If you have a cologne or aftershave that she enjoys, put some on. Put on a comfy robe. Being fully dressed is not suitable, but your naked desire could be threatening. Then make last-minute preparations of the space. Have massage oil or lotion and personal lubricant within reach, and spread a clean towel on the bed. Light the candles. Mental preparation is even more important: breathe deeply and try to cultivate a calm, loving attitude and a sense of devotion.

~

"All right," thinks Martin, already going through possible props in his mind. "This sounds like major fun."

~

Connection

Invite your goddess into the place you have prepared for her. When she emerges from her bath, ask if you may dry her off and help her slip on her robe. Smiling, invite her to the prepared bed.

Now the ritual itself can begin. We suggest you begin with soulgazing: it intensifies intimacy by creating a feeling of closeness and sacredness. Sit across from one another as you hold hands and breathe together, visualizing energy flowing back and forth between you with each breath. You might imagine a huge energetic erection crossing the space between you and filling her up more with every breath. (This is a sure-fire way to increase your presence!)

Touching

Invite her to recline on the bed. Undress your beloved slowly, then begin to touch her gently, perhaps on the face. Stroke her hair. Slowly, attentively, move on to other parts of her: neck, arms, hands, belly, legs, feet. Use oil or lotion if you like. Talk to her as you caress her—tell her about her skin, her hair, her eyes, about how it arouses you to see and touch her. Don't conceal your lust; use it to energize the connection. Kiss her, touching your lips to many parts of her body. Do all this without expectation of response or thinking about a goal—she is simply to receive your attention. But do welcome any show of emotion and arousal from her. Stay present—try not to get lost in the details of doing all this "right." (At this point you may not have to imagine an erection to stay present!) Allow your sense of humor to be part of this process: Your goddess enjoys your light-heartedness and laughter.

Maintain an awareness of her heart center as you touch her. Feel your loving energy flow out through your hands and lips to her; feel her soaking it in. Put your hand on her heart, attune your breath to hers and connect through soul-gazing at any point during the ritual. Her breasts are external manifestations of her heart; caress them with this in mind.

≈

Steve wonders whether Kate will go for this part; if he knows her, she'll be in a hurry for the action to move to between her legs. "Maybe if I do it just right," he thinks wistfully.

≈

The Yoni

When you feel it is time, move on from gentle exploration of the rest of her body and bring your attention to her yoni. Sitting to the side of your beloved will allow you to maintain a close connection with her as you softly, gently communicate love and appreciation through your gaze and your words. Begin to explore the soft folds of the outer part of the yoni with one hand while the other hand rests on her heart or belly. Use lubricant as you wish, even if she has plenty of her own—it can add to the sensuality of your touch. Before entering the yoni with your finger, spend time with the clitoris, using gentle and varied strokes. Find out what kinds of touch she likes on her "pearl;" don't assume you know. You can ask directly, but be careful not to pull her into an excessively verbal, analytical mode. Often it's better to just try a lot of different pressures, speeds, and directions, and let her body language tell you what you need to know. You can also use your mouth and tongue on the clitoris (lubricants are non-toxic and taste fine), though it's more challenging to maintain a heart-to-heart connection with her while you do this.

Sacred Spot

After a time of exploration of the outer part of the yoni, when you can sense your goddess's readiness, move inward to make contact with the sacred spot on the roof of the vagina under the pubic bone. Use the utmost care. Begin to coax it with gentle strokes, pausing often. Many variations in pressure, pace, and direction of stroke are possible and desirable. A curling, come-hither motion of the finger works well, either down the center or slightly off to one side of the midline. Side-to-side rocking and circular motions can be interspersed. Try placing your thumb lightly on the clitoris at the same time that you stroke the sacred spot with your middle finger; or use your other hand on the clitoris to make a kind of counter stroke. Let your goddess's responses guide you; encourage her to tell you what she is feeling. If she wants to make sounds, encourage this by joining in the sound with her.

We should mention here that it's okay for your beloved to touch you for her own pleasure. Don't allow her, however, to start "doing" you. This ritual is all for her. This part is particularly difficult for many women; it's important for her to learn how to purely receive, fully surrendering without worrying about taking care of you.

Remember: There is no goal of orgasm, only of pleasure and connection. As soon as you start focusing on achieving a goal, she'll be able to tell you're no longer present, and she'll start to lose her connection to her shakti. That said, it's perfectly fine, in fact quite likely, for her to have orgasms during this exercise. Don't forget to look into her eyes and breathe with her. By penetrating your lover with your deep presence, confidence, and trustworthiness, you are helping her surrender more deeply to love. This masculine quality is far more powerful than any knowledge of specific technique.

Continue your loving attention to the yoni and sacred spot for many minutes, stopping to rest whenever either of you wishes to. But don't let your attention or connection lapse, and continue your ministrations until the allotted hour has passed. Energy may build and release through several cycles. Often the experience is not the familiar one of arousal and orgasm to which the two of you are accustomed, but something very different.

Emotions

Many emotions may arise during your connection. Try to stay with them, feel them in your body, breathe through them, and encourage her to do the same. Don't concentrate on, or analyze your emotions now, however. Stay in the moment, feeling what you feel. This is a powerful experience—laughing and crying are not uncommon forms of energy release; angry outbursts may also occur. This is fine, and nothing to take personally. You are both entirely free to feel whatever you feel within this hour and in this room. Observe, be present, honor, share, breathe, and try not to judge either yourself or your partner.

Amrita

It is possible that your beloved may experience ejaculation, or amrita, during sacred spot connection. Amrita is considered to be a special blessing to lovers.

Often a considerable quantity is released (one reason for the towel). Remember, it's expelled from the urethra, but it's not urine. It doesn't necessarily occur during a typical orgasm, although it's usually associated with an energetic release. Of course, it's perfectly okay if she doesn't ejaculate, too.

Finishing

Conclude your connection with a gentle embrace with full-body contact. You may be highly aroused, but it's important to refrain from intercourse just now. Absorb the energy you feel by breathing it up and allowing it to spread through your body. Choosing not to seek release from intense sexual arousal may well be a new and unfamiliar experience—trust us, it's good for you, and as you continue with your erotic weekend, its benefits will become clear. Be aware of your beloved's glow. Let her know in words how you have felt and received her shakti. Spend some time in silence as well. You will find that a great deal has happened within you and between you in the last hour.

⌒

THE COUPLES AWAKEN THE GODDESS

Steve and Kate

After reading through the assignment, Steve easily overlooks the admonition not to let the desire to perform well become a distraction, and is already planning to do the assignment with masterful perfection. After all those years of college and law school, he's focused on getting "a good grade." Kate is just plain anxious about the whole thing. Despite her stated eagerness for sex, she likes to be in control, and is not at all sure about being the receiver. But after a little discussion, they agree on a time for the assignment, and she leaves to run a couple of quick errands so that Steve has a chance to prepare. He gets busy collecting the things he needs to make their bedroom a proper space and arranges it all very nicely, even draping a beautiful, big silk scarf of Kate's over the television. He runs a bath with scented bath oil for her. But it becomes tepid while he waits and waits for Kate, who comes in, laden with shopping bags, a full 25 minutes after the agreed-upon time, apologizing non-stop.

Suppressing his irritation, Steve drains the tub and runs another bath for her. Kate gets in for a quick dip while he puts on the music he has selected, and he returns with her robe. As he leads her to their bed, she notices and comments on how nice the entire bedroom looks. "He has really gone to a lot of work," she thinks, but somehow this increases her apprehension.

"I know that you're still angry with me," says Kate as they settle on the bed for soulgazing.

"No honey, it's really all right. I want to find out what can happen with this." He looks deeply into her eyes and smiles. This makes Kate even more anxious. Suddenly she gets up and exclaims, "I can't do this!" Wrapping her robe tightly around herself, she goes over to the desk, sits down, and won't look at his puzzled face.

"Sweetie, what's wrong? We're just supposed to do the soulgazing, which we've already done, and then I get to touch you, and make you come a zillion times, and you know how to do that." Steve tries to keep his words and tone as rational and reassuring as possible, since he can tell that Kate seems to be losing it.

"No, this is totally different!"

"What's different about it?"

"I don't know! It just is. Stop analyzing me! I feel like I'm under a microscope."

At a loss for words, Steve wonders, "What in the hell am I supposed to do now? I need some help here."

Here is what David would tell Steve:

Kate is really scared right now. You won't be able to reason her out of this. You have to go hold her and tell her that it's okay for her to be frightened. Remind her that it's difficult for her to open her heart, since she has been wounded. Then show her that you'll take care of her and her heart if she is willing to give it to you. The key is to connect her enormous sexual energy to her heart. You're doing a great job, but you have to forget about trying to accomplish anything other than making this a safe and loving experience for Kate.

Steve slowly gets up and crosses the room. Kate is still facing away from him; her head is in her hands, elbows on the desk. Gently, he slips his arms around her and holds her to his chest from behind.

"I know this is hard for you, sweetie. You feel really vulnerable doing this. I'm going to take good care of you, I promise. I love you so much!"

Kate turns with tears in her eyes. "You do, don't you? I feel so silly not letting you!" Steve pulls her up to standing, and gives her a long and tender hug.

"Come on, let's try it again," he says, leading her back to the bed. Kate sits across from him and allows him to take her hands, feeling strangely shy, but more willing to try letting his love in.

Steve begins to touch her with real tenderness and awe. She feels the difference, and her heart opens toward him. He caresses her belly and her breasts, and tells her how much touching her turns him on. He holds her eyes with his gaze, and she can feel the truth of his words; for once, she forgets to think about being too heavy. By the time he begins to touch her sacred spot, she feels as if her heart, and her whole being, were wide open to him. As vulnerable as this makes her feel, she stays with it, and has several spine-tingling orgasms, and begins again to cry, this time with relief. Steve, feeling intensely protective of her, cradles her in his arms and rocks her as they end the session.

Charlie and Nicole

"I do love a challenge," says Charlie, who's been reading aloud to Nicole. "But I have to say, just reading this homework assignment is getting me hot. How am I ever going to keep from jumping your bones after all this build-up?"

"I knew you wouldn't take this seriously," Nicole says, her voice trembling. "There's nothing in it for you, so you don't want to do it for me."

Charlie puts the book down. "I never said that, and I didn't mean it. I actually think it sounds pretty interesting. Why are you getting upset, sweetie?"

Nicole is clenching her jaw, and doesn't answer. She thinks it's going to be hard—that he'll get bored and start joking around. The idea of him treating her like a goddess is just too far-fetched for belief.

As Charlie sets up the room, Nicole marches grimly off to the bathroom, as if she's going to her own execution. But Charlie pays no attention; he is into it. He loves games, and this strikes him as a particularly good one. After he gets together the gels and lubes and puts on Bolero, he hurries back to the tub, holding a big towel for her as she steps out. He dries her off gently and thoroughly, then enfolds her in the robe he has at hand. Not being Mr. Aesthetic, he hasn't done much with the room, but he does have the bed turned down and the pillows placed neatly for soulgazing. Nicole is fluttery and anxious, but the fun he's having doing all this begins to lift her spirits.

Once Charlie begins stroking and touching her, he's amazed by how satisfying it is to focus completely on Nicole's pleasure. He can feel her unwinding and beginning to respond under his touch, which fills him with unexpected happiness. He's never been one to use his fingers on her yoni, but once he starts exploring it, especially her sensitive clitoris, he finds he likes it, especially her obvious response--she gets really wet. But as soon as he slides his finger inside to search for the G-spot, she suddenly stiffens and then, rolling over and hiding her face, begins to cry. He is taken aback, but instinctively withdraws from her yoni, pulls her into his arms, and holds her, rocking and hushing her softly. "What's wrong, baby? It seemed like you were really getting into it…"

Nicole has just been flooded with repressed memory: An older cousin had backed her into a stairwell once, pulled down her pants, and shoved his fingers inside her while keeping her pinned against the wall. She'd tried desperately to keep out of his way ever after, but he still managed to catch her alone a few more times and repeat the assault. Almost as traumatic as the physical abuse were the words he'd say to her, and the looks he'd give her during family gatherings. She had been too ashamed to ever tell anyone. Now, at last, she tells Charlie.

Appalled and sorry, he holds and comforts her as she cries. He's enraged thinking about Nicole being abused, imagining such a thing happening to his own daughter—but realizes this is not the time to express this. He remembers the image of the warrior lover, and when she is calm again, he gently kisses away her tears.

"I'm so sorry that someone did that to you, baby," he whispers in her ear. "I'm here with you now, and I love you." Charlie slowly resumes touching first her skin, then her breasts, and finally her yoni. Staying on the outside, he looks deep into her eyes. Seeing that she is still connected to him, he says, "I'd like to touch you inside now. Is that okay with you?"

Nicole sees the love in his eyes, and suddenly is overwhelmed with the depth of her feeling for this man. "Yes! Let's try it again. I'll just keep looking at you." Very delicately, Charlie slides his ring finger (he has the thought that the middle finger will be too strong) into Nicole's yoni, and begins to slowly massage the roof, feeling the sacred spot gradually swell beneath his finger. Nicole is able to stay with him and to stay relaxed. When he puts his thumb on her clitoris as well, she begins to moan and move her pelvis more strongly into his hand. She's astonished to feel herself approaching a huge orgasm—the first she's ever had this way, and one of the strongest she's ever experienced—and she cries out, letting Charlie see all her pleasure. Once they've finished, they lie together quietly for a long time, Charlie feeling so proud of his ability to comfort and please her that he completely forgets about his erection.

Martin and Linda

Martin sets up their bedroom beautifully, transforming it with pretty cushions from the living room, scarves from Linda's drawer, and the props he acquired in anticipation of the weekend. He chooses a couple of their favorite CD's, then switches their order in the CD player several times. Then he lights a stick of incense, puts flowers on the towel he's placed in the middle of the bed, and checks that all his body potions are at the ready.

Linda floats in from her bath looking every inch the goddess. She's wearing the necklace he gave her for their tenth anniversary, with its large amber pendant between her breasts. He admires her openly: "Wow! Shakti is in my bedroom!" He leads her to the bed, they sit across from each other on the pillows, and effortlessly begin to soulgaze. Thirty seconds in, tears are running down Linda's cheeks—she loves him so very much. He assists her in reclining, making sure that she is perfectly comfortable, then begins. As if he had all the time in the world, Martin languidly pleasures every inch of her body.

Every touch is electric, and Linda is soon awash in pleasure; she's deeply aroused even before he begins to touch her clitoris. As he moves inside and contacts her sacred spot, she gradually feels a new sensation of fullness and then an urge to bear down. She lets go as she hasn't done in years, and experiences a rippling, full-body orgasm during which she ejaculates for the first time ever. Martin is awed and inexpressibly pleased by her response, and strokes her head and neck slowly as she comes back to earth, asking her to tell him when she's ready for more. He feels the reawakening of his ability to access the wonderful sexual desire he has for his woman and to be the key for new levels of pleasure for Linda. When they finally wander out to the kitchen and look at the clock, they cannot believe how much time has passed

Bob and Paulette

"Oh for God's sake—not like that!" exclaims Paulette. Bob has begun stimulating her clitoris, but his touch is clumsy and uneven, somehow too rough and too tentative at the same time. "That's not even..." She doesn't finish her sentence because Bob immediately pulls his hand away and sighs, pulling his robe more tightly around him. Paulette feels sorry for having snapped at him, but also frustrated. "How can I ever get him to do what I need?" she wonders irritably.

Lana would answer her question like this:

This is not about you getting him to do anything, Paulette. Your job is to stop trying to control the entire sexual scene between you and Bob. His awkwardness has a lot to do with your constant criticism of his efforts. And it's your fear of surrender that keeps you in judgmental mode. If he is ever going to be the man you want him to be sexually, your warrior lover, you are going to have to risk letting him explore your body inexpertly, and to learn from your non-judgmental responses.

David would also take this opportunity to give Bob some advice:

Paulette criticizes you because she is a strong woman, and needs to feel that your strength matches hers. It's how she tests you. So it's important not to withdraw from her criticism, nor to react defensively to it. Try responding to it with humor and see what happens.

Bob gets up and walks purposefully across the room, leaving Paulette on the bed feeling guilty and miserable. She sees him rummaging around in his briefcase, and wonders what he could possibly be up to. He finds what he's apparently looking for, and returns to the bed with it: a wooden ruler. Paulette is mystified.

"This is for you, Paulette," Bob says solemnly. "The nuns found it useful to help me learn better handwriting. Just whack me on the knuckles with it whenever I'm not touching you right."

Paulette bursts out laughing. "Here, give me that." She grabs the ruler from him and gives herself a whack on her naked thigh. In a mock stern tone she says, "You get back to work this instant, young man! Right here!" She points imperiously at her yoni with the ruler, and starts giggling again.

Bob gives her a sly grin and settles back onto the bed. He lightly places his hand on Paulette's mons, and looks at her with a mixture of longing and hesitancy. Paulette lays her hand on top of his. "I'm sorry," she says. "Please go ahead. I want you to touch me. We'll figure it out together." She holds his gaze while she slowly spreads her legs.

Bob begins to stroke the outside of her yoni, but he's still rather tentative. Paulette keeps her hand on his as she turns and stretches to reach the KY on the nightstand with her other hand. "I think this might help now," she says. He opens the bottle, and a big blob plops out right on her belly. Bob cringes, but Paulette laughs and scoops it up and slathers it on her yoni. "The more the merrier!" Now it's Bob's turn to laugh as he starts working the slippery gel all around her vulva.

Paulette puts her hand back on his; Bob pauses again, and looks at her, but sees that she's relaxed and smiling, and begins to slide his middle finger along her clitoris, as she gently guides him with her hand.

"Ooh, yes, that's nice! You can do it a little harder and faster... aah!" Paulette begins to rock her pelvis, as Bob, emboldened by her response, changes to a circular movement around the clitoris. "Oh, yeah, I like that a *lot*," she intones, now in a deeper voice, arching her back and rocking a little faster. "I want you inside me now!" He shifts on the bed so he can use his left hand on her clit from above while he slips his right middle finger under the pubic bone along the roof of her vagina. He feels the nubbly tissue of her G-spot and strokes it outward each time his other hand strokes the clit upward, all the while watching Paulette's face and feeling more confident and excited.

"Oh my god!" Paulette suddenly stiffens and bucks uncontrollably with an intense orgasm. "Wow," she breathes as she comes down from it, "that was fabulous."

Bob's hands are still in position on her yoni. "Lots more where that came from, darlin'. The hour is still young." And he begins to stroke her sacred spot again, slowly now, placing his left hand between her breasts. Paulette looks at him with surprise, and makes no move to stop him.

NIGHT

- Have a bite to eat: you're probably starving!

- Sit down together to talk about what happened. Debriefing a sexual encounter is, for many people, a totally new concept, but it's an invaluable exercise in intimacy and communication.

- We give you a couple of hints about talking about it below, and illustrate the process with the four couples who are doing the weekend with you.

- After your talk, you're on your own. Some of you may want to go for "extra credit" and return to the assignment, or some variation of it. We still recommend you defer intercourse, but you have lots of other options.

Talking About It

You've seen how our fictional couples—who illustrate some of the most common patterns we see in our workshops—have managed the assignment. Their problems, reactions, and triumphs are quite typical experiences of people who go through this potentially life-changing experience, which is just the first of three assignments designed to help you find your own way to a more ecstatic, heart-centered sexual practice.

Of course, you, unlike these couples, did not have the advantage of doctors at hand to set you straight if your encounter started to get off-track, and you can't talk afterwards with a circle of equally buoyant, stunned fellow participants. Your most important resource in processing what went on in that hour, is right there beside you. The two of you will want to talk about the assignment, your sensations, feelings, and reactions. It's important that you share your feelings in a loving way, not only while you are pleasuring and being pleasured, but after the session is over. You don't want to let the wide-open conduit of feeling that has opened between you close again. In doing the assignments, you're not only trying out a new framework for sex and refining your techniques, you're also reawakening the delicious sense of closeness and union that you had together at the beginning of your relationship.

By this point in your life, you know how easily an originally ecstatic fusion of souls can become obscured. You have also now had a glimpse of how to find it that place again, and make it a sacred, loving space in which the two of you can heal and rejoice.

THE COUPLES TALK ABOUT THE ASSIGNMENT

Steve and Kate

Lying on the fluffy rug and colorful cushions in their living room, Steve and Kate talk in a desultory, dreamy way as they continually, casually touch one another. Both are sipping wine and feel fantastically relaxed.

"You know what I honestly don't get?" Kate says, swirling the wine in her glass. "Why I resisted so hard. Now it just seems so…unreal. You know what I mean?"

"Oh, yeah." Steve answers. "It's like it gradually dawned on me, 'Hey this is Kate! And me! She's sooo naked and all I want to do is make her feel as good as possible.' I mean, that's heaven."

"Too bad I was such a jerk. I really am sorry that I treated you that way."

Steve rolls closer and nuzzles her neck. She smells so good. "You were anxious. It's scary for you, letting me see into your heart. I mean, now it seems like I always kind of knew that there was some secret garden that I couldn't get into, but that it had anything to do with how you felt about sex—that's something I never would have guessed—you're such a goddess/woman! I know you so much better than I did a couple hours ago." He's starting to choke up a bit.

"Ohhh," Kate murmurs. "You're my big strong lover. I don't need to feel nervous that I'm going to be left alone, do I?"

"Hell, *no*," answers Steve, from somewhere deep inside her thick, shiny hair. "You've always had my heart. It's just so incredible to find out that you *need* it."

Charlie and Nicole

"Well, who would have thought it?" said Charlie, coming up suddenly from deep beneath the surface of the big hotel pool. He pulled himself up onto the deck and sat beside Nicole, stretched out in a lounge chair near the edge.

"Thought what?" she says, distracted from her recollections of their time together. She can still feel his fingers inside her, driving her crazy.

"Who would have ever thought that not getting off could be so much fun. I thought it would be like playing doctor—lame kid stuff, you know? But I got such a charge out of just making you smile." He looks into her eyes and they kiss, ignoring the other people around the pool.

Nicole settles back, laughing. "You think you were surprised, huh? *I* went through a made-for-TV movie in an hour: I hated the whole idea, then I sort of gave in because *you* were being so sweet, then all that awful stuff about Joey came up. It really was like a movie started rolling in my head." She stops for a second and takes a deep breath. "But I could handle it, because you were there. And, then, of course, the big event!" She gives him a lazy, teasing smile. "Did I mention, at all, that that was nice?"

"Lady, I did get the impression that you were pleased." He stretches out on the warm cement, closes his eyes against the sun, and smiles to himself, a happy man.

Later, walking around the grounds of the resort in the twilight, talking softly, they feel very much "in love." Charlie, though is still very aware of "needing" sex.

Martin and Linda

"Boy howdy," says Martin as he and Linda begin to awaken from a short, sweet nap. "Here I am sleeping next to a goddess. Not that I didn't always think you were divine, my dear...." He stops to kiss her breasts, one by one.

"Well let me tell you, the goddess is one happy deity right now." She sighs and stretches as Martin's tongue wanders over her chest and neck. "I think she may be in the mood to grant all sorts of favors."

"It was enough just to be there, baby," he answers. "God, I can't tell you how I felt when you came like that—it was like some sort of natural force just letting loose."

Linda becomes serious, tearful. "Where has this been all these years? Where have I been? I feel so good right now I can't even describe it—why didn't I know about this?"

Martin caresses her tenderly, reverence in his every movement. "Well now you know. Now *we* know. We're not going to be forgetting anytime soon."

Bob and Paulette

Sitting and talking after a sumptuous dinner, Bob and Paulette hold hands across the table. Bob has been glowing ever since this afternoon.

"Well," he says, smiling. "Do we dare talk about it? I've been dying to tell you that I liked the ruler bit best."

Paulette giggles self-consciously. "That *was* fun, wasn't it? I just felt like I'd been such a bitch...."

Bob cuts her off by leaning forward and putting his finger on her lips. "Don't talk about a goddess that way. It's sacrilege."

She appreciates the joke, but is determined to have her say. "I honestly didn't realize how controlling I am, or why. I always thought I couldn't let go because you weren't 'doing it right.' I really blamed you. God, it must have been awful for you."

Bob takes both her hands in his and holds them tightly, holding her gaze with his. "Listen to me. Loving you has been only joy to me. You're the love of my life, and today was one of the greatest days ever. Right now, I am so incredibly pleased with myself that I can't even begin to tell you. I feel like going out and conquering a civilization or two!"

They both laugh.

"Oh, but what it will be like, weeding the dahlia bed with Ghengis Khan?"

Day Two has been the Day of Shakti. You've spent all day honoring female sexuality—he has given pleasure and she has received it. This has pleased Shakti, and empowered Shiva. On Day Three, the tables will turn, and you'll honor male sexuality. Shakti will return Shiva's favors.

Don't forget that you and your beloved have only one day left to find or make meaningful gifts that you'll exchange at the end of your weekend! Your gift can be a poem, something you have crafted or found, anything but something bought. And you must include words, either written or spoken, in your presentation.

Day Three

Pleasuring Him

DAY THREE

SPECIAL INSTRUCTIONS

Women, this is when you return yesterday's favor. Spoil, indulge, worship your lover as you never have before. You know what he likes—now you will give it to him. Make your bedroom a testament to his phallic beauty.

Men—let your woman lead you on a journey of sexual self-exploration. Let her show you how to make love for hours, control your sexual energy, delight in new erotic sensations, and experience whole-body orgasms. This is your day to experience pleasure as you never have before, in the arms of your beloved.

Suggested Schedule

MORNING:

- Men, sleep in if you wish to.
- Women, make preparations to honor Shiva in your lover.
- Greet each other with Namaste.
- Connect your sexual selves with Yab Yum.
- Read *What You Need to Know About the Male Sexual Response*.
- Master the *PC Muscle Awareness Exercise* together.
- Learn how to get your sexual energy flowing in sync with the *Touch Hands Exercise*.

NOON:

Enjoy a leisurely lunch in bed. Ladies, feed your man his favorite food. Don't worry, you're a sex queen, you can make a burger and fries sexy if you have to.

AFTERNOON:

- Do *Honoring Shiva*, your structured sexual assignment for the day.
- Rest. Indulge in a little nap together if you like.

EVENING:

• Dine at your leisure.
• Spend some time talking about the assignment, as you did yesterday.

NIGHT:

• End the day with *Puja*.

MORNING

• Namaste on awakening
• Yab Yum after breakfast
• Then dive into the following:

WHAT YOU NEED TO KNOW ABOUT THE MALE SEXUAL RESPONSE

Male sexual response, because it is so easily observed, may seem like the topic you least need to know about, but there are several lesser known aspects that deserve more attention, and those are the points we'll be discussing here. First, let's cover some of the important details.

Male Anatomy

The erectile tissue of the penis is organized into three compartments: a pair of *corpora cavernosa* ("cavernous bodies"), on the sides of the penis, and a *corpus spongiosum* ("spongy body") around the urethra and the glans, or tip, of the penis. The corpora cavernosa are much longer than you may realize—they extend under the scrotum and on back into the perineum, so, in fact, only part of the penis is outside the body. When you're erect, you may be able to locate the erectile tissue back between the scrotum and the anus. (Men! Want a ten-inch lingam? You already have one!) The corpus spongiosum terminates around the urethral bulb, a crossroads of muscles, nerves, and ducts in the perineum just below the prostate and deep to the scrotum. (This area is a neglected erogenous zone, and an interesting spot for erotic stimulation.) These compartments of the penis are spongy because they consist of a network of blood-filled spaces called *sinusoids* that have the marvelous capacity to expand when the proper signals command their muscular tissue to relax and allow more blood in. The basic mechanics and plumbing of an erection is actually pretty simple—spongy tissue filled with blood under pressure.

What about the prostate gland? You've undoubtedly heard of the prostate: it's been in the news a lot lately, especially since several celebrities and politicians have been open about being treated for prostate cancer. Most people seem to connect the prostate with old age and disease (not only cancer, but also the more common benign enlargement that makes urination slow and difficult for older men and often requires surgery), and have only the vaguest idea of where it is and what it is for (other than keeping urologists employed!). The other thing the prostate seems to be famous for, at least among men, is the indignity (the subject of many a crude locker-room joke) of having it examined: because of its anatomic location, doctors use a gloved finger in the rectum to check it. Because the prostate is involved with orgasm and—like the G-spot in women—is very sensitive, stimulating it either through the rectum or by pressing on the perineum can be very exciting.

Actually, the prostate is an internal male sex organ: it produces much of the fluid content of the semen, and thus has an important function in orgasm and ejaculation.

It's important to know your anatomy if you're going exploring here. The male sacred spot is easiest to stimulate through the rectum, the same approach (but with a lot more loving tenderness!) the doctor uses. A lot of men, perhaps understandably, are pretty apprehensive about this, though. So it is possible to get a similar, though less intense, effect by accessing the prostate through the perineum. It requires a good bit more pressure, because the floor of the pelvis is a fairly substantial sheet of muscle (the PC muscle we've discussed earlier), and you're going through this tissue to deliver pressure to the prostate.

He Has a Sacred Spot, Too

Remember our discussion yesterday of the G-spot and female ejaculation? The vestigial glands around the female urethra are embryologically related to the prostate and, like the prostate, produce acid phosphatase. We think it makes sense to think of the prostate as the *male* sacred spot. This makes it easier to understand the profound but more subtle quality of erotic sensation derived from stimulating the prostate compared with the tip of the penis. It is well worth exploring for couples who seek to broaden their sexual horizons and deepen (no pun intended!) their sexual connection.

Speaking of the PC muscle, this is another aspect of male anatomy that deserves more attention than it commonly gets. Women are routinely urged to tone their PC muscles, especially if they've gone through vaginal delivery of a baby. It's important for restoring pelvic support and bladder control, and it's also important for their sexual function, since good PC tone and control can really enhance a woman's pleasure, not to mention that of her man. But a strong PC muscle is also vital sexually in men—it enhances the accumulation of sexual energy, and it's critical to the development of ejaculatory control. More on this later.

Male Physiology

Yesterday we covered the sexual response cycle in women, referring along the way to the much more obvious male cycle. Arousal phase for the man means erection, which corresponds to lubrication in the women; the second phase is plateau, the excitement zone where sexual energy builds; then comes orgasm and ejaculation, followed by the resolution phase, which in men—but not women—entails a refractory period, during which it's not possible to get an erection again. All this appears very straightforward. In fact, that's one of the biggest problems with it. By going "straight forward," many men (and consequently their women) miss out on a number of wonderful opportunities to make sex richer and more satisfying.

AROUSAL

Now, the arousal phase, getting an erection, is what people commonly refer to as male *potency*—a term loaded with implications for the male ego, and, therefore, typically men's greatest concern when it comes to sexual function—are they going to get it up or not? But consider this: erection is not something that involves a lot of skill—you get one or you don't. There's not much we can do to control the arousal phase (as any mortified 14-year-old with a hard-on in geometry class can tell you), so making your worthiness as a man depend on whether you can get an erection is fairly absurd. Of course, our saying it's absurd probably won't change the low self-esteem of a man with erectile dysfunction (the currently accepted medical terminology for what used to be called impotence). Fortunately, there's a lot of excellent treatment now for E.D., so far fewer men need to accept this blow to their ego (and its often devastating effect on their love lives).

Erectile Dysfunction

There are a lot of reasons for losing or not being able to get erections. Back when we were in medical school, in the 1970s, the psyche got blamed for most of it, and organic problems were considered relatively unusual and typically related to obvious disease processes. In the intervening time, there's been a great deal of investigation into erectile dysfunction, and it's become clear that there are many more organic causes of erectile failure than was previously thought. Which is not to say that there are *no* psychological reasons—there certainly are—but we now understand the biology of sex, and sexual troubles, much better. It's not all in a guy's head, anymore.

One of the first things a doctor is likely to think of when a man complains of problems with his erections is a low testosterone level. For both men and women, testosterone is "the hormone of desire," and reduction in it often leads to diminished interest in sex. This can lead to erectile inability in an indirect way—if you feel little desire, you are much less likely to engage in activities that lead to erection, which may affect your capacity to become erect. Mostly, though, the problem with low testosterone is one of desire. The great news about this biologic cause is that, if you feel you're losing interest for no particular reason, you can easily get your testosterone levels tested. Replacement therapy with a patch or gel is readily available, and it works.

Medications are another thing the doctor needs to pay attention to when a guy has E.D, because they are a likely cause, and one that's easily treated—perhaps by substituting a different drug, or lowering the dose, or even reconsidering the need for drug treatment at all. (Of course, a guy has to report the trouble to his doctor: many docs aren't in the habit of asking about sexual side effects.) Antidepressants in the Prozac family are among the most common drugs leading to sexual difficulties, which can range from loss of desire to E.D. to difficulty having orgasm. Blood pressure meds also commonly cause erectile dysfunction, and lately a number of cholesterol medications have also been implicated. This raises the interesting question of what is really causing the E.D.: Is it the medication itself (and some of these drugs do have a direct effect on the erectile mechanism), or is it underlying vascular disease? There is increasing evidence that the well-known age-related decline in erectile function is really a manifestation of the subtle (or not-so-subtle) dysfunction of blood vessels that is characteristic of people with high blood pressure, diabetes, obesity, high cholesterol, and of smokers and people who don't get enough exercise. And this makes a lot of sense—erection requires an exquisite responsiveness of blood vessels in the corpora of the penis, so those with less responsive blood vessels are bound to have problems.

Viagra

Fortunately, Viagra and its newer competitors, Cialis and Levitra, have made a huge difference for men with these problems. Viagra has an incredibly elegant and specific effect on the chemical mechanisms of blood flow in the penis that has absolutely revolutionized the treatment of E.D. Contrary to what many people seem to think (judging from the jokes one hears about it), it has no direct effect on mood, perception or hormones. Viagra is not an aphrodisiac. It does not make you "horny," except as a placebo (if you expect it to be an aphrodisiac, it may well act like one), or as a secondary effect to becoming a more confident lover. It can't *give* you an erection, or increase your desire, or make you bigger or harder. If an ordinary guy having no trouble with erections takes Viagra, nothing changes. He feels exactly the same. That may seem sad, but it's actually one of the great things about the drug. The old treatments for erectile dysfunction involved injecting a drug into the penis, producing an erection that was totally independent of any sexual stimulation. But Viagra works in such a way that it integrates seamlessly into normal sexual relations, so you don't have to stop and go off to the bathroom to inject yourself and come back with this Frankenstein erection independent of how aroused you feel. Viagra works with and depends on how you feel—it just helps the plumbing work right.

⁓

"Well, that's all good to know," Bob thinks. "I really had no idea how the stuff actually worked, and the idea that all this time it's just been my sinusoids not filling up is sort of reassuring. It's not me, it's my plumbing." The thought makes him smile. "I wonder how it'll work for me?"

⁓

Viagra, the Wonder Drug—It's Not Just Good for Your Sex Life!

Human beings—especially male human beings—are always on the lookout for possible aphrodisiacs, and over the course of history people have tried out some pretty amazing concoctions. Even today, some rare species are endangered for precisely this reason: Desiccated tiger penises and powdered rhinoceros horn are still extremely valuable commodities in some parts of the world. Viagra has apparently begun cutting into these markets, taking some of the pressure off the animals, so there's one more reason to like it.

As great as Viagra is, it doesn't always work for everyone. However, there are vacuum devices that draw blood into the lingam, medicated pellets in the penis tip, and of course the injections, all of which are definitely effective. The important point is that erectile problems are very treatable and should not be a cause for despair.

Psychological Factors

What about psychological reasons for erectile problems? One of the biggest is loss of self-esteem. (We already alluded to this when we talked about the Desire dimension.) Losses and humiliation in other arenas of life—particularly in a man's work life—can cause men to feel so inadequate that their sense of failure washes over into their sex lives, where it may cause lasting difficulties. Another major cause is depression. (Some people would classify this as an organic cause. Many psychiatrists view depression as basically a physical illness.) Depression can have a very profound effect on sexual desire, and loss of libido is, in fact, one of the criteria for diagnosing depression. Treating it, with therapy and/or the right drug, is very important to restoring sexual energy for the man and his lover.

Yet another common psychological cause of erectile dysfunction is conflict with your partner. Men, like women, simply can become too hurt or angry to make love. This is not voluntary, conscious withholding of sex, but the body expressing outraged feelings. In much the same way that injured muscle overrides conscious control by going into spasm, the physical mechanisms of the erectile response ultimately take orders from the emotional core—not from the conscious mind. Old, negative teachings about sex are just as relevant for men as they are for women. "*This is wrong, this is bad, sex is dirty*" messages can create enough internal static to derail arousal. There's nothing like an inner lecture from Sister Mary Alice's warnings to ruin the moment.

Spectatoring is another culprit. You may recall this phenomenon from our discussion on Day Two of what holds women back from great sex: where you observe yourself having sex, almost as if you've split into two people, a doer and a watcher. This is often related to fear of erectile dysfunction in men, and can actually cause it. Men who have had episodes of dysfunction may be so worried about it happening again that they constantly monitor their performance; a man who has the mental habit of checking on "how he's doing" can develop erectile dysfunction as a direct consequence of his performance anxiety. Spectatoring—judging yourself—easily becomes a vicious circle of monitoring and failure, and it's a pretty sure way to interfere with sexual response.

Although treatment for a psychological erectile problem typically involves counseling to develop insight into its cause, there are other approaches that are more direct. Masters and Johnson developed "sensate focus," a body-centered and non-verbal approach that has enjoyed tremendous success. It is at the root of many of our exercises, which are designed to teach you how to let go of thoughts of goals and accomplishments in favor of experiencing and communicating sensations. The more you can quiet the mind's distracting, counterproductive chatter, the more you can be "in the moment," feeling what you feel and attending to what your partner feels. Nothing is more erotic than "Right Now!"

PLATEAU

The plateau phase is all about building and containing energy. Unlike the arousal phase, this is a stage where you can, with practice, develop skills that can make sex really extraordinary. Mastery of the flow of sexual energy through the body can also help enormously with the very common disorder of this phase of male sexual response—premature ejaculation, which we define simply as ejaculating before you, or your partner, desires it. One reason premature ejaculation is so common is the early conditioning most men get from masturbating. It's not that self-pleasuring is bad in any way. The problem is the usual combination of circumstances: intense sexual urges, little privacy, and a great desire not to get caught. Naturally, self-pleasuring becomes a furtive activity, one that a guy wants to get over with as quickly as possible. Since young guys tend to masturbate a lot, they undergo a pretty intensive Pavlovian conditioning process, effectively training themselves to get from arousal to ejaculation ASAP. As such, they become habituated to ejaculating quickly, and that can be quite difficult to overcome later on, when they finally do have plenty of time, privacy, and a partner. Slowing down and controlling ejaculation requires unlearning a highly ingrained habit.

All well and fine, you're thinking, *but how does a person do this?* The basic method is really quite simple: You just practice letting energy build and subside, build and subside before allowing yourself to go over the edge into ejaculation. This is an astonishingly effective practice that very few men in our culture ever try out. The idea that you can get really excited and then let yourself cool down a little and then get excited again—the idea that you can play with that and learn to work with your sexual energy—is a very important thought, and one of the pillars of our program.

❧

Steve is fascinated. He sometimes comes too soon with Kate, as he did with his previous girlfriends, and now his refractory period has been getting longer. He always used to be able to get it up again so fast that it hadn't mattered—he could always keep her happy in the meantime with oral sex—but lately this has been taking longer. Nagging worries about these issues have contributed to his avoiding Kate recently. Sometimes it's been easier to keep churning through work from the office than to wrestle with his anxieties about performance—and with the idea of what Kate might say if he disappointed her. The prospect of learning ejaculatory control—which he's beginning to think might solve his problems—both intrigues and cheers him.

Another crucial idea in developing ejaculatory control is moving sexual energy around the body. There is something very *focusing* about arousal. An erection tends to concentrate your attention on the sensations in your pelvis to the point that you sort of forget that the rest of you is even in the room. But if you move your attention to other parts of the body when you're sexually aroused, you can actually *spread it out* throughout your whole body. This will help you control ejaculation by diminishing urgency and, at the same time, increase the total sexual energy circulating through you. As you move the energy, it grows, because that's how chi works. When you finally choose to ejaculate, it's better: stronger and longer and more intense and pleasurable. This is one effect that makes learning to do what you want with your energy worth it. People who know about this talk about whole body orgasm and super orgasm, and they are not exaggerating. And it isn't even hard to learn. You really only have to be able to do three things:

1. Control your breath. Yep—back to good old breathing. It's that intimate connection between breath and energy, between voluntary and automatic body functions that we talked about earlier. By now you've had quite a bit of practice using your breath to send energy to different parts of your body, what with soulgazing, Yab Yum, and the other breathing exercises.

2. Control your muscles. By this we mean learning how to relax certain muscles (like the abdomen, thighs, and buttocks) while contracting others (like the PC muscle). There's a tendency to tighten all your muscles as orgasm approaches, which tends to further focus, rather than spread, the build-up of sexual energy. So learning how to differentiate the various muscles and only tighten the ones that need to tighten is a useful skill.

3. Control your attention. This is the most important of all, and in fact under-lies the other two. If you can't pay attention to what you're doing with your breath and your muscles, you won't be able to do what you want with them. And it's a basic rule of consciousness that energy follows attention, so as you learn to move your attention around yourself (and your partner, with

whom you become a single system during sex), you'll be able to move the energy where you want it to go, too. (Later this morning you'll do the PC Muscle Awareness Exercise, another Feldenkrais® movement lesson, which combines all three of the above skills into one lesson.)

ORGASM AND EJACULATION

Finally—the big O! That's what it's really all about, right, the holy grail of great sex—fantastic orgasms? Well, no, not exactly. Don't get us wrong: orgasms are great, and the more (and better) the merrier. But don't make the mistake of putting all your eggs in this basket—you'll miss out on a lot that way, especially if you're one of those men (meaning almost everyone in our culture) who believes that male orgasm necessarily entails ejaculation.

What's that? you say. *Orgasm without ejaculation? Coming without* coming? The very idea that men can have an orgasm without ejaculating is surprising to Westerners, but it's well understood in the East. The Tantric masters realized that orgasm and ejaculation are not *exactly* identical, and not *necessarily* linked in men, any more than they are in women. Unlinking them is not some mystical trick, like snake charming or floating in the air over your meditation mat or something; it's perfectly possible for ordinary Western guys to achieve without any great spiritual transformation. You can have your cake and eat it too.

We hasten to clarify at this point: the kind of orgasm you have when you don't ejaculate is different. Rather than the series of contractions every 0.8 seconds so well documented by Masters and Johnson, the non-ejaculatory orgasm is an experience of a continuous streaming of energy. We like to think it may be equivalent to vaginal (versus clitoral) orgasm in women. Sadly, we aren't aware of anyone who's had both non-ejaculatory male orgasms and vaginal ones who could confirm this!

Multiple Orgasms—They're Not Just for Women Anymore!

What's especially great about the non-ejaculatory orgasm is that it does not come with a refractory period. This means that you can have an orgasm, stay erect, drop back to plateau, have another orgasm, and so on. The multi-orgasmic experience men envy women for can now be theirs.

Riding the Wave

So, how is it done? Basically, it's simply an extension of the techniques we discussed above for ejaculatory control. You practice approaching orgasm and backing off until you have a good sense of how close you can get to your "point of no return," ease off, and then try to do it again. As your control over this process becomes more delicate and precise, you will at some point encounter a sort of window or gateway that opens up, right at that "point of no return," that allows you to pass through, as it were, into an entirely new realm of energetic experience. An analogy we like to use is that of surfing—with the right skill and timing, you can catch a wave of energy and ride it, with little effort of your own, just enough to stay in the wave without cutting out (going back to plateau level) or wiping out (ejaculation).

If you're more of a scientist than an athlete, you might prefer the image of orbiting a black hole, where you can catch tremendous energy radiating just outside the event horizon, but have to avoid getting sucked in by the powerful gravitational force. It's actually quite interesting as a sort of game (men usually love to engage this sort of challenge), and playing it successfully involves developing a really refined awareness of your sensations, and control of those three things discussed above—breath, muscle tone and attention. With practice, the non-ejaculatory orgasm can last for quite a long time. We don't think Guinness is keeping any records on this, but several minutes is not that unusual.

⤴

"A several-minute orgasm," thinks Martin, who's been reading with growing excitement. "Well, well, well." Being able to keep going for hours is another attraction of mastering ejaculatory control. He knows for a fact that Linda will be an enthusiastic collaborator. He turns down the corner of the page and decides to talk with her about it before the assignment.

⤴

Because maintaining your balance on the edge of ejaculation, on the crest of the wave, is fairly challenging at first, it's best to start working on it in masturbatory sessions, with or without your partner. When you want to bring it into intercourse—and you definitely will—you'll need your lover's informed cooperation. This can become part of your ongoing project together, another aspect of your intimacy, and one that opens the door to basically endless exploration together.

Practicing Non-Ejaculation

At this point in our workshops, there tends to be a certain restlessness among the men. What do we have against ejaculation, anyway?

⤶

"Damn straight," Charlie says to himself as he reads along. "If there's one thing in life that doesn't need improvement, it's coming."

⤶

Denying oneself ejaculation sounds like abstinence, some sort of grim punishment, to most Westerners. Surely your reward for making nice and foreplay and making sure she has her climax, etc., is that thrilling ten second release of tension. Isn't coming the whole point? Not necessarily. Many Eastern traditions teach that men who ejaculate are depriving themselves of the most important benefit of sexual communion—an increase in their overall level and quality of energy, life force, prana, chi, whatever. And there is indeed much to be said for this practice, whether you engage in it occasionally or on a regular basis.

Of course, even if ejaculation is perfectly healthy (which we believe it is), it's still quite obvious that it does change your energy, at least temporarily. It's not hard to get most men to agree that their energy is pretty depleted immediately

To Come or Not to Come

Classical yogic and Taoist thinking place great emphasis on abstaining from ejaculation: it is viewed as a reckless squandering of one's vital energy. These Eastern teachings strongly urge the man to forgo it for long periods of time—to engage in sex and intercourse to rouse and increase one's energy, but not to release it for weeks or even months at a time. There's plenty in the old texts about the benefits to a man's vitality and health and ability to get things done that accrue from these ascetic practices. (Remember the colonel in *Dr. Strangelove* who's obsessed with holding onto his "vital bodily fluids" because he thinks that every ejaculation brings him closer to death?) We are, however, unaware of any scientific evidence that might support this view.

after ejaculation. The question is, how long does this effect last? Are there subtle effects on a man's vitality that persist after the resolution phase, after he's had that traditional post-coital cigarette and snooze? And how do these effects compare and contrast with what happens if he should choose not to ejaculate? The answer appears to be quite variable from individual to individual. Many men have tried non-ejaculation and find little difference in their vitality (although the wives of some of these men will contradict them, having noticed important differences in the quality of their presence and attention). Many other men, however, have been very impressed by the change in their overall energy, and by important qualitative differences in how they carry themselves into the world—not only in their love lives, but also in business, parenting, friendship, and so forth. So we recommend that every man give the practice a fair try to assess its potential benefit for him personally.

Blue Balls, Prostate Trouble and Other Worries

All right, but what about blue balls? That always comes up at this point. Isn't it unhealthy to get very excited and not ejaculate? There is surprisingly little medical literature on this phenomenon, but it's a widespread concern. Here's our take on it: Some men do experience symptoms of pelvic congestion after becoming aroused and not ejaculating, a kind of heaviness and aching in the perineum and testicles. Whether this occurs on a given occasion has a great deal to do with the circumstances, specifically with how a man manages his sexual energy. If you generate a lot of energy and are frustrated in your attempt to discharge it, then you are likely to suffer the consequences of blocked energy. If, however, you have learned how to circulate energy, how to spread it out through your body and exchange it with your partner, and it is your intention to refrain from ejaculating (so that frustration is not part of your experience), you are unlikely to have trouble.

Another worry of some men is prostate infections. Those of course are real, and a real nuisance, and no one wants them. And it seems that there may in fact be a causal connection between a *sudden change* of sexual habits and risk for these infections. Going abruptly from, say, daily ejaculation for years to no ejaculation at all seems to cause some men to experience congestion in the prostate gland, which may be associated with development of infection. The key words, though, are "suddenly" and "abruptly." The human organism has a tremendous capacity to adapt to changing conditions, and much of this functional flexibility is the doing of the glandular system. The glands, including the prostate, adjust very quickly when things change. But adaptation takes time, so if a man has had his prostate in high gear and then suddenly stops ejaculating at all—say his girlfriend dumps him and he's too depressed even to masturbate—his prostate may become congested and irritable for a while. Interestingly, the same thing can happen in the opposite situation. After six celibate months go by, if the same guy falls in love with an incredible woman and they hardly get out of bed for a week, his long-suffering prostate may get irritated again until, one more time, it adapts completely to the new regime. This is predictable, if you think about it— anybody who's gone into the gym and tried to make up for years of inactivity in two hours or who's plowed into a high-fat meal after weeks of strict dieting knows that abrupt change is asking for pain.

Finally, if you're still anxious about hurting yourself by not ejaculating as often as you're accustomed to, recall that there are quite a few men, monks for example, who *never* ejaculate, and many of them live to a ripe old age with no more prostate trouble than anyone else. "Backed up semen" cannot hurt you.

RESOLUTION PHASE AND THE REFRACTORY PERIOD

We've given ejaculatory control and non-ejaculation (with or without orgasm) a pretty hard sell to all of you, and one of the reasons is the refractory period, that interval of time following ejaculation during which a man is unable to enter the arousal phase (get an erection) again. A particularly important thing to know about the refractory period is its relationship to aging. Almost as predictably as the eventual need for reading glasses, the steady lengthening of the refractory period is just something that happens as a man ages. It may only be a minute or two for a teenager, while a typical healthy guy in his forties may require 15 or 20 minutes. By the time a man reaches eighty, it may be as long as a couple of days! Thus, ejaculatory control assumes greater importance the older you get. Another strategy for assuring that you can continue to have all the sex you want (and your partner wants) as you get older is taking Viagra and, presumably, its newer competitors. Though not labeled for this purpose, it appears to be notably effective in shortening the refractory period. This could be a significant boon for the older man who wants to be sexually active more often, and also to any man who suffers from premature ejaculation—if he does ejaculate, he may be able to recover sooner and not totally disappoint his goddess.

We've just introduced a good bit of new information about male sexuality, plus a couple of pretty radical ideas concerning the male orgasm. We've found that a lot of men are very skeptical of these ideas, attached as they are to their familiar patterns of sexual experience and behavior. Still, there are many potential rewards for men from ejaculatory control. The most accessible one, the thing every man can benefit from, is getting to know his sexual energy better, learning to separate himself mentally from this idea that sex is about the goal of ejaculation. The attentiveness you need for this cannot be anything but nourishing for your lover and your connection.

Your assignment for this afternoon is designed to give you a chance to try out some of these new concepts in the context of your newly developing intimacy and heart connection. There's no obligation to make a permanent change, but we think you'll both find the exploration interesting, challenging, and enjoyable. But first we'd like you to do two exercises:

- The PC Muscle Awareness Exercise mentioned above.
- Touch Hands. This is an exercise we developed for our couples workshops that will give you a chance to get your energy flowing again, and to explore how you negotiate energy exchange with one another non-verbally.

PC Muscle Awareness Exercise ⦙·⦙9

The pubococcygeus muscle forms the floor of the pelvis, and serves a number of important physiologic functions, especially those related to eliminative functions. It also has a role to play in sex—it contracts reflexively during both male and female orgasm, and it can be used intentionally to increase the pleasure of sex, by both men and women. The better the control you have of your PC muscle (not just strength but also ability to differentiate it from other muscles in the area), the better you will be able to enhance your own experience, and that of your partner as well.

This exercise to improve the use of your PC muscle is an Awareness Through Movement® lesson based on the principles of body-based, organic learning of the Feldenkrais Method®. To get the most out of it, you should approach it not as a workout of your muscles, but as an exploration of the way you control your movement, relying on your curiosity to guide you, rather than your diligence. Do the movements that are suggested with the minimum amount of muscular effort and the maximum amount of attention to the *feeling* of what it is like to do them. Make sure you are comfortable, and only do what is easy. If there is any discomfort or strain, stop and rest, then start again and do it more slowly, more gently, with even less effort than before. The important part is not how much you can *do*, but how much you can *sense* of what you are doing: the less you do, the better you will be able to sense.

1. Lie on your back, preferably on a carpeted floor or a mat or some other firm padded surface. You might want a small pillow or pad under your head, not too thick or soft, just enough to bring your head forward to align it with your spine as if you were standing. Bend your knees and stand your feet flat on the floor, a comfortable distance apart, where you feel the least effort necessary to keep the legs upright.

2. Spend a moment sensing the area of your pelvis. Think of the pelvis bone itself, and also of the various muscles that attach to it (it's okay if your

knowledge of the anatomy is vague, just feel what you can feel inside yourself), the bones that connect to it (the thigh bones that meet the pelvis at the hip joints in the front, beneath the groin creases, the spine that joins it in back), and the internal organs cradled by it.

3. Also notice your breathing. Don't try to breathe "correctly" or in any particular way. Just notice what your ordinary breathing feels like, what parts of you move when you breathe, how breathing affects your contact with the floor behind you, how your pelvis moves (if it does) when you breathe.

4. Now, very slowly and gently, contract your PC muscle, and then release it just as slowly. Your PC muscle is the muscle you would use to stop urinating in midstream. For women, it's the muscle you tighten when you do Kegel exercises after childbirth. If you tighten it very hard, you will also tighten your anal sphincter, but don't tighten it that hard, just a little bit, much less than the full amount you could do. Try to make this contraction of the muscle smooth and continuous, and the relaxation equally smooth.

   Repeat the cycle of contraction and relaxation a number of times, making sure you rest briefly between each cycle so that each contraction is a fresh, new, intentional action done with awareness. You can gradually increase the fullness of the contraction, so long as it can be done smoothly and slowly, without straining or becoming uncomfortable in any way. Then take a rest and do nothing special for a few moments.

5. Now turn your attention to your breathing again, and begin gently to exaggerate the enlargement of your abdomen each time you inhale. Let your belly get full and round (without straining), as if you have a balloon expanding in all directions in your belly. When you exhale, it's just letting go of the effort of inhaling. After a few breaths like this, rest and breathe normally.

6. Then begin to exaggerate the contraction of the abdomen each time you exhale. Now the active part of breathing is emptying the air out, which you do by gently squeezing your belly smaller, drawing it in evenly in all directions. The inbreath is a (more or less) passive result of letting go of the effort of breathing out—you expand and let air in passively when you stop pushing it out. Rest again after a few breaths like this.

7. Begin to breathe the same way again, contracting the belly to breathe out, but this time also contract the PC muscle in the same rhythm. Try to time it so that you begin contracting the PC just when you begin exhaling and contracting the belly, you finish contracting both at the same moment, you begin relaxing the PC and the belly to breathe in at the same moment, and you finish relaxing both at the same moment. Rest and breathe normally after a few cycles.

8. Now reverse the coordination, contracting the PC each time you inhale and expand the abdomen, again paying close attention to the precise timing. Take your time, make the movements small and slow enough that you can be sure you're doing exactly what you intend to be doing. Then rest again.

9. Extend your legs fully on the floor. Contract your right buttock muscle slowly and smoothly but not too powerfully, and relax it just as slowly and smoothly. Notice that your pelvis rolls a little to the left when you do this. Repeat this a few times. Then do the same with the left buttock, rolling the pelvis a little to the right. Then contract both buttocks at the same time and release them several times. Gradually increase the fullness of the contraction, without straining or disturbing the smoothness of the movement.

10. Keep both buttocks comfortably contracted for a little while, and while they stay contracted, contract and release the PC muscle several times before you release the buttocks. Repeat this cycle several times, then rest.

11. Contract and release the PC and both buttocks at the same time, and release them at the same time and the same pace, carefully coordinating the timing so both movements are exactly synchronized.

12. Then reverse the coordination, so that you're contracting the PC while you're releasing the buttocks, and vice versa. You may find this harder to do, and that you make a mistake and start contracting both together again. That's okay, just stop and try again, going slower and reducing your effort till you get it the way you want. Again, it's getting the precise timing right that's most important, not how many times or how strongly you contract your muscles. Then take a good rest, with your knees bent and your feet standing.

13. Hold your knees in your hands, feet off the floor, one knee in each hand and knees comfortably apart from one another. Your knees will be over your belly or chest somewhere. Find where the weight of your legs is balanced by the length of your arms with the least overall effort. In this position, relaxing as much as possible, contract and relax the PC muscle slowly a number of times.

14. Then bring the knees closer to the chest by bending the elbows a bit, and each time you do that, contract the PC in the same rhythm, relaxing the PC when you let the knees go back to their original position by letting the arms lengthen. Repeat this cycle several times.

15. Then reverse the coordination, so you relax the PC when you bend your elbows and bring the knees into the chest, and contract it when you lengthen the arms and let the knees go away from the chest. Pay careful

attention to the timing as you repeat this a number of times. Then let go of your knees, put the feet on the floor, and rest.

16. Go back to simply contracting and relaxing the PC muscle now, and gradually speed it up. Make the contractions very quick and light, and find out how quickly you can pulse your PC without getting mixed up and distorting the quality of the movement.

17. Then slow it way down, contracting and relaxing the PC muscle so slowly that you could take several slow, full, belly-expanding breaths before you complete even one cycle of PC contraction-relaxation.

18. Just rest on your back. Sense the pelvis now, and compare the sensation with what you felt at the beginning of the lesson. Can you feel anything different? How is your breathing now? Slowly get up and walk around, see if you can sense any difference in how your pelvis participates in your walking.

Touch Hands ☺ 10

We developed this exercise for our couples workshops to teach a type of non-verbal communication that is related to sexual exchange in interesting ways, to continue familiarizing participants with the feeling of energy flow in the body, and to energize the group after sitting for a time listening to lectures. We often prescribe it for couples who get trapped in verbal debates that prevent their getting as close as they'd like to. In the workshops, we have people do this exercise with several people of the opposite sex, and this usually gives couples useful insight into their interaction with one another.

The basic stance and movement are derived from the two-person form of the Chinese martial art Tai Chi, which is a game or competition known as *Push Hands*. Briefly, the idea in Push Hands is for each partner to serve the other's growth and skill by trying to "uproot" him; that is, to force him to move his feet from their original stance. Skill in Push Hands consists of the ability to remain rooted to the earth through one's feet while remaining relaxed and flexible enough in the upper body to absorb, evade, transform, and reflect back the energy coming from one's partner, and to sense his vulnerability to being uprooted. It is not about size and strength at all.

In Touch Hands, we don't try to uproot our partners, but we do send our energy, and receive theirs as well. We stay rooted through our feet and legs, but loose and sensitive in our upper body to respond easily to their intentions and to communicate ours clearly.

We use the most stable Tai Chi stance (it's similar to an archer's posture, so it's called the bow stance) to connect ourselves to the earth, a very light but sensitive connection of the hands to our partner, and a basic rhythm of movement shifting weight from the back foot to the front foot. This forms a kind of bass line, drumbeat, or pulse upon which the improvised movements of the arms and upper body play (see illustration).

1. First learn the stance and movement by yourself. Stand with your left foot forward, pointed straight ahead, and your right foot back and pointed out to the right about 45 degrees. If you're of average height (let's say 5'6" or so), there will be about two feet (that is, 24 inches!) from the tip of the left big toe to the back of the right heel, and if you draw a line through your left foot the long way, it won't come close to touching the right foot: it should miss the right heel by a good six inches, so that your feet are separated not only front to back but also sideways to give you the best stability. (This is not a ballerina pose with one foot directly behind the other). Bend your knees a little bit, let your spine be long, and your low back relaxed.

2. Now begin to shift your weight back and forth, from the left to the right foot and back. Do this by bending and straightening your knees and hips alternately. Your feet remain completely flat on the floor (so your ankles will need to bend and straighten too), your spine remains long and vertical, and your entire body above your legs (that is, your pelvis, abdomen, chest, and head) glides effortlessly forward and back. When you go forward onto your left foot, you straighten the right hip and knee to push you forward, while you bend your left hip and knee to accept the weight. When you go back on your right foot, the bent left hip and knee straighten a bit to push you back, and your right knee and hip bend to accept the weight. Breathe easily, take your time, and spend a few moments getting the feel of this basic, back and forth rhythmic movement.

3. Then stand in the same stance facing your partner, so that your left feet are parallel, a few inches apart, with each one's toe even with the other's heel. Place the backs of your hands touching each other, so lightly that if there were butterflies between them they wouldn't be crushed, but firmly enough that they couldn't escape.

   Begin to glide back and forth with one another, adjusting to one another's rhythm until you find a tempo that works for both of you, all the while maintaining the same degree of light pressure between the backs of your hands. You're not pushing with your hands, but with your feet on the ground. Think that you're moving from your center (the center of energy in martial arts is the lower abdomen, which is also the body's center of gravity).

Touch Hands.

4. After you have done this long enough to feel that it's easy and natural, change your hands so that your fingertips are touching with the same lightness as before with the backs of your hands. (You may want to reverse your legs now and again during this exercise if they get tired with the same foot forward all the time.) Start gliding back and forth again, and this time one of you (let's say the woman) should begin to move her hands around. This is a freestyle movement, and can be anything that strikes her fancy—hands up or down, one hand forward and one back, large or small movements.

The idea is to make it interesting and fun for the two of you, maybe a little challenging, but not with the idea of defeating him in any way. His job is to follow you, maintaining the same light contact between the fingertips, not crushing the butterflies but not letting them escape. Find out where you can go with your hands without disturbing the basic rhythm of the pulse, the steady back-and-forth weight shifting. You can and should vary the speed of the movements of your hands and arms, have them do different things from one another, use turning movements of your trunk, anything you can think of, so long as your feet stay on the ground and you continue the basic back and forth rhythm (though it's okay to change the tempo of the basic movement).

Try doing this with your eyes closed, and notice any difference in the quality of the experience compared with having the eyes open. (Many of our students are surprised to find that it becomes easier and more enjoyable with their eyes closed.)

5. Then reverse roles (and reverse feet if you want). The man leads the movement, establishing the tempo of the basic gliding back and forth (and changing it when he wants), and moving his hands about in interesting ways, while the woman follows, trying to maintain the same light contact of the fingertips the whole time. Try it with your eyes open and with your eyes closed. After a minute or two, pause and rest.

6. Return to the same stance and basic rhythmic gliding with fingers touching. This time, you're to do the hand and arm movements with *no leader*, or more precisely, you'll see what it's like to lead and follow simultaneously. This is actually a very subtle thing, and requires a great deal of presence and sensitivity to the energy of the moment. You must be receptive enough to feel the very slight change of pressure and intention in your partner's hands and body, yet creative enough that *some* movement will happen that is varied and interesting to both of you. You need to be both active and passive at the same time, yet neither dominant nor submissive. (Perhaps it is now a little clearer how this relates to the sexual connection.) Be sure to try it with the eyes both open and closed.

7. When you've explored this to your satisfaction, let it go, and come to stillness. Thank your partner, perhaps with a bow and a Namaste, and spend a
   minute talking with each other about what you noticed with this exercise,
   particularly as it relates to acting versus sensing, controlling versus remaining passive, sending versus receiving energy.

AFTERNOON

Now you're ready for a long, delicious afternoon putting what you've learned
about male sexuality to work, your second major assignment: *Honoring Shiva*.

Men, you need to give your goddess some time and space to get the room
ready, so go meditate or stretch, take a walk or even a run, shower up or take a
bath, and get ready to be pleasured.

Ladies, read through the assignment, and prepare to take your man on a
journey he won't soon forget.

HONORING SHIVA

Yesterday, you and your partner honored Shakti. Today, equipped with a new
understanding of male sexual responses, and techniques that can help your man
go places he's never been before, you are ready to honor Shiva, the male energy
that sets the female essence free.

How often do we, as women, honor our lover's male energy? Most of us were
startled by our first glimpse of an erect penis (Ohmigod! *That's* what they look
like?!) and we may still find the sight of our lover's lingam a bit alien, even a little
frightening. Just the way it goes from docile to rampant makes it seem as if it has
a life of its own.

We don't have anything weird like that. Our major sexual organs are hidden
away safely inside, where we don't see them or even think about them unless they
give us trouble. How many of us gave our uterus a thought until our first period?
Who thinks about her ovaries and fallopian tubes until they malfunction?

Things are so different for boys and men that you probably can't fully understand your man's feelings about his sexual organs. Since the penis and scrotum
are outside the body, vulnerable and revealed in all their workings, he identifies
with them more strongly than you could know: "My penis, myself" is the general
idea. It's hard for us women to imagine boys' typical anxieties in a locker room,
and the self-conscious agonies of a guy who's missing a testicle mystify us. We're
likely not even to notice this horrible disfigurement until he points it out.

This great difference between men and women results in the lingam being unloved—except by its owner. Today, your assignment is to change that. Your mission, and we hope you decide to accept it, is to awaken the sleeping lingam, to explore its sensual delights, and to call on Shakti to connect his lingam energy to your man's heart. In the process, you will also have the opportunity to help your lover explore controlling his ejaculation, and possibly even begin to learn orgasm without ejaculation.

As you learned yesterday, it is usually easier to give sexually than to receive. This goes double for men, who quite understandably focus on performance and accomplishment—that's what most of a man's life in our culture is about. You may have had the sense that your man has doubts about his energy, or his sexual skill, or even his anatomy. Most likely, he does. Only you can allay his doubts.

The assignment is to devote one hour entirely to giving him pleasure, without intercourse or reciprocation. Your purpose is to reawaken him to the world of sensation by playing with his sexual arousal, and to help him discover the power inherent in open-hearted connection with his goddess.

＊

"Hmm," Paulette says to herself. "That book about the *Kama Sutra* I brought might come in handy...."

＊

To make this hour all it can be, you must consciously bring all Seven Dimensions of love to the experience, just as he did when he pleasured you:

1. Biologic: touch and caress the lingam and scrotum lovingly and creatively.

2. Sensual: create pleasure through all the senses.

3. Desire: put forth feminine sexual polarity—your loving, accepting energy and appreciation of his masculine presence.

4. Heart: transmit heart energy so he can feel your generosity and loving connection.

5. Intimacy: communicate openly, honestly; reveal your desire to give pleasure.

6. Aesthetic: enhance awareness of radiance (his and your own) and gratitude.

7. Ecstatic: cultivate a sacred quality to your connection; be mindful of the ritual aspect of the experience.

YOUR ASSIGNMENT, STEP BY STEP

First off, know that you can do this. You know his responses so well already—you'll just be taking your competence further and perhaps adding to your repertoire along the way. As Shakti, you are the ultimate source of pleasure; you can create heaven on earth for your man.

☙

As she lies on the hotel room couch reading, Nicole is still glowing with love and appreciation for yesterday, and is eager to do for Charlie what he has done for her. It strikes her that her expectations about sex with him have changed radically in a very short time.

☙

Preparation

Creating a proper space for this ritual is very important and can be a wonderfully creative experience. You want to make the space a refuge from the world, a frame within which there is nothing but love. Remember that the environment must appeal to all the senses—sight, sound, touch, taste, smell, and sense of movement. Let your imagination run wild as you create a space fit for a sultan. Hang scarves over lights, find exciting or soothing music, put your perfume on the pillow, ensure that there will be no interruptions, make the bed a sumptuous throne. Place towels on the bed if you plan to use oil, and have massage oil or lotion and some lubricant within reach. Consider putting fragrant flowers near the bed and around the room. Have iced fruit juice or wine and lovely glasses at the ready. If you think he would appreciate it, have a soft robe for him at hand. Bathe or shower and perfume yourself to be ready for him. Arrange pillows on the bed for soulgazing.

When your man arrives, send him off to bathe while you complete your preparations. Dress yourself in something easy and flowing, or wear nothing but a scarf and earrings! While you await your beloved, think about why you want to pleasure him and focus on your purpose—creating joy within him.

⌒

"Oh great," Kate thinks reflexively, *"I have to let him see me naked in day-light again."* But she remembers his awed reaction to her body during yes-terday's session and lets go of her worry... a little. "Well, one good thing is that today I'll be the one in control."

⌒

Invitation

When your lover emerges, greet him with a smiling face and offer to dry him off. Ask him if he would like a robe, and if he would, help him on with it. Lead him to the waiting bed, letting him see the appreciation in your eyes.

Soulgazing

Seat him on one of the pillows you have placed on the bed, then seat yourself opposite him. Sit across from one another holding hands and breathing together as you look into each other's eyes. Imagine that you are seeing into the heart of this man and allow him to see into yours. Visualize that you are sending him loving energy with every exhalation.

Touching

Invite him to lie back on the bed, arranging the pillows for his comfort. Begin to touch his head and face, taking time to caress each feature as if you were trying to memorize his face with your hands. Use your lips, hands, hair, and breasts to touch him as you proceed to slowly explore his whole body. Use lotion or oil if you like, and hum or whisper words of love as you tantalize every part of his phys-ical being. Suggest that he let you know when something you do feels especially good. Gently encourage him to relax and let all this loving in. Do not allow him to reciprocate except to touch you for his own pleasure. If necessary, playfully forbid him to "do" you.

There is no goal, and active response from him is not expected or even desired. If his lingam becomes erect, fine. If not, fine. If he gets an erection and it goes away, that's fine, too. You will not be having intercourse, no matter how much either of you may want to.

Connecting With the Heart Center

As you touch this wonderful person, your lover, keep your heart open. Imagine that you are radiating heart energy through your skin to him. Know that you are turning him on in the most profound sense, that with every touch you are lighting him up with love. Keep your gazes connected. Do not let him sleep—he is so deeply relaxed and soothed by now that this could happen! Let him be both at ease and aroused—this is a novel experience for most men. Discourage him from making any effort, and attend to any tension you feel in his body with gentle caresses and soft murmurs.

About Duration

Be aware of any tendency, in either of you, to hurry to a climax. Allow your lover to let his energy build gradually as drifting along in a stream of pleasure with you beside him. Also be aware that he may become overwhelmed by the experience of your giving to him, and have a strong emotional release. He may cry or shout or laugh; he may feel sad or angry as he recalls past sexual times that were humiliating or even shameful. He may even grieve for all the pleasure he has been missing out on before today. Welcome all emotion—do not take anything personally. In this room, for this hour, he is free to feel and express whatever comes up for him. Breathe, stay focused on your beloved and keep pouring love into his heart. Demand nothing.

Pleasuring the Lingam and Scrotum

When you feel that it is time to touch his "wand of light," do so with the utmost love. Most men have never had their lingam really *loved*. It is your privilege to introduce him to this wonderful experience. As you touch the lingam, spend time with the shaft and base, but even more with the tip and its rounded edge. (Lubricant adds greatly to your man's pleasure during this part of the ritual.) The rim of the glans is dense with nerve endings, and for most men it's the focus of sexual excitement—the summit of heaven. Carefully explore the "v" on the underside with gentle fingertips or your lips and tongue. Use your fingers and thumb to encircle the rim, twisting around the tip while your other hand holds the shaft. Move the skin firmly and lovingly along the shaft. Most men like a tighter, more vigorous touch here than you would think, so don't be too delicate about it. Explore the sensitive scrotum and testicles with varying touch. Caress and massage the part of the lingam that is hidden under and behind the scrotum, too. This is his sacred spot, and it may require quite firm pressure externally to elicit a pleasure response deep in the prostate. And don't hurry. There is a lot to play with, and you have plenty of time.

Tea for Two

There is a simple but wonderful treat that you can give your man, ladies. First, ask him to disappear for a few moments into the kitchen to make you a hot cup of your favorite tea while you prepare yourself and your bed for lovemaking. When he returns with the steaming liquid, take the cup from him and have him lie down on the pillows. Take a sip of the lovely brew, swallow, and kiss his eyelids—he will be surprised to find that your mouth is pleasantly hot. Next, sip and kiss his ears, his nose, his mouth and neck. Work your way down his body, pleasuring his nipples, putting a little hot tea in his belly button and sucking it out, and finally take the tip of his lingam into your hot mouth. He will love it, and you will wonder why you never thought to do this before!

Even as you explore your partner's body, stay connected with the soul and heart. Speak words of love and desire. Gaze into your lover's eyes when you can, and remember to often rest one hand on his heart. The more you can help him feel the heart-lingam connection, the more vivid, profound, and lasting his experience will be.

～

Linda sighs as she stops reading for a moment. "This will be just like the old days," she thinks dreamily. She and Martin used to spend whole afternoons in bed, playing sexy games together. "Except, of course, for the no intercourse part. We never would have thought of that."

～

Exploring Ejaculatory Control

Allow your man to build energy, but help him contain the energy and spread it throughout his body, rather than striving for orgasm and ejaculation. Watch him and stay very attentive to his experience; encourage him to tell you how close he is to orgasm. Ask him to ride the edge of pleasure and to let you help him experiment with taking the energy to several peaks, backing away from release each time. It is even possible that he will have an orgasm without ejaculation.

The whole-body stimulation you have been giving him, and your loving cooperation in riding the waves of pleasure, create this potential. You can additionally help him control the ejaculation reflex by stopping all stimulation as he nears climax and applying firm pressure to the perineum (the area behind the scrotum) until the energy dissipates a bit. Touching other parts of his body—legs, arms, feet, hands, head—may also help him decrease his concentration on the sensations in his genital region. Remind him to breathe deeply, to relax his muscles, and to imagine the energy flowing upward to his heart and head.

After several peaks, you both may be ready for him to experience conscious ejaculation. If and when this happens, stay connected through your eyes and maintain awareness of the connection between your open hearts. He'll probably be vocal when he comes; don't be shy, sound out with him! Welcome his fluid; play with the silken liquid before you gently remove it with a cloth.

Alternatively, you may decide together to finish the connection without ejaculation, quite possibly a new experience for both of you. If you do this, he will have more energy to bring to your next session together.

Finishing

Conclude your connection with a warm, full-body embrace. Remember, though, that no matter how sexually aroused you both may be, there is no intercourse. Exchange energy with your breath, you heart, and your eyes. Bathe in the radiance of your beloved. Tell him what it was like to be his goddess and pleasure him. Allow him to rest and absorb the experience.

THE COUPLES HONOR SHIVA

Steve and Kate

Steve is a little ambivalent about this exercise. On the one hand, he's really looking forward to being pleasured by Kate, but on the other, he's worried about coming too soon. Kate has never said anything to him about this, but he still feels a bit inadequate about his lack of control, and he really wants to learn how to do better. He's been doing PC exercises diligently since he first read through the book.

Kate greets him wearing only a scarf around her head and absolutely nothing else but perfume. She's a bit shy leading Steve to the bed, but his wide-eyed delight, not to mention his instant erection, makes her feel more confidently goddesslike—and rather wanton. Since it's become clear just how big a turn-on her naked body is to him, she's starting to think that she actually does look pretty good.

She throws herself into her job, and he's soon moaning as she rubs her oiled breasts over his skin.

"Katie..." says Steve. He wants to share his doubts with her, but is struggling now with his growing arousal.

"What, baby?" she grins at him as she teases him by brushing a nipple across his cheek.

Steve hesitates—he's not used to feeling this vulnerable. "I really want to work on not coming so fast. We've never talked about it, and you've always been really great about it, but..."

Kate pauses in the midst of her playful seduction, suddenly turning serious. "I know you hate coming so fast, honey, but you always take such good care of me, so I never wanted to complain. Besides, I was afraid I'd hurt your feelings, and I didn't want to do that."

"So can we work on it? Like try the stuff in the book?"

"You bet! I was planning on it anyway," she replies with a mischievous grin, and turns to reach for a bottle on the nightstand. She liberally douses him with lubricant, and begins massaging his scrotum and penis, pushing his legs apart so that she can begin her sweeping upward strokes on his perineum. It isn't long before she can sense him tensing up in a way she knows well. "Should I stop for second, baby?"

"Do that one more time—not quite so much pressure." She complies until he urgently asks her to stop. She does, and begins trailing her fingers down from his groin to his toes and back up again, stopping to massage his feet a little along the way.

"Oh man," Steve gasps. "That is so good. I was right there, just about to tip over."

Kate has been watching him closely, and feels very much in tune with Steve's level of arousal. A few moments later, she senses that it's safe to start stroking him again, and this time uses the twisting motion. She remembers to spread the energy out from his genitals, and uses one hand to make light, quick outward strokes on his arms and legs, and reminds him to focus on his breath. She also reminds Steve to let the muscles in his belly and thighs relax when they start to tense by signaling him with her touch. She's surprised how excited she's getting with all this, and is beginning to really want him inside her. But she stays faithful to the assignment, and once again brings him within an inch of climaxing.

"This is so fabulous!" says Steve. "I'm really starting to get the hang of it."

Still with one hand on his lingam, Kate places the other hand on his heart. "You're doing great, baby. I want you to go ahead and come this time, but stay with me." She begins to stroke him again, holding his gaze with her own. She feels an incredible sensation of expansion in the center of her chest, and her breasts feel swollen and somehow powerful in a way that's completely new for her. Slowly she increases the cadence of her strokes, and gradually Steve's energy climbs. He continues to look into Kate's eyes, acutely aware of her awesome beauty and the intensity of their connection. As he approaches the point of no return for the third time, it is much more slowly than he has ever done before, and he has time to remember to relax into it as he finally comes with a deep, throaty moan. The contractions are unbelievably powerful, and continue for much longer than he thought possible. He has a quick thought about his PC muscle and the benefit of the exercises he's been doing, then is back with Kate, relaxing slowly under her loving gaze.

Kate has found the whole thing incredibly erotic and she curls up next him, giggling a little to herself.

"You're such a good student. It's just a pleasure to have you in my class."

Charlie and Nicole

Charlie can hardly wait for the hour to begin. The exercises so far have been good, great even, but getting so excited yesterday without release is wearing on him. He has no plans whatsoever for exploring non-ejaculation, as the whole idea sounds crazy to him. Why would anyone want to get it on and not come? Trying to make it last sounds like fun, though. He doesn't want this to be over before time is up.

The idea of Nicole devoting herself to his pleasure fills his mind—she's never been into exerting herself for him. In fact, he can't think of anyone who ever was. Which, now that he thinks about it, is sort of sad.

When he gets out of the tub, Nicole meets him in full goddess mode. She's tied a scarf around her breasts but is otherwise naked. She's a knockout, he thinks, just as she was on their wedding night.

For her part, Nicole is feeling generous and sassy—and very divine. Being active and in control is something really different, and she finds the prospect exciting. As she leads Charlie to the bed—no surprise that he didn't want to put on the robe—she thinks about yesterday and hopes that she can make him feel even half as good as he's made her feel.

As they soulgaze, each keeps a hand on the other's heart, and Nicole begins to sense a sort of warm fizzing sensation where her hand touches

Charlie's skin. She's thrilled by this new ability to detect energy-flow, and asks Charlie if he can feel it. He is mesmerized by her beautiful face right in front of his and replies that he can. In fact, he suddenly overcome by how much he loves this woman and his eyes well with tears that Nicole gently licks from his face.

As she moves toward his lingam, he wonders how she'll touch it, and is totally surprised when she begins to kiss and explore it with her tongue. It's been a long, long time since a woman has done this for him. Back when he was dating, he'd always felt that his girlfriends didn't really like doing it—they'd gone down on him just to make him happy. But here is Nicole, humming to herself and turning around to wiggle her bottom at him! He's exquisitely aroused and so enchanted by her playful, lightheart-ed mood that he loses track of his reactions and comes perilously close to ejaculating after just a few minutes. When he incoherently asks her to stop, though, she turns back around and gently kisses his face and strokes his hair until he calms down.

Nicole is high as a kite on the feeling of being completely in charge, and exercises her power by taking him closer and closer to climax. She's turned on by having this big, forceful guy, her guy, begging for mercy, testifying to the intense pleasure she's giving to him. This, she thinks, is what it's like to be a goddess.

Finally, they agree that he's had all he can stand. She takes him past the point of no return and he ejaculates powerfully, shouting into a pillow to keep from startling the people in the neighboring rooms. Nicole strokes him affectionately as he stops thrashing and plays idly with his softening penis while keeping a hand on his heart.

A weight that's been there for years has just lifted.

Martin and Linda

As Linda makes last-minute preparations, Martin lies in the tub inhaling the scented oil she put in for him. He's anticipating an experience as pow-erful as hers the day before. He's savoring every moment of waiting for it all to begin. He's also thinking about orgasm without ejaculation. He once met a guy in college who talked about being into some kind of mystical sex and claimed that he could come without coming. Martin and his friends had argued about whether this was possible and decided the guy was full of it. Still, the idea that there was some better kind of orgasm out there had preoccupied him for months. Finally, he's going to figure it out.

He's nearly trembling with excitement as she leads him to the bed. She's wearing the amber pendant again between her gorgeous breasts and she has that radiant smile lighting her face. Martin thinks, "What a blessing she is in my life!" They begin the now familiar soulgazing and sweep into a deep connection. She invites him to lie back and begins gently stroking his head and then, after cradling his face in her hands, touches his eyes, ears, nose and lips. Then she runs her tongue luxuriously over his closed eyes, and reaches for the massage oil. She rubs it sensuously between her hands to warm it, and applies it to Martin's belly and thighs with slow, kneading strokes, working all around his genitals but not quite touching them yet.

"You trickster!" says Martin with a grin.

"Tsk, tsk, let's not be impatient. I have a whole hour to work on you, remember?" But Linda relents and gently takes hold of his lingam, which is half-erect.

She takes her time with it, caressing, kissing, loving the gradual expansion in her hands. Soon he's fully erect, and Linda reaches for the KY, and slathers him with it. She strokes him alternately gentle and firm, slow and fast; she uses two hands, then one; she explores his perineum with a variety of pressure. Martin has his eyes closed, and is now urgently thrusting his pelvis in time to her strokes. After a few minutes, Linda notices that he's clenching his jaw, and senses that he's not with her.

"What's going on, sweetheart? What would you like me to be doing?" she asks.

"Exactly what you're doing. But… something's wrong. I don't know— the feeling's gone. I want this so damn much! I don't get what's happening at all." He looks away from her with frustration.

Here's what David would advise Martin right about now:

You're trying too hard, Martin. You love her so much, but you're too eager for what's coming, and you're forgetting to connect with her energy, with her heart. She's tapped into the life-force, Shakti. Maybe you were a little intimidated on some level by her response yesterday—the full power of the goddess can be overwhelming. But Shakti is tender, too. Look into her eyes and let her pour her love into you. All you need to do is let it in.

Martin, who's been squeezing his eyes shut, gently pulls Linda to him, breathes deep, and looks into her eyes, where all he sees is boundless love. He begins to relax into her radiance, continuing conscious breathing and letting all the muscles he's unconsciously tensed loosen. Linda breathes with him, smiling down while touching his face and head and throat. She reminds him that all he needs to do is lie there and enjoy himself. As she works her way slowly down his body again, he turns her a bit so that he can touch her wet yoni, which gives him an instant jolt of energy. He feels her power running through him and his erection returns. Now she can feel that he's letting her goddess energy in, and she revels in her role of bestower of blessings. She returns to the work of pleasuring him with lascivious gusto.

It doesn't take long for Martin's energy to build this time. He signals Linda that he's close to orgasm by laying his hand over hers and squeezing his request for her to slow down. She instantly backs off, keeping a firm grip around the base of his shaft, while slowing the movement of her other hand on the head of the lingam to a snail's pace. Martin continues to guide her with his hand, mostly keeping her still while he moves his pelvis smoothly into her grip. She puts a hand lightly on his throat as tiny screams begin to emerge from it; she can literally feel the energy coursing through him as his eyes open wide, his chest expands with deep, full drafts of breath, and he finally cries out with a long, continuous note of pleasure. He continues to move his pelvis with slow, controlled undulations, though, and the energy continues to flow, seemingly from his lingam up through his center and out the top of his head. It goes on and on, to the amazement of both of them, as they continue to hold one another's gaze while Martin rides the wave of ecstasy. He has no idea how long it has lasted when he finally decides to let it subside and rest.

Martin starts laughing. "Do know what just happened? Do you *know*? I came without ejaculating. Oh. My. God. This feeling just built up down there and it's like I pulled it up, all the way into my throat and out my head. It's all true—what a trip! Oh baby, I don't know what to say."

"Don't say anything, honey. You can just let it be. It was awesome for me too."

She holds him in her arms, and they rest together quietly for a long time.

Bob and Paulette

Even though the book tells him not to worry about performance, Bob does. He nervously popped his first dose Viagra a couple of hours ago, and he is cautiously optimistic about how things will go (he didn't tell Paulette that he'd had a pretty good erection the day before when he was pleasuring her).

Paulette is anxious, too, as she carefully prepares the room. She's concerned that Bob is worried about having an erection—which of course he is—and that if he's disappointed he'll feel awful and she'll feel as if she's failed him. Readying herself in front of the mirror, she thoughtfully takes inventory of the changes time has made in her body and doesn't much like what she sees. Can Bob still honestly think she's sexy?

Both make an effort to set aside their fears as Paulette helps Bob dry off, gets his robe, and leads him to the bed. The translucent red and pink scarves she's draped over the shades make the glow from the lamps warm and flattering, and she feels better about her body. Bob's murmurs of appreciation, and the way he admires her breasts as they begin soulgazing, buoy her even further, and she forgets to be self-conscious.

To both their relief, his lingam begins to stir as soon as she starts stroking his skin—something she hasn't seen for many months. Whether it's the Viagra itself working, or his hopes for it, or both, he couldn't care less. He feels more sure of himself than he has for a long time. Relieved of this oppressive worry, he finally relaxes and lets himself simply enjoy what Paulette is doing, which is very interesting. She fills one palm with lubricant and spreads it with great care over his lingam, scrotum, and perineum, and into the creases where his thighs and groin meet. Then, gazing steadily into his eyes—she's propped his head up slightly so that he can see—she tries out some of the massage techniques from her *Kama Sutra* book. She holds his erect lingam tightly in both hands and begins sliding one hand down toward the base while using the other to pull and swivel around the rim. She asks Bob to tell her what he likes as she varies her touch—sometimes coming down with one hand over the head of the lingam and the other on the shaft, at other times stroking up from below the scrotum and all the way to the tip. Bob is trembling with pleasure, and she's having a wonderful time playing.

She begins to feel him tensing and his breath gets faster. She's looking forward to bringing him to joyful orgasm when he suddenly says, "Can you slow down a little, sweetie? I'd rather wait, I think." Astonished, but competent as ever, Paulette shifts gears and presses firmly at the base of his lingam and down below his scrotum. She feels him slide back down the wave, away from coming, but his erection doesn't fade.

As she leans forward to kiss him, his brilliant, serene smile goes straight to her heart and the tears start to roll. "There's always tomorrow," he tells her jauntily, which makes her cry harder. She is gladdened beyond words by his confident masculine energy, and amazed by the feminine energy she feels flooding through her heart.

EVENING

You've learned more about each other's bodies (and your own!) than you ever have known before, you've pleasured each other as you never have before, and most important, you've expanded your sexuality consciousness in ways you could never even have imagined before your Long Erotic Weekend began.

Time to curl up in each other's arms and talk about your experience. Take a nap, and then talk some more. When you're ready, do the Puja Exercise, an intensely intimate connection that will bring you even closer together, and prepare you for tomorrow, when you will put it all together and take it home with you.

TALKING ABOUT IT

You may feel as if there's nothing to say about what just happened, but it's vital that you share your impressions with each other. Your experience of sex and of each other is in flux, and you need to be in close communication not only during the exercises, but at other times, too. You're probably feeling things moving around inside you—share that with your partner, and encourage him (or her) to tell you what's happening inside.

You're probably finding that all sorts of things—memories, old misunderstandings, things you always wondered about—are coming up for both of you. Enjoy to the utmost the intimacy you've created by communicating about things you've never talked about before, or that you've only been able to discuss in a limited, stilted way. Use the loving energy that you've banked over the last two days to clear out some of the emotional clutter from your relationship. Notice how easy this becomes when your bodies are relaxed and your hearts are open.

One of the deepest lessons you can take away from this weekend is that when we make love, that's exactly what we do—we generate love itself, and that immense good feeling between us can make emotional walls that seemed impregnable melt away like ice in the sun. Free and open communication is just one more blessing that great sex—ongoing, sustainable, repeatable erotic ecstasy—can bring to life.

$\backsim$

THE COUPLES TALK AFTER THE ASSIGNMENT

Steve and Kate

"You know what?" Steve says, stepping out of the shower behind Kate. (They've used up all the hot water soaping each other.)

"Nope." Kate starts to dry her hair, but Steve takes the towel away and begins doing it for her.

His voice is quiet and low. "I came too soon the first time we ever did it, and I've always felt bad about that. I really let you down, and I feel like you've been pissed off about it ever since. Not that I blame you. I mean, what a way to start a relationship."

Kate looks up from under the tangle of her wet hair, surprised. "Steve, this is total news to me."

"You're kidding," he says, standing still.

"No. Honest. Didn't you realize how sloshed I was? I must have drunk a whole bottle of champagne myself." She takes his face between her hands. "I swear," she says tenderly. "All I can remember is you getting irritated with all those buttons and starting to rip them off. Oh, yeah—and wondering whether I was too queasy to sleep. You thought I was *mad*?"

"Well, yeah."

"You knucklehead! Besides, that glitch—such as it was—is history. You ride the wave with a flick of my tiny hand." She's feeling gay and generous and playful, and starts snapping the towel at him.

"You will pay for your disrespect to Shiva, my dear," he growls, and tackles her so they land on the bed.

Charlie and Nicole

Charlie lies on the bed happily scratching his belly as Nicole comes in from calling his parents to check on the kids.

"How are they holding up? My folks, I mean." He grins.

"Your mother sounded fairly together, for her, but she says Morgan and Carter have been fighting since breakfast." She sighs, looking distracted.

"They're there. They're fine. We're here, and we're *very* fine. Don't think about it."

"Well, yes. But..."

"No 'yes, but.' You are my goddess and I love you with all my heart, and all my lingam, too, and we have one more day before we have to be parents again. Put them out of your mind, 'O radiant one."

"That's easy for you to say," Nicole says, falling back into a tone Charlie knows all too well.

He pulls her close and runs his hands over her skin. "Yeah, it is. Which is why you should listen to me say it. We need to figure how to keep them from wearing you down so much. They're not as fragile as you think."

"Nature gave children mothers because if they just had fathers, none of them would live," Nicole says, poking him in the side.

"Yeah, and she gave mothers lovers so they wouldn't drive themselves nuts over the kids. Seriously, you've got more sparkle in your eyes than you've had since Morgan was born. I'd really like to see it there after we get home. What we were doing this afternoon...." For once he's at loss for words.

Nicole lies back stretching her naked self luxuriously. "Yes. I was rather magnificent, if I say so myself. And I *do* feel frisky—all this energy stuff seems to be working. I was thinking maybe we could get in some tennis before dinner."

"And have to get dressed?"

Martin and Linda

Martin returns to the bedroom from rustling up a snack in the kitchen. He's prepared sliced apples and various cheeses and two glasses of white wine, one of Linda's favorites. He sets it down carefully on the bedside stand and offers her a pretty napkin with a flourish. "My dear."

"Oh, how sweet of you," she says, propping herself up with pillows. "I could get used to this."

"You should," he replies, settling down with his own plate. "We're going to need to do a lot more fooling around from now on. We've got this whole new, well, country to explore."

"As long as we don't get too goal-oriented," Linda says. "We're not looking for the Northwest Passage."

"You mean, as long as I'm not. Point taken." He kisses her under the ear. "I just have to remember to raise the goddess' energy, and then feel it. And oh, does it feel good."

"But it's so natural to want to *get* somewhere. I mean, that's what our jobs are like, and then we come home and there's so much to get done, and the kids are everywhere you look, and...."

"All the more reason for having a place and time to recharge, right? We are going to work on that. I don't know about you, but I feel as if I've got enough juice to rearrange our lives next week," he says. "Maybe I can get it done Monday."

"Ah, that's the magic orgasm talking," Linda replies, smiling.

"Absolutely. And the prospect of more and more of that with you."

Bob and Paulette

"I have been such a fool," Bob says, sitting out on their patio with Paulette. Her feet are in his lap, and he rubs them gently while they talk.

"Well, of course, dear," she says sweetly, parodying herself. "But which particular foolishness of yours do you have in mind?"

"Being shy about getting the Viagra. Things could have been better a year ago—no wonder you were so irritated with me about it."

She looks thoughtfully up through the tree branches above them to the sky. "It wasn't missing the sex, so much, you know—though I did miss it. It was more worrying that you were shutting down, giving up. Shutting me out."

"I am so sorry," he says, taking her hand.

"Oh, it was just as much my fault. I get all bossy when I'm upset, and you're too sweet to tell me to go jump in a lake. Which you should, you know." She takes a deep breath. "On the other hand, if things hadn't gotten so bad, we might never have done this program and never had this afternoon. Or yesterday afternoon. If you'd run to Jerry and gotten the pills right away, we would have just gone on as before."

"Which was fine, but..."

"But we would have never known what we were missing."

"Well, we're not going to miss it any more," Bob says with decision. "So little time, so much ecstatic sex."

NIGHT

FINISHING THE DAY: PUJA

Puja is a Sanskrit work that means ceremony or worship. This exceptional exercise has been a powerful experience for couples in every one of our workshops, and we want you to enjoy the impact of this exchange as well. In our groups, there are two circles: the men are on the outside facing inward and the women face outward, each opposite her man. After each connection in the exercise, the women move left to a new partner. We give verbal instructions for each dyad as they hold hands and face one another. Sometimes eyes are closed and some individuals are able to keep their eyes open as they look at each partner in sequence. There is emotional beauty and intensity in this exercise and often some tears.

In your case, you will be able to have the benefit of having all the varied experiences with your own mate; you will see him/her in different life stages and be able to send your life energy as you imagine yourself as different personas as well. Allow yourself not only to concentrate on sending emotional energy but also to be the receiver—to be as open as possible.

Begin by standing opposite your partner. Bow in Namaste, acknowledging the light in them with your own light. Take the hands of your beloved, and look into their eyes.

Women, see before you the boy that this man once was. Imagine that you are a favorite aunt, his grandmother, or an older woman friend that loves him unconditionally. Send him caring, love and appreciation for his hopes, dreams and vulnerability. Men, be the boy, one who is unsure, sometimes afraid, lonely or sad, and receive this love. Allow the nurturing, caring and wide-open appreciation that is flowing towards you to enter into your heart.

After you have sent this energy, ladies, give your partner a forehead kiss and prepare to receive. Men, take your partner's hands. See before you the girl that this woman once was. Pour love, caring, and appreciation into her as if you were her father, grandfather, or favorite uncle. Notice her vulnerability, her fresh awareness of life and her dreams; send her loving protection and delight for the girl she is. Women, let this love into your heart, let it fill you and soothe any fears. Allow this older man who loves you and wants to keep you safe to have a special place in your heart.

Men, when you have sent this love, kiss your partner on the forehead to complete this phase of the exercise. Bow to one another in Namaste. Stand together in the Tai Chi stance, and play Touch Hands for a while, with the woman leading. When you feel complete, gently come to stillness, separate to stand facing one another again, and begin the next stage.

Women, take your mate's hands. See this man before you—someone with responsibilities, who has tried to be successful and sensitive, strong and yet open, and bless him with your appreciation, your recognition of his strengths and the belief that he can become even more truthful and loving. Men, let this appreciation in. Allow this wonderful, giving woman to send her energy into your being. Women, when you are finished sending, kiss your man on the lips and prepare to receive.

Men, hold the hands of this woman before you, someone who has tried to nurture so many others, who has taken her responsibilities very seriously, who has tried to be strong and loving, nurturing and compassionate. Bless her with your admiration, your recognition of the goodness in her and the belief that she can become even more truthful to her core. Women, allow this man to send his appreciation of your efforts into your heart, let yourself be seen in this way.

Now, gentlemen, kiss your woman on the lips to complete this phase, and once again bow to one another in Namaste.

Stand again in the Tai Chi stance, and play Touch Hands, this time with the man leading. Continue until you feel complete, then come to stillness. Separate from one another, and prepare for the next stage by holding hands.

Women, see before you a part of God—the divine in human form. Know that this man has within the highest good, an aspect of the sacred, and send your love for this radiant being directly into him through the hands that you are holding. Men, let this radiance show, claim what she is seeing, and allow your sacred nature to be strengthened and bathed in this energy streaming toward you. When you are finished, ladies, kiss the palms of your partner's hands, and prepare to receive.

Men, see the Goddess before you, the light and the radiance in her being. Understand that she carries a part of the Divine in her and send your love to that aspect. Women, allow yourself to seen in this way, claim the beauty of that part of God that dwells within. Receive the love and the energy coming towards you, knowing that it will strengthen this sacred aspect of your being. Men, when you are finished, kiss the palms of your Goddess to complete this phase of the exercise. Stand in Tai Chi stance and play Touch Hands with no leader.

Now, place your right hand on your partner's heart (see illustration). Cover their hand with your left hand. See this wonderful person before you—the child, the adult, the sacred being. An individual so complex and so simple, so ordinary and yet so divine. Allow the radiance to show in your face as you look at your beloved. See the beauty in the face looking back at you. Send this person heart energy, sustenance for any problems or difficulties ahead. Make their heart grow beneath your hand, receive the loving energy flowing back to you, and allow yourself the luxury of being overwhelmed. Kiss—with all your beings.

⌒

THE COUPLES END THE DAY WITH PUJA

Steve and Kate

As they begin Puja, Kate quickly becomes overwhelmed when Steve sees the young girl in her. He assumes the image, in her eyes, of the older man who loved her unconditionally—her dead father—and that vision fuses with that of the real man standing before her. He sees the sadness and vulnerability—

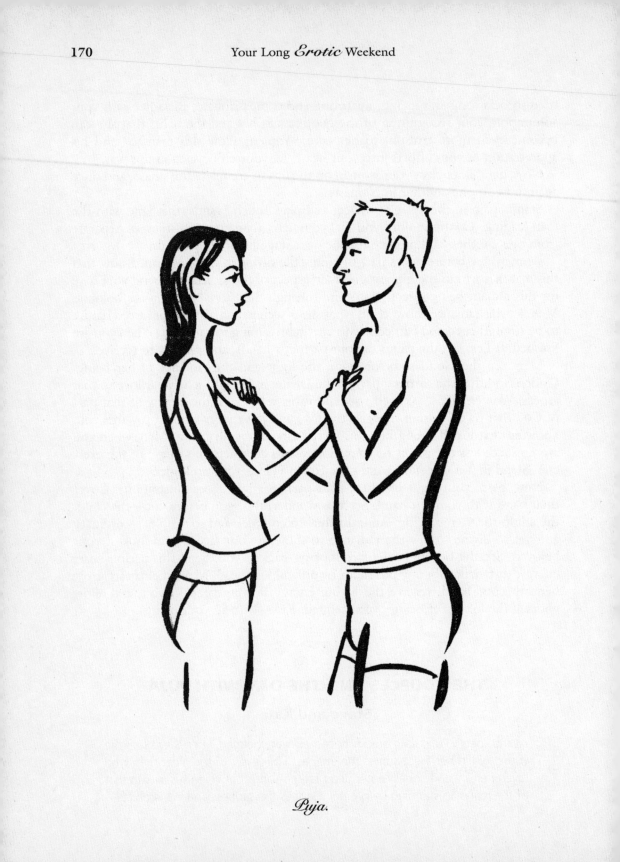

Puja.

and the love—in her suddenly-young eyes. Waves of melancholy mixed with relief wash through her as she recognizes that her heart is at last fully open to the man she loves.

Charlie and Nicole

As he and Nicole look into one another's eyes, Charlie sees how she embodies the strength and sexiness of a woman who has recognized her own power. He is awed by this, feeling a shift in himself as he engages this more confident woman. Nicole radiates self-assurance, clarity and sexiness as the grown woman who has finally claimed her sexual maturity.

Martin and Linda

As they stand touching hands, seeing one another in one persona after another, both bask in each other's divine nature. Martin has a vision of Linda as goddess, no longer disguised by depression—the amber pendant between her breasts seems to glow with her power. She sees the god in him, radiating a masculine energy that magnifies her own. Both finish the exercise feeling that they've glimpsed a truth that had been concealed.

Bob and Paulette

Paulette has a sudden sense of Bob as a man—she had almost entirely lost track of his masculinity, his separate maleness. The familiarity born of a long marriage falls away, and she sees him anew. Bob warms himself in her unobstructed female radiance. When he envisions her as the goddess, he realizes that the hardened, pinched feel of their relationship has vanished, and he feels himself sinking into their love like a warm pool.

Day Three has ended, and with it 48 hours of honoring the Shakti and Shiva in you. Time to relax, cuddle, and restore your energies, to be ready for the most glorious day of all—Day Four, in which you learn to integrate the male and female energies of the love goddess and the warrior lover. You will also create a detailed plan to carry what you have learned into your normal, everyday life, with all its stresses and demands, so that sex continues to nourish you in your relationship far beyond the end of your Long Erotic Weekend.

GIFT REMINDER

Don't forget that you and your beloved will exchange gifts tomorrow! If you haven't done it yet, you'd better get busy finding or making meaningful gifts to mark the end of your weekend! Your gift can be a poem, something you have crafted or found, anything but something bought. And you must include words, either written or spoken, in your presentation.

Day Four

Putting It All Together and Making It Last

DAY FOUR

Suggested Schedule

MORNING:

- Sleep in together. Everything you do today, you do together, as one.
- Revisit your Seven Dimensions of Sexual Energy Inventories.
- Learn about the tools for *Maximizing Your Seven Dimensions of Sexual Energy*
- Develop a *Good-for-Life Sex Plan*. Fill out the form together. Seal the deal with a kiss.
- Arrange your beautiful space together.

NOON:

- Go out for lunch. Let others wait on you as a couple.
- If you need to take a break and finish preparing your gifts for one another, do so now.

AFTERNOON:

- Prepare for the final assignment by reading *Seven Dimensional Sex*.
- Take a long bath or shower together. Let yourself be carried away in the union of energies—we provide suggestions if you want them.

Now that you are both relaxed and sexually tuned in to each other, it's time to bring everything you've learned this weekend into play. That's Play, with a capital "P." Enjoy *Seven Dimensional Sex*.

You should both be relaxed and satisfied; indulge in a little nap together. Take a little time to examine, in the light of your new experiences, the beliefs that might limit you from creating the kind of sexual future you have envisioned.

EVENING:

- Dine at your leisure. Make it a romantic dinner of fine dining and drink—the best you can afford. You deserve it.
- Present each other with your gifts. Be prepared to be blown away by your love, devotion, and desire for each other. Celebrate your oneness as a couple, and pledge to make your sexual happiness a priority from now on.

MORNING

- Namaste on awakening.
- Play Touch Hands.
- Review your questionnaires on the Seven Dimensions from Day One. Go through each dimension point by point together, and identify the ways you've changed over the course of this weekend. Talk about the ways in which you can continue to boost your scores in each dimension. Make a list for your Good-for-Life Sex Plan.

MAXIMIZING YOUR SEVEN DIMENSIONS OF SEXUAL ENERGY

You've "worked" your way through several exercises and two full-scale assignments designed to show you that the erotic can be an inexhaustible source of joy and vitality. By now, you have seen how very obtainable that wealth can be for you and your beloved as well as what a blessing for the future of your relationship. One more assignment awaits you, but before that final lesson, revisit the Seven Dimensions questionnaire with which your journey began. Your responses will look much different to you now—so much has changed!—and you'll find that you have developed insight and motivation to become stronger in all Seven Dimensions of love. Much that may have seemed irrelevant three days ago (*What does having a "stingy heart" have to do with hot sex?*) now makes more sense.

Our questionnaire has not been validated by a university study, but it is pretty good at assessing issues that come up again and again in sexual counseling and therapy. While every person is unique, there are only a limited number of themes underlying sexual experience. We designed the questions to reveal the dynamics of a wide range of common problems, so some of the questions may really ring a bell for you, while others don't have any personal significance. Every single score isn't that important. What *is* useful is to look back through your responses and find your highest scores—the dimensions you were strongest in—and the lowest. Here is where you will need to give special consideration to the tools for those dimensions.

Knowing your strengths reveals where you will naturally help your sexual connection without even having to think about it—although the tools in your strong suit may give you some additional ideas. In the weak areas you can focus on what will open your awareness to sexual energy in this realm and perhaps allow you to rely on and acknowledge your partner's contribution.

Don't, for heaven's sake, feel that you have to be perfect in every dimension—that's just the curse of perfectionism sneaking in again! You, will, in the end, always have strengths in some dimensions and weaknesses in others. No one is completely balanced, nor should they be—that is the beauty of being in a relationship: You get to utilize your complementary strengths.

These tools are designed to help you continue to alter habitual ways of behaving that might get in your way in the weeks and months ahead. Some are for you as an individual, while others require that you and your partner work together. In practice, they will interweave and overlap. When one partner succeeds in, say, giving up anger about one thing, the freedom and relaxation created will inevitably cause shifts in the relationship that both partners will feel, and that will, in turn, trigger further changes. No man, as they say, is an island—especially when that man (or woman!) is in a committed relationship. There are three steps to using any of these tools:

1. First, you'll need to become aware of what you're already doing, and notice your existing patterns of thought and action, especially those that tend to occur automatically and unconsciously. (This is not so easy, since our habits are by definition out of our awareness.)

2. Second, you'll need to be able to imagine, and then actually do, something new and unfamiliar. That will undoubtedly feel somewhat awkward, but that's to be expected. Be patient and take it in small steps and your new behavior will become more comfortable.

3. Third, you'll need to practice the new pattern, so that it can ultimately become as natural and automatic as the old habit was.

This will not happen without conscious desire and intention and action. Remember that all this may sound like work, but there's a lot of fun and satisfaction along the way. And a lifetime of multidimensional loving is definitely worth it!

THE TOOLS

Biologic

- Learn how to ask and respond to questions about what you and your partner are experiencing during sex.

- Get new ideas about what is possible and what seems worth exploring from outside sources like books and videos. (You'll find a list of materials we like at the end of this book.)

- Consider getting checked out clinically for issues of hormone deficiency or imbalance, medical conditions, and/or medication issues that might be relevant to your sexual function.
- Begin and continue a program of physical conditioning that includes toning and flexibility around the hips, knees, and pelvis, including the PC muscle.
- Schedule regular "training sessions" with your partner to consciously develop new lovemaking skills. Structure your explorations; be curious and scientific—and don't forget your sense of humor.

Sensual

- Become aware of the amount of time you spend "in your head," and begin to decrease it in favor of time spent just noticing what sensations you are having in your body at any given moment.
- Be quiet together.
- Play "Sense of the Week," either alone or, better yet, with your partner.
- Get new ideas for expanding sensual pleasure from books and videos.
- Agree to make a given lovemaking session especially erotic in one sense.
- Learn partner massage and practice it regularly.

Desire/Lust

- Acknowledge and honor whichever partner is "the keeper of the flame" of desire.
- Make a conscious decision to give up your anger about one thing.
- Practice deliberately building the sexual charge between you in little ways throughout the day.
- Work to increase the masculine-feminine polarity in your relationship.
- "Cut a deal" to establish a contract about sex for the next month.
- Men: Practice non-ejaculation from time to time.

Heart

- Spend time paying attention to the body sensations around your heart in various circumstances.

- Imagine that you can open or close your heart at will, and decide to spend the next two hours with an open heart.
- Create a surveillance system for the Stingy Heart. Yours that is—not your partner's.
- Exchange with your partner lists of five things that would open your heart if your partner did them.
- Change something just for your partner.
- Write a love poem to your partner.

Intimacy

- Notice your tendency to need to be right, and practice consciously letting go of this in favor of being close.
- Cultivate an attitude of curiosity about your partner. Try to learn one new thing about him or her every week for the next month.
- Practice non-verbal communication—for example, Touch Hands.
- Schedule 30 minutes once a week to share your thoughts about life and each other, with each of you having 15 minutes to talk without interruption. Support your partner in this by asking him or her to "tell you more" about his or her feelings, keeping clearly in mind that "it's not about you."
- Make love with your eyes open and the lights on, and really connect. Take small steps toward this if it is hard at first.

Aesthetic

- Concentrate on perceiving the radiance in your partner—see if you can increase it. Imagine your own radiance. Believe that you have it.
- Become aware of the curse of perfectionism and the habit of criticism, and do what you can to let go of them.
- Notice one beautiful thing each morning, noon, and night for a week.
- Create a beautiful place in which to make love.
- Learn how to say Namaste to your partner and mean it deeply. Learn how to receive this blessing, too.

Ecstatic

- Make love as if it were a sacred ritual.

- Make your bedroom into a temple for the practice of this ritual—even if only for that session.
- Develop skill in the art of soulgazing.
- Use Tantric imagery consciously and by mutual agreement during lovemaking. For example, imagine that your energies are circulating with your combined breathing as if through one being.
- Study Tantra books and tapes. Better yet, attend a course in person. Practice what you learn.

While many of the tools are self explanatory, several of the ideas in each dimension need some elaboration.

BIOLOGIC DIMENSION TOOLS

- *Learn how to ask and respond to questions about what you and your partner are experiencing during sex.*

The Golden Rule of Sex! Clearly, this is one of the very most important skills for achieving extraordinary sex, or even satisfactory sex. You must learn to ask and respond to specific questions. Not only do you need to ask for information from your partner, but you also need to be able to give your partner feedback. When your partner asks, "Do you like this? Is this good for you?" then you have to be willing to check in with your sensations and your desires and respond in a helpful way. This is especially important when you're trying out new things—some you may like, some you may not, so if you withhold your reactions from your partner, you're not going to get to where you want to go.

The most helpful information comes in the moment, and concerns specifically what is happening at that moment. A lot of people will only talk about lovemaking afterwards, when the mind has had time to start plowing along in its old grooves. This type of sexual post-mortem tends to yield vague, generalized observations. If you wait until later, you're likely to fall into the "I always...," "you never...," "Women do this...," "Men do that..." traps. If you want something fresh and useful, give your partner information about what you *feel*, not what you *think*.

- *Schedule regular training sessions with your partner to consciously develop new lovemaking skills.*

Structure your explorations; be curious and scientific—and don't forget your sense of humor. We recommend doing this once a month at the beginning, and then maybe once a quarter. Many lovers have resistance to this tool: it seems too planned, a bit like going to class. However, the skills you will develop and the clarity of your feedback will get you an "A" in the course. Having some new moves and making certain what you are doing to your partner really works is definitely worth the effort in scheduling. You did some of this yesterday and the day before in your assignments: You were finding out, "Does he like this?", "Does she like it when I do that?", and "That didn't go over so hot, but this other thing really rang her chimes." This is great information to have, and, as you know from recent experience, these sessions can be erotic and fun—it's hardly dry laboratory research!

This brings up a general point about attitude. Be curious. Try not to box your partner in with your expectations and assumptions, but rather, welcome change and exploration. The essence of love is supporting the growth of your beloved. An open-minded, curious approach lets your partner know that you honor his or her ambitions to expand and become an even better lover.

- *Consider getting checked out clinically for issues of hormone deficiency or imbalance, medical conditions, and/or medication issues that might be relevant to your sexual function.*

This is so obvious that it goes without saying, but it's so important that we are, in fact, saying it again. If you suspect that any sort of biologic change is problematic, get it checked out—fixing these issues is often easy.

SENSUAL DIMENSION TOOLS

- *Become aware of the amount of time you spend "in your head," and begin to decrease it in favor of time spent just noticing what sensations you are having in your body at any given moment.*

The key to enlivening the sensual dimension is getting out of your head. Evaluating, judging, questioning, considering, thinking, analyzing—getting wrapped up in these modes instead of in feeling is the problem to work on. Much of what you've been doing the last few days has been about exactly this—getting back into your senses, and you've felt the results. It will take attention and effort to continue to sharpen and expand this part of your awareness. Become an artist— someone who treasures the sensory experience of life.

- *Be quiet together.*

One particular practice that can help you focus on your senses is to stop talking. Of course, we're one hundred percent for communication, but no one said that has to be strictly verbal. We're all very skilled with words, of course, and language is a huge part of our lives, but in our culture it often displaces our awareness of sensation. Using language puts you into a part of your nervous system that isn't conducive to feeling, to being present. Some special types of language, like poetry, may encourage feeling, but ordinary language takes you into that left-brain mode of analyzing and speculating and out of the holistic, perceptive mode of the so-called right brain. Silence, in this context, can indeed be golden.

- *Play "Sense of the Week," alone or, better yet, with your partner.*

Playing Sense of the Week is an enjoyable, effective practice for bringing sensory awareness into your day, and requires very little time or effort. It goes like this: One of you picks a sense for both of you to indulge for a week, and you post it on the refrigerator or the bathroom mirror. Then you both make it a point to notice the impressions that come to you from that sense as you go about your business for the week.

So let's say that one week the designated sense is hearing. Both of you will do things like buy new music, listen to natural sounds like the singing of birds and the wind in the leaves, tune in to the rise and fall of voices, pay particular attention to background music when you go the movies or watch television. You call each other's attention to sound when you're together, and talk about what you've heard for a few minutes at the end of the day.

The next week, the other partner will choose a different sense—touch, or smell—and your assignment is to notice things that appeal to that sense each day. If it's touch, you may register the feeling of everything from a child's hair, to the varied textures of the clothes in your closet, to the sensation of water on your skin when you step into the shower in the morning; if it's smell, you might take a side trip to the perfume counter at the mall, or notice the smell of the cut grass outside your office, or pay special attention to the aromas in the produce section at the grocery store. Of course, you can also incorporate your new favorite sense in your lovemaking. This game will make you more sensual; in addition, it will help calm and quiet your mind while adding to the sum total of pleasure in your day.

- *Get new ideas for expanding sensual pleasure from books and videos.*

It is *not* cheating to turn to books and videos for ideas and instruction, and of course it can also be a lot of fun. We're not recommending pornography, which is often worthless for practical lovemaking and a turn-off for most women. Rather, we're talking about intelligent, well put-together materials—we list a number at the end of the book. It's empowering to watch a an erotic massage video and realize, "Hmm, I could do that." Good ones show you things you can use, like how to touch the perineum, or oral sex techniques you've never thought of. And it's enlightening just seeing what other people do: "Whoa, they're using *lots* of oil. Now he's using a feather—that might be interesting. I could try moving my hands like that next time." You can pick up lots of ideas.

Books can be great, too. There are serious technique books out there that are very good, such as *The Bedside Kama Sutra*. There are also many that are more playful—*101 Nights of Great Sex*, for instance, may not give you any deep insights, but it's chock-full of ideas for sexual pleasure and fun. And that's what the sensual dimension is all about.

DESIRE/LUST DIMENSION TOOLS

• *Acknowledge and honor whichever partner is "the keeper of the flame" of desire.*

Desire is the "must have" dimension; without it, nothing happens. This is why you must honor the one who's the keeper of the sexual flame in your relationship. Because of this person's desirous energy, your connection continues to flow. If you are the low-desire member of your dyad, you need to realize that what you have been resisting is actually an asset.

• *Make a conscious decision to give up your anger about one thing.*

Grudges, anger, and persistent irritability all kill desire. If you are in the habit of holding on to hurts, treasuring those past injustices, you are creating a chasm between you and your partner. In order to not have to cross the Grand Canyon before you get into bed with your partner, you will have to consider which angers need to go. And, truth be known, there are plenty of irritations that we hang on to purely out of habit. They do not serve us any longer, except to continue feelings of spitefulness and separation. You may have been *right*; you may have been completely justified, but is that worth extinguishing the heat of love? It is time to give them up and get on with the wonderful business of loving.

• *Practice deliberately building the sexual charge between you in little ways throughout the day.*

Another important fact about the desire dimension is that you need to "feed the stream," keep the currents of desire circulating. Lovers who've been together for a long time generally can't rely on the thrill of the unknown to spark desire, so keeping it alive and burning requires attention. One practice that can help amp up the charge is sending each other Love Arrows—private looks and smiles that say *I want you*, anytime, anyplace, as little unexpected reminders of what you have between you. You can also try what we call the IV Kiss (or Conscious Kiss). This is when, instead of the nice little peck on the cheek or quick lip-brush that's expected, you slow the kiss down, look into your lover's eyes, and kiss like you mean it. Soften your lips, maybe dance around with your tongue a bit, gently catch your lover's lower lip between your teeth. This is great sexual first aid, and it only adds a few seconds to your morning good-bye or evening hello. The concept here is to allow yourselves to experience desire without having to consummate it—you're putting money in the bank for later.

- *Work to increase the masculine-feminine polarity in your relationship.*

We do see quite a few couples in which both partners are weak in desire. They may be very loving and romantic, spend time together, kiss and hold hands, tell each other everything, but neither is, by nature, very lusty. Those couples need to focus on ways to increase the polarity between them—the king-and-queen, quarterback-and-cheerleader, Shiva-and-Shakti push/pull that drives the world. It's often invigorating to be a bit flashier in your gender identity. You can do this in humorous, lighthearted ways, by doing a little role-playing, or in physical activities like dancing (especially Latin dancing like tango) that embody the male/female difference very clearly. Polarity generates desire.

HEART DIMENSION TOOLS

You've heard a lot about the heart dimension being the fulcrum of sexuality—the crucial dimension that turns "having sex" into "making love," and many of the exercises you've been doing have centered on the heart. You've felt the warm, wide-open satisfaction of keeping your heart open. And it's not that challenging to have an open heart when you're spending a weekend doing nothing but making love. However, it is a challenge to remain openhearted out there in the world. This isn't an easy thing to do—religious adepts spend years in prayer and meditation to reach the blissful state of continuous open-heartedness. We are asking you to begin that worthwhile practice with your special partner—your beloved—in order to reap the immense rewards of being able to fully open your heart during all of your sexual encounters.

- *Imagine that you can open or close your heart at will, and decide to spend the next two hours with an open heart.*

Start trying this on easy occasions—going to lunch with a dear friend, attending a wedding, having a romantic dinner together, spending time with children. Monitor yourself for negative, judgmental, ungenerous thoughts, and when you detect one, push it gently away and settle back into the sweetness of your loving, appreciative heart. Once you can stay openhearted for two hours, challenge yourself with longer periods of time, or more difficult circumstances. It will become easier over time to drop into that state of unruffled happiness and serenity whenever you wish. During lovemaking check in frequently to your heart space and make certain that this area of your chest is warm, soft and open.

- *Create a surveillance system for the Stingy Heart. Yours that is—not your partner's.*

It's very important to keep track of whether you're in a stingy-heart space, as we so easily slide into that ditch. It's so very common, so very human, to think, *Well, yes, I want to open my heart and give love and all that, but you, my so-called partner, didn't do X yesterday, so I'm not doing Y today, and it serves you right.* That's counting, that's keeping track, that's miserly activity, and it closes the heart, slams the doors right shut. When you find yourself thinking like this, remember that keeping score, however petty or subtle your scorekeeping may be, will give you only bitter satisfaction, not juicy love.

- *Exchange with your partner lists of five things that would open your heart if your partner did them.*

This is a very simple, straightforward little exercise that often has quite amazing results. Your partner may dream of things you never in a million years would have guessed, things that you may be happy to give. Lana had a surprise some years ago when she and David exchanged lists. He'd written, "Exercise with me." That he wanted her to come out and play with him had never, ever flashed through her mind. She doesn't particularly like sports; he is an enthusiastic tennis player, and generally athletic. But since then, she has learned to play tennis and to ski, and so they've found some things to do together that they both enjoy. For David, this has been an indication that Lana really loves him—she's willing to try new things to give him pleasure. But until he let her know, she would never have guessed that taking ski lessons would warm his heart. We tend to think of things like poetry, gifts, celebrations and flowers being signs of love, and they are, but anything we do to make our beloved happy is a gift of love. It all flows from generosity, which is what the heart dimension is really about.

INTIMACY DIMENSION TOOLS

- *Notice your tendency to need to be right, and practice consciously letting go of this in favor of being close.*

The need to be right all the time—the compulsion to win the argument or point out the mistake or explain the better way—is one of the biggest killers of intimacy around. So if you are strongly attached to being correct—which is just a manifestation of the need to win—recognize the choice you are making. Do you want to be right or do you want to be loved? You learned from your parents and in school and at work how important it is to have the right answer—this is how we distinguish ourselves from other people in a competitive setting. But it's not conducive to a great love life. In fact, it's destructive to intimacy.

- *Schedule 30 minutes once a week to share your thoughts about life and each other, with each of you having 15 minutes to talk without interruption. Support your partner in this by asking him or her to "tell you more" about his or her feelings, always keeping in mind that "it's not about you."*

Scheduling time to talk is a pretty common recommendation in relationship seminars and programs, and it's good advice. It is simply amazing how we can go for days and weeks without really talking, without finding out what's going on inside the person we love most in the world. Establishing a regular time to exchange thoughts, observations and musings will go a long way towards bridging the gap that our too-busy lives create. If you can't do half an hour, then make it 15 minutes. (No matter how busy you are, you've got a free quarter-hour in the week somewhere.) Set a timer for seven and a half minutes, one of you talks until it goes "ding," and then it's the other's turn. Fast, simple, and very, very helpful.

What will make this tool work is good listening. This is listening without commenting, and without saying, "Well, yes, but...," or "Are you sure you're being reasonable?" No, this is listening, taking it in, nodding, and saying things like "Okay," or "Wow," or "Hmm. That's interesting. Tell me more." Or even, "Okay, now here's what I think you just said...." These formulas may sound simplistic, but "mirroring back" truly works—therapists use this technique all the time. And if you've ever talked to a good counselor or therapist, you know what an incredible relief it can be to talk to a sympathetic person who really *listens*. You don't have to be a therapist to do this for your partner, you just need to maintain an attitude of curiosity.

"Tell me more" is a very good phrase to remember. It's the perfect response when your partner says something that makes you feel defensive. Instead of assuming your lover meant to criticize you, assume instead that there is some valuable information in what he or she is trying to express, and say, "Tell me more about that." And then when he or she says a little more, say, "What else?" Your attitude is one of curiosity. You don't have to be defensive about every passing comment, and you'll sometimes find that, as your partner continues to talk about that particular issue, he or she will work it out and let loose of it, winding up with something like, "Well, maybe I've been a little bit over-reactive about this." That's *so* much better than if you had said, "You know, you're being hypersensitive and defensive and you shouldn't feel like that. Stop feeling like that!" Intimacy vanishes with that attitude.

"It's not about you" is another useful mantra—this time a silent, interior one—for these situations. Often our partner will express him or herself, out of frustration or irritation, with a personal criticism or attack, or perhaps because of our own hypersensitivity, we hear it that way. Either way, it's seldom helpful to respond in kind. If instead we can train ourselves to look for the feeling being expressed underneath the attack or criticism (hurt, sadness, whatever), we can choose to respond to that, and transform a potential argument or fight into an opportunity to understand one another better. Remembering to tell yourself, "This is about *his* feeling vulnerable, not about me," goes along way toward increasing intimacy.

- *Make love with your eyes open and the lights on, and really connect. Take small steps toward this if it is hard at first.*

This is one of those small step/giant step tools. It's so simple: leave a light on so you can look into your lover's eyes while you make love. Soul-gaze, in other words, while you connect physically and you begin to merge. True intimacy is about revealing your whole self and not holding back; this is the physical demonstration of that desire. Also, watching what's going on can be an incredible turn-on. Use candles or cover the lampshades with cloth if you like—the last thing you want is glaring light or a clinical atmosphere.

AESTHETIC DIMENSION TOOLS

- *Concentrate on perceiving the radiance in your partner—see if you can increase it. Imagine your own radiance—believe that you have it.*

You've been working on radiance, a new and possibly strange-sounding concept, in many of the exercises and certainly in the assignments. Since this was all so unfamiliar to begin with, you'll need to continue to practice perceiving radiance in your lover and letting your own light shine. Use the exercises—soulgazing, Puja, Yab Yum, Heart lingam and yoni, to keep reminding yourself that your partner is a radiant being, and that you are, too. You can increase that radiance by remembering to look for it and honor it. When you can see another person as a radiant being, as a part of the divine radiance, that person becomes beautiful, and your whole attitude changes.

- *Become aware of the curse of perfectionism and the habit of criticism, and do what you can to let go of them.*

Perfectionism truly is a curse. The pursuit of excellence is a virtue, of course, but insisting on perfection is guaranteed to yield unrelenting dissatisfaction. This not only interferes with our ability to perceive beauty and radiance (since we are always on the alert for flaws and shortcomings), it also prevents us from expressing them (since we're always issuing judgment and criticism). It also robs us of our willingness to try new things. This is particularly so for women, who tend to get so wrapped up in their looks that when you mention the word aesthetic they start thinking "me, my body, imperfect, arggh!" And what's so sad about this is that, when you ask men what they most want from their women, it's always the same thing—they want her to let go. Women: Wrap a fringed scarf around that imperfect part of you and forget about it for a while.

Criticism is the twin of perfectionism and together they extinguish the joy of many sexual encounters: "*I don't look good when I'm on top, my belly hangs out.*" "*Can he see my cellulite from that angle?*" "*What if she doesn't get off on what I'm doing?*" On and on and on we go, until we have sucked the entire encounter dry of any spontaneous energy. If you cannot help being critical, at least apply the balm of humor and tease about your own sensitivity: Then you can share a laugh about the impossibility of being flawless.

- *Notice one beautiful thing each morning, noon, and night for a week.*

Share your "beauty moments" with your beloved, and you create a circle of beauty for the two of you to live in. The source of this circle of loveliness surrounds us day and night, yet we often fail to notice it and, even more commonly, fail to share the awe with our beloved. When you both call attention to the erotic, the exquisite, the extraordinary, you have enriched both of your lives and brought forth the lovely sensuality that permeates our world.

ECSTATIC DIMENSION TOOLS

- *Make love as if it were a sacred ritual. Make your bedroom into a temple for the practice of this ritual—even if only for that session.*

These two go together, as you've seen in the assignments. As you've already seen, honoring the sacred aspect of love is an enormously powerful way to expand your experience of sex. Incorporating ritual into lovemaking is an excellent way to underscore this sacred aspect in our consciousness. Ordinarily, we don't allow much room for ritual in our lives, for doing things in a dignified, patterned, elegant sort of way. Rather, we hustle from one practical task to the next, depleting our energy, and then unwind with passive entertainment. Ritual refocuses our souls.

Sacred ritual requires a sacred space. Perhaps when you think of sacred spaces you picture Greek temples, Angkor Wat, the Sistine Chapel—impressive and awe-inspiring monuments. But a sacred space can also be small and private and unique to the two of you: a tiny household altar, a beautifully prepared bed, or a place in your bedroom that honors the two of you with photos, vacation tokens, and objects recalling sweet memories.

To create a sacred space, you need to ask, "What will set this space apart from the everyday?" If you were walking into a temple or church or mosque and you didn't know what it was, how would you know that it was sacred? What would you notice? Peace, quiet, cleanliness. Order. There might be water or soft music, there might be wonderful fragrance, like incense or flowers. There could be candlelight or shimmering stained glass windows. Everything would be carefully, deliberately arranged to be as beautiful and serene as possible.

In order to make your bedroom a space into which you invite the divine, you will want to pay attention to all of the senses to evoke a spiritual atmosphere—a place for sacred loving. A lot of our bedrooms are like the family room: You've got the kids in there, the dogs, the cat, the exercise equipment draped with clothes, a basket of laundry waiting to be folded. You've got the television; maybe even a computer in the corner reminding you of the noisy world outside. Not exactly an environment that promotes a sacred feeling. So you'll probably want to make some changes in your bedroom. This doesn't mean you have to totally redecorate, though. You may use candles, or fresh flowers, or maybe put up beautiful sensual prints. Perhaps you'll cover the TV with a lovely scarf. The details are up to you, but the first step is to say, "We're going to pay attention to making the sacred part of our sexual connection. We're going to deliberately make our space more serene."

- *Develop skill in the art of Soulgazing.*

Soulgazing is our favorite ritual for moving into the sacred together. It is certainly not the only way to do this, but when practiced, it can be a very efficient way to enter the ecstatic dimension. Spiritually, it's probably not important whether you sit just so, with the left palm up and right down, or whether the television is covered or not. What is important is the intention involved in beginning the ritual of Yab Yum or Soulgazing, or in beautifying your room in preparation for lovemaking—you are committing to calling forth the ecstatic, the divine to be in attendance during your sexual exchange. Your consciousness makes a vast difference in the quality of your experience. That's really what ritual and sacred spaces are about—the transformation of consciousness.

THE COUPLES REVISIT THEIR QUESTIONNAIRES

Steve and Kate

Kate winces as she looks back over hers. "Well I aced the Biologic, for sure. But Heart, 4; Intimacy, 4; Aesthetic, 3. God. Where do I start?"

Steve's supportive and completely into the project at this point. "Well, which one do you think is most important to you?"

Looking back over the individual questions, Kate says, decisively, "Intimacy. My heart feels more open—some of those answers would be different now. Same with Aesthetic—I'm feeling better about my body, for one thing."

"I should certainly hope so," says Steve, running his hand over her bottom.

"But telling you everything? Not criticizing or being judgmental? That's hard. We're all *about* arguing."

Steve laughs. "True enough, but maybe we can tone it down. I'm just as bad. Repeat after me: '*Tell me more* about that, dear.'"

"And you. What about that Heart dimension?"

"I know, I know. I will take Valentine's Day seriously forever after this weekend. I swear. And watch for my stingy heart acting up. We both need to count less, but I'm just going to watch out for my own little shriveled, stingy heart."

"Yup. Do you still feel like we have sex more than make love, though?" Kate asks with some emotion.

"No, no, and no. And if I start feeling that way again, we'll talk. Deal?"

"Deal," Kate replies.

Charlie and Nicole

"Well my scores were so awesome to begin with..." Charlie begins. "Except for, let's see, Heart, Intimacy, and Aesthetic, of course," Nicole counters. Their banter, though, is friendly as they lie side by side on the bed, reviewing their questionnaires.

"So which one should I work on, do you think?" he asks her.

"Heart, hon. You have a great big heart, I know that. But lots of times you don't let me see it."

"Okay," he says, thoughtfully. "How do I do that?"

"Little presents would be nice. Flowers once in a while. Remember that time when we were engaged and you sent me all those yellow roses? I loved that."

"Let me write this down," Charlie says, pulling out his electronic organizer. "That's not much. What else?"

Nicole feels a world of possibility opening up. "Help more with the kids? Ask me what I want to do? I'll have to think about that."

"Okay, that all seems doable." He picks up her sheets. "Oh, girl."

"I know. Depressing, isn't it? 4, 4, 3, 2. But I feel we've made headway with a lot of things, don't you?"

"Absolutely," he answers.

"But probably Desire will be the hardest once we get home. You know, our old pattern. You want it all the time, I don't."

"Yeah, well right here it says that you should give up your anger. So could you stop being mad at me all the time?"

Nicole pinches him lightly. "If you don't piss me off, I could. But really, I think I do need to take more responsibility for my own happiness. It's not like you're an ogre keeping me locked in a closet, is it?"

"Not hardly. And when you get into your sexual Shakti self, it is *so* great! What do you think about this Conscious Kissing thing? Could we work on that? Maybe right now?"

Martin and Linda

"Sensuality and the Ecstatic, that's what I need to beef up," says Martin. "I need to get out of my head—all the work and money stuff grinding away in there all the time."

"Yeah, and some of these games sound like fun. I'd love to do this Sense of the Week thing... and this one about just doing things because they feel good. Remember those wine-tasting parties we used to go to?"

"They weren't that expensive, were they? And you give such great back rubs. God, what you were doing to me yesterday felt incredible!"

Linda brightens as they think of ways to hold onto this great feeling. "Yeah, I could try to find that oil we used to like...."

"And we both need work on the Ecstatic. I love that Yab Yum position—I really can feel your heart lingam penetrating me. I'd like to try making love like that..."

"Great minds work alike. I worry some about those antidepressants, but I do think that I need them and they haven't spoiled the fun this weekend, that's for sure. Maybe if we attend to these other things, that side effect won't really be a problem. I was thinking of how we could make our bedroom more of a temple—I've been wanting to make it feel more exotic, anyway, and this give me the perfect excuse. We'll just have to find another place for that damn ironing board," Linda muses. "Oh, and study Tantra books—that I want to do for sure."

"More Shiva! More Shakti! More chi!" Martin chants. "I'm for it. And more radiance all around."

Bob and Paulette

"Well, Problem one for me is already fixed, it looks like," said Bob, lightly. "Oh, that little blue pill."

"But you've still got to work on Desire. You got one point in that category!" Paulette points out. "But maybe the Viagra will help some of that. I mean, it must have been such a downer, not knowing how it would go every time."

"Amen," Bob agrees. "I could do more of this stuff, though, like Love Arrows. And I could be the one to start things once in a while."

"I'd really like that," Paulette answers. "And you know what I'd like us to do? This idea of thirty minutes to talk every week. Maybe if it were on your schedule...."

"I'd see it as a real item that needs to be accomplished," Bob finishes for her. "I'd be willing to do that. And what about your test, ma'am?"

"Well, I'm not that great in Biologic or Aesthetic. First of all, I need to take your example and do something about this lubrication thing."

"That KY is great stuff." The engineer in Bob appreciates a well-designed product. "We should definitely keep that around."

"Yeah. Now that we've gotten over being so embarrassed with each other about it. We've been so ridiculous, haven't we? And then, Aesthetic. Do you think I criticize too much?"

"Not to be critical," Bob says, smiling, "but you can be a bit of a perfectionist."

"You're right, darling. I'd really rather be appreciating radiance. I'm going to start this practice of noticing something beautiful morning, noon, and night. And sharing it with you." Paulette's gaze softens as she turns to face Bob.

"Okay, I'll do it too and I'm starting right now," he says. "Your lips are beautiful." And he leans over to give her a slow, lingering kiss.

As you look for the particular tools that will help strengthen you as a multi-dimensional lover, don't forget that all the exercises in this book are available to you. The task of changing your beliefs about sex, about your body, your lover, your life, may seem daunting, but it will feel less so if you remember that simple physical practices nurture the process. The body and mind and heart all change together: Something as simple and quick as a daily session of Yab Yum or Touch Hands can gradually open your heart and expand your spirit further than you can imagine if you let them.

MAKING IT LAST: A GOOD-FOR-LIFE SEX PLAN

We hope that at this point your sex life has expanded beyond anything you imagined, your relationship is at perhaps its highest point ever, and that you're buoyant and happy and filled with the energy of life itself. How great!

And a big question has begun to loom: How do you keep this good thing going once the weekend is over? This is the perennial question of all the couples who do the sexual enhancement program. You're here, now, in the refuge from the world that the two of you have created, but soon this interlude will be over and you'll be running full tilt again, taking care of all the people and things that you're responsible for. You've changed, your connection has changed, but out there the world is just the way you left it. How can you keep from sliding back into old patterns?

Here's what we know works: You become businesslike and create a structure in which your new erotic connection can flourish. You establish a new division—The Good Sex Division—of the "company" that is your relationship, and together work out a Good-for-Life Sex Plan for your new joint enterprise.

The Business Model

This may seem to be the strangest of all the new thoughts about sex we've presented to you—the idea that you need a business plan to help you sustain the joy you've found during these three days. Remember, though, that the challenging and unique experiences we've taken you through have all been highly structured—it's much easier to let go within clearly defined boundaries. Structure will help you take these changes into the everyday as well. It has worked extremely well for hundreds of couples.

Why use the business metaphor? Because most of us have a good understanding of business, which is, basically, about getting things done. The sort of planning that goes on in business is an effective, refined process for accomplishing goals, whatever those goals might be. What will most help you sustain and develop the nourishing sexual connection you've established is commitment to a well-defined plan of action. Hence, the Good-for-Life Sex Plan. The two of you will fill it out together—or you may find that completing it separately and then putting your heads together works for you—and, finally, you will both sign it to indicate that you have agreed on each item. At that point, the plan becomes a contract between you, to be reviewed and renegotiated monthly.

The Good-for-Life Sex Plan

Vision/Mission Statement: _____

_____

_____

Goals: _____

_____

_____

Capital: _____

_____

Budget (time): _____

_____

_____

Specific Tasks and Responsibilities:

Daily: _____

_____

Weekly: _____

_____

Monthly: _____

_____

Special commitments:_____

_____

Policies and Procedures (consequences):_____

_____

_____

Bonus for exceeding goals: _____

Board Meeting scheduled for: _____

Signature:_____ Signature:_____

Elements of Your Good-for-Life Sex Plan

STATEMENTS OF VISION AND GOALS

Every new enterprise needs a vision statement, a formulation of the ultimate, overriding purpose for which the division was created. We're asking you to make a vision statement as a couple, a statement about what you intend your sexual connection to be. For example, "We want to have a vibrant, sexual connection that's manifested and felt by both of us throughout the rest of our lives together." Your statement need not be as fancy, of course, but it should be inspiring and sweeping.

Some people in our workshops find it more helpful to put this statement in present tense, as if they're speaking from their fulfilled vision. A statement of this type might be: "Our sex life is rich, rewarding, and pleasurable for both of us, and a source of nourishment in our lives." The point is to feel uplifted and committed when you read the vision.

The second piece, once you've worked out your vision statement, is to hammer out your goals. This statement is more specific, because you need to be able to determine whether you've achieved a goal or not—that's what a goal is. A vision statement is the expression of an ideal, which may not even be actually achievable on this planet in this lifetime. But when you set goals, you want to be able to determine, based on objective observation, whether you have achieved them or not. Still, these goals should be overall intentions which will carry you forward—we'll get down to the specific, day-to-day aspects of your plan later.

A goal statement might look something like, "We will be competent as lovers." This could then encompass several subsidiary goals: "We will understand what each of us wants and likes sexually," "We will take care of medical issues that we've neglected," etc.

CAPITAL

Every new division needs some capital to get rolling. The Good-for-Life Sex Plan's capital may not be cash, but rather investments that will help you reach your goal: books on sex that you think are useful, a good sensual massage video like *Tantric Massage Video* (see the reference list) that would help you both give and receive massage, a CD player for erotic music in your bedroom. You might also want to start a fund so that you'll have the wherewithal to have a whole weekend together every two or three months. Your capital is what you decide to invest in this division.

TIME AND BUDGET

Of course, money is not usually the limiting factor for this new division whose business is creating a satisfying sexual connection. It's in finding time that most of us run up against our real trouble "funding" our sex lives. Since time is the limiting resource, finding time and setting priorities is what most of this process is about. In business terms, this is fundamentally a budgeting process. We ask you to go into quite a lot of detail about how you budget time to be together. We have made many suggestions about activities that show a good return on investment, things like kisses, glances, and messages that do not take much "time currency," but that do have a significant impact on your bottom line—the accrual of positive energy in your relationship's account. When you take a look at the way you currently budget your time, you'll almost certainly find quite a few opportunities to improve your division's efficiency and productivity!

SPECIFIC TASKS AND RESPONSIBILITIES

Here is where you get down to the nitty gritty of the management of your new division. What specific actions need to be taken to meet the goals you've set? What kinds of activities, of the many that you've come across here (and others of your own devising), do you want to make sure to include in your plan? How often do they need to be done? Who is responsible for doing which tasks? All include appropriate delegation of responsibilities, and provisions for accountability. We suggest that you divide these up into daily, weekly, monthly, and special commitments—even though your initial agreement will just cover the first month.

Let's start with the present moment. What can you do every day to feed your sexual energy? We've talked about some of the tools you can use, including sending love arrows, giving a full body hug, or kissing consciously once every single day. Those are easy things to put on the list and set a time for. Agree to soulgaze for two minutes every morning, before you do anything else, or right after you both get home from work. Two minutes—everyone can manage that. Or sit in the Yab Yum position together each morning for 10 or 12 conscious breaths. You have lots of practices and tools now—decide on one (or more) that you both enjoy to reach your goals.

Be creative and flexible about this, and try to keep the responsibility evenly divided. You might say, "Why don't I be responsible for us doing soulgazing on the odd days, and you can do the even days." Because *someone* does need to make sure you fulfill your commitment daily—otherwise it's too easy to forget and then let it slide. And if your connection becomes only one person's "job," that partner will most likely resent it.

The weekly commitment is where the rubber really meets the road. It's in the context of the weekly plan that you actualize the major operations of your new sexuality division. So, you might each agree to initiate sex once a week, or twice a week. The numbers matter much less than the commitment to making sure sex happens. And it's important that the plan provide for each partner to initiate at least some of the time. This means that the more passive, lower-desire partner will sometimes have to step up and take charge, even if this is an unfamiliar and perhaps somewhat uncomfortable role. Less-assertive partners take note—the pay-off for being the initiator is that you get to call the shots for that session. If you're a romantic type and you love flowers and music and ambiance, well, great—you set it up. If, on the other hand, you're more into the level of lusty energy the two of you can generate, then you might say, "I'm going to pick a time of day when we're not tired or sleepy, and when I initiate it's going to be a matinee—an afternoon encounter." You call the shots; you get to arrange things the way you want.

Monthly, you can agree to give yourselves a real sexual treat: "I'm going to make sure that sometime this month we have a whole morning together with no distractions." And remember that in this contract, at all levels—daily, weekly, monthly—the partner who does not initiate agrees to go along and help fulfill the terms of this mutual commitment. An example of a special commitment might be to agree that next winter the two of you, and only the two of you, are going to finally take that trip to Hawaii, and you'll resist all impulses to go with friends, or to take Aunt Elsie or Uncle Fred, or, heaven forbid, the kids. Put it in your contract and then make sure you do what you need to do to make it happen.

A Word on Scheduling Sex

We know what you're thinking—we've heard it over and over again in our workshops. "Making an appointment for sex?! Having to do it at a certain time?! Like we've got to write it on the calendar with the dentist's appointments and Little League games?!"

Yes. You have to write it on the calendar. And then you must keep the appointment. This, busy people, is how you manage the rest of your life, and now, as you're trying to manage your sex life, you're going to use this very valuable tool called scheduling to make sure that making love doesn't get lost in the fray.

"But that's so unspontaneous!"

It's very romantic to think that the two of you might be overcome with lust while at opposite ends of the house (one paying bills, say, and the other emptying the dishwasher), rush into each other's arms and make mad, passionate love on the dining room table. But, come on, how often does that happen? You want to get more sex going in your lives? Then you are going to have to actually have sex, and this is the best way we know to make sure that happens.

"But what if we don't feel like it right then?"

Do it anyway. You need to explore the energizing power of sexual connection, and what it feels like to start from zero. You're going to make sex a responsibility for a while, until your new commitment becomes part of your lives.

"It'll take too long!"

How long, really, does sex take? We're not saying you have to do a full-on Tantric session every time—although it's good to try for that every so often. You just need to get together, and the better you get at connecting your hearts and souls, the more quickly you can make great sex happen.

Any more objections? We thought not.

Policies, Procedures, and Bonuses

Every company has "What if?" policies—a set of contingency plans. This is where you spell out the accountability in your company, the consequences for not keeping up one's end of the deal. What if one person misses initiating on a particular occasion? This is not an occasion where you just say "oh well" and then forget about it: That would not be businesslike. Rather, if either of you fails to fulfill a commitment, that person must make it up to the other. What that person will do is specified here, and it can be whatever you like. Of course, it is better not to make the consequence a punishment, but more an activity or time that will enhance your connection. If he fails to keep a date, for example, he must go with you to a gallery opening and at least pretend not to be restless. If she forgets a commitment, she must go with you to your favorite sports bar and watch a game and have a beer with you. The specifics of what you do is up to the two of you, like the rest of the plan. Put your heads together and create your own "loving penalties."

Finally, you'll designate a bonus: A reward for both of you if you exceed your "production quota" in a given month. A special dinner out, a drive to the beach, some new gadget you've both been wishing for. You've worked hard at changing the old habits, and, you deserve it!

ONLY FOR A MONTH

Okay, so now you're probably thinking: "Aww, come on. How can we possibly commit to something like this forever?" You couldn't, and you aren't. The plan you create today is good for one month. That's all. *Of course* a "forever" plan would fail before it began. Your reaction would be, "Un-huh. Sure." You'd never get started on changing your lives: You probably wouldn't even start discussing it.

But this is for just one month. For a month, you can say, "I'll commit to initiate sex once a week," and do it. You can tell yourself, "I'm willing to do Yab Yum twice a week, and I can come up with a conscious kiss every weekend. What the hey? It's only for a month."

This doesn't mean that you fold your division at the end of the month—not at all. You are committing to a long-term project when you sign this document, but you are agreeing to *this* particular plan for just 30 days. When the contract expires—and this is one of the terms of the agreement—you will have a board meeting.

You schedule this meeting, put it on the calendar and commit to it. At your board meeting you'll review the preceding month, modify the plan in whatever ways you agree on, and renew for another month.

Please note that the meeting of the Good Sex Division is limited to its particular business—no talking about the kids, or what needs to be done to the house or your new neighbors or anything else off-topic. You'll just talk about how the Division is doing. Go over your plan point by point. Are you meeting your goals? What do you have to change about the plan to make it work better? Were you overly ambitious in your sales projections? Or can you expand production?

Another point. We'd like to caution you against analyzing how the division is performing until the board meeting. If you say things like, "Oh you know, last night when you initiated sex, you did a lousy job," you're tearing your new enterprise apart before it has a chance to live. So don't get too critical or worried before you have a chance to collect some data. The business analogy is again useful here: Imagine that you were starting a division selling a new widget and you said after a week, "We didn't sell the 10,000 widgets we expected to sell!

Shut down the division!" That reaction would be pretty drastic, and a mistake. You've both invested time and energy and capital in this program, so you want to give it some life. A better attitude is, "Okay. I'm just collecting data." And then when the board meeting rolls around, you can say, "I loved it when you did... it was really fun and let's do more of that." And if somebody goes above and beyond—bonus!

So get to work on your contract right now, keeping in mind a couple of things we've noticed over the years as we've watched couples go through this process. One, there tends to be one person who is wildly ambitious and says, "Let's go for it. We'll have sex five times a week! We'll soulgaze twice a day, three times on Sunday! Let's transform our relationship completely!" And the other partner usually responds this way: "No, that would be setting ourselves up for failure. If we say we'll do all that, for sure it's not going to work." So you have the exuberant person and the conservative one. Watch out for that dynamic and try to work out a reasonable compromise without getting into an argument.

Another possible glitch is that some people get very concerned about signing their names—generally these are the attorneys in the workshop group. They worry because this makes it seem like they are really committing. They *are* committing. The reason we put a signature line at the bottom is to make this a contract, not a series of vague ideas about what you might do if you feel like it and have the time.

But most people, we find, start to see the logic of doing this once they start putting words down on paper and really sink their teeth into it. It turns them on because they recognize that, wait, here is a way to make this nebulous love stuff really *happen*.

THE COUPLES DEVELOP THEIR PLANS

Steve and Kate

Since they're both such verbal people, they tear into the project, squabbling happily over the choice of words at every turn. They decide that job one is curtailing Steve's "after-school" work in the evening and weekends.

"I know it's hard to say 'no' to those hot dogs," Kate says, "but you need set some priorities with your time. What use would it be to have a down payment all together but we're splitting up?"

Steve, startled, looks somber, and says, quietly, "Don't even say that."

He agrees not to bring work home at least two nights a week: Tuesdays and Thursdays, nor on the weekend. He, in turn, wants to make their bedroom a Sacred Space—one in which no arguing or sarcasm is allowed. Kate gets excited about setting up an "altar" to make it even more special.

Steve has another idea. "I'd like for us to set up some of those 'training sessions' they talked about. If you'd be willing to help me with that control thing...."

"You bet! I'd be delighted," she says, kissing him. They agree on the last Sunday of every month and pencil it in.

"Okay, so what are we going to do every day?" Kate asks. "You know, I really liked that Touch Hands thing. It was fun, and I felt like I was in touch with you without talking."

"Good one," he agrees and they begin to wrangle amiably about who will be responsible for which day.

They have a particularly good time with the policies and procedures section. After much teasing, they agree that if she messes up, she has to work out with him; if he does, he has to go shopping with her, no complaining allowed.

Charlie and Nicole

Charlie is delighted by the contract idea. He's eager to get Nicole to commit to sex every day, or at least every other day, plus lots of soul-gazing, Yab Yum, and exploration. He's especially excited about getting some books and videos they can study together.

Nicole has come to appreciate his enthusiasm more over the weekend, but she is cautious about making commitments she's not entirely comfortable with.

"We could never keep up that pace," she says, when they get to the "weekly" line and Charlie spells out his plans. "I'd feel overwhelmed, then I'd get cranky, you'd get pushy and we'd be right back where we were." She thinks for a moment. "Well, not *exactly* where we were," she says, smiling.

"You're such a banker, hon," Charlie says. "Every time I deal with a bank, it's the same: 'Nope, can't take any chances, can't go for broke, need more collateral.'"

"Yeah, well we have to be like that or all you crazy entrepreneurs would clean us out and bankrupt yourselves in the process."

"You know, I really don't think making love more than once a week is going to bankrupt either one of us...." Negotiations are stalling out.

Here's how we might help Charlie and Nicole out at this impasse:

"First of all, you two, stop generalizing. This is about practicalities, specifically what you're going to do, not your personalities.

"Second. Nicole, you need to think in terms of learning to start sex from a neutral place. Even though you may not feel like it, every time it's your turn to initiate, you'll do it, because you know sex is good for you, for Charlie, and for the relationship. And, of course, because you promised. You've seen how great sex feeds both of you, and you need to keep that happening in your lives.

"Also, you'll want to commit to initiating frequently. By taking more responsibility for your connection, you'll take some of the pressure off Charlie, plus learn where to find your sexual energy when it doesn't seem to be anywhere. And don't forget that the initiator gets things her way.

"Charlie, an important opportunity for you here is to start getting yourself out of the role of 'the one who's always after it.' Your tremendous energy is a blessing in your relationship, but now you have the opportunity to explore the experience of being seduced. Once you have this plan finalized, you won't have to worry about when you're going to get to make love to her. You'll be able to relax.

"Let us make a final suggestion. Decide how many times a week you will have sex. Then, Nicole, you commit to being the initiator more often than Charlie. And don't forget to agree on how you'll use tools to feed the stream."

Charlie, now thoughtful, asks Nicole if four times a week would be too much. She makes a counter-offer of three times, and he agrees—this is not as often as he'd like, but it's better than he's been doing the last couple years. With some lingering reluctance, Nicole proposes that she initiate twice a week (Tuesday and Saturday); she is thinking that, since she is going to be initiating quite a bit, she will use her prerogative to make certain that Charlie pays attention to Sacred Spot massage which was so important for her. Charlie, still a bit confused about this part, will initiate only once (Friday). He will send "love arrows" at least three days a week, and Nicole will make sure that they soulgaze every morning, with special attention to perceiving each other's radiance. Charlie writes it all down and reads it aloud to Nicole as she nods in agreement; both feel that they can definitely commit to this for a month. They sign and hug.

"Wait a minute!" Charlie says. "What about the kids? What if one of them wanders in? You know how much home-alone time we have."

"I've been thinking about that. One little word: lock. On our bedroom door," Nicole answers. "They can still interrupt us, of course, but they can't just barge in, and of course we'd unlock when we were ready to sleep.

"My wife, the genius."

Martin and Linda

"Time," Martin says, looking over the form. "I see this as being all about how we find the time to keep this feeling going. Maybe that's our goal."

"That's my main concern, too," Linda answers. "And we can't just say, 'We'll make more time for us.' How many times have we said that over the years. We need to really spell it out."

They settle down to mapping out schedules for daily, weekly and monthly encounters. A number of ideas for finding five minutes here, an evening there begin to emerge from the discussion: Getting into a carpool for getting their youngest to school rather than Linda driving out of her way every day; picking up more healthful prepared meals instead of cooking every night; trading Saturday-night stay-overs with their youngest one's best friend, and letting the two older kids watch videos in the rec room instead of insisting on homework one night a week.

"And you know what I've been thinking about?" Martin asks. "A massage table in the bedroom. They have ones that aren't that expensive. That could be our capital investment."

"And our bonus, too. When we exceed expectations—his and hers massages!"

"It might come in handy at other times, too," Martin suggests.

"It might at that."

Bob and Paulette

Bob and Paulette decide easily on their vision and goal statements— Paulette, thinking of the recent changes in her lubrication, includes "Take care of all medical issues" when they formulate the goal. They also agree quickly on who will initiate sex and how often, and on feeding the stream with love arrows, conscious kissing, soul-gazing, and so on.

"But," Paulette says, "I don't see us remembering to do all those, do you? How realistic is it to think we'll keep it up?"

Bob considers this briefly. "I see what you mean. But what if we make specific plans for all that, too? Put it on the calendar if we need to?"

"What, like you send me love arrows on Monday, Wednesday and Friday, and I take the other days except for Sunday, which we'll alternate?"

"Don't laugh. It might work, and after a few weeks I bet it would get to be a habit. Let's try," Bob said, starting to draw a calendar on the back of the form. As a construction supervisor, this kind of planning is second nature for him, and as they discuss who would be responsible for what, he neatly begins filling in the squares.

Paulette suddenly sees the cheerful, competent, take-charge guy she'd married sitting before her and her heart seems to turn over in her chest.

"Okay, and since we're dreaming, you know what I've always wanted? A fireplace with gas logs in the bedroom. And a furry rug. And maybe one of those little fountains. I've always thought that it would be so romantic to be all warm and naked in front of the fire, with the sound of trickling water. I think it's something I read about in a novel."

"Okay! That is something I can get into," says Bob, who writes this down, too. He likes nothing more than a project around the house.

⌒

Does the prospect of filling out your own contract fill you with dread? Are you tempted to skip ahead? Don't! This task is crucial to the future of your Magnificent Sex life. We've devoted time to this exercise because it creates the framework for sexual success. It relieves the anxiety of not being able to take your experiences forward from this weekend into your everyday life, and gives you a document by which to measure your success. Your reward for hashing out your contract? Coming up next, the two of you will finally experience sex in all Seven Dimensions!

NOON

If you need more time to finish your gift for tonight, do it now. Agree on a time to get back together for your "homework."

AFTERNOON

This is it. It's finally time for you and your partner to put it all together—all the knowledge, attitudes, and skills you've acquired in the last three days. In this, your final assignment, you get to go all the way—in every sense. You'll use all you've learned, plus all the energy you've built up working through the previous exercises and assignments.

- Prepare your love space for *Seven Dimensional Sex*. Set out the candles, oils, and towels, and create the mood for elegant, exceptional connection
- Put away your contract and read about the mutual pleasuring you are about to experience
- Then make beautiful love together
- Rest a bit in each other's arms.
- Examine your limiting beliefs together.

"Oh, do I have energy," says Steve. 'I cannot tell you."

"You don't have to, baby," Kate answers, sitting down on his lap. "We've haven't thought about another thing for days, and here comes the big payoff."

She gets up, goes into the bathroom and starts to run water in the oversized bathtub. The tub is the reason they'd leased this condo, but they haven't used it together much. "You coming in here or not?"

You've practiced awakening first Shakti and then Shiva in the two preceding assignments, encountering the quality of one type of energy at a time. Now you are ready to fuse the awakened power of these energies in the ecstatic sexual union of male and female.

"Alrighty then," says Charlie. "I gotta admit that the other homework was pretty incredible, but this is the real deal." He pauses and looks up. "So, you think we can keep flying high?"

"Frankly?" Nicole replies. "I think we can do anything. Look at the amazing stuff we've worked through. I've had two once-in-a-lifetime experiences in two days, and even the hard things have helped bring us closer than I think we've ever been." She ruffles his hair and kisses his cheek. "Just look at the difference in us."

"Does this mean you want to go three for three, then? We still have a ways to go with those candles, don't we?" he says, starting to look around.

SEVEN-DIMENSIONAL SEX

You've undoubtedly experienced a number of firsts over the weekend, but this will be the biggest. Many of our workshop participants have described this assignment as being something like losing their virginity—with the significant difference that this time around they knew what they were doing.

"Oh, Lord, the first time is the last event in my life I'd want to replay," said Linda, pretending to shudder. "It was unspeakable. What was your first time like?"

"Mmm, what's that phrase? 'Nasty, brutish, and short.' With a girl I'd known for maybe two hours. In a backseat, naturally, although I almost didn't make it there from the front. But I have to admit, I'm probably as excited now as I was then." He pauses. "It's weird, isn't it, that something we've done—what?—at least a thousand times has turned into this awesome, just-can't-wait event? It's gotta be some kind of trick."

"Oh, yeah," says Linda. "They've tricked us into remembering who we really are."

This is a wonderful thing about human beings: When we put our minds (more accurately, our hearts) to it, we can transform ourselves so thoroughly that something we've done for years feels brand new.

We're confident in saying that sex will never be the same for you again. The ultimate reason for that is not any specific technique you've learned, or your deeper knowledge of your lover's body and responses, although those things are profoundly useful. No, the final cause of the glorious expansion of your sexual connection is that you have learned how it's possible to love in all Seven Dimensions.

⌒

Paulette sits on the sofa in their room with her feet up, while Bob lies with his head in her lap, reading out loud, commenting as he goes.

"I want to get to the 'how to' part," he says, flipping ahead. "Ah, coming right up." He looks up at Paulette. "You know, this would look pretty funny to somebody who hadn't been through it. The idea of people married as long as we've been learning how to make love!"

"But that's just how *you* felt at first," Paulette answers, and then stops. She's trying to be vigilant about her habit of criticizing, but she just caught herself saying, "I told you so" in different words. It's going to take time.

Bob doesn't take it that way. "No kidding. I told myself I was just humoring you. I'd put myself out and do something because you wanted it, and—to be honest—to get you off my back. That seems so long ago to me. Does it seem that way to you, sweetheart?"

Paulette is still amazed by his ease and steady good humor, and by the easy way talk flows between them. Now that they've regained their sexual optimism, she recognizes that both of them had been shutting down parts of their personalities for some time. The difference in Bob's mood makes it clear that he had been as discouraged as she had been by their long sexual drought.

Now, so much more than sex was flowing between them, unhindered. It felt so good to be close again.

⌒

YOUR ASSIGNMENT, STEP BY STEP

Getting Ready

Preparation: Share the preparation of the room. Agree ahead of time on the general division of tasks, but surprise each other with the specifics. Let your generous heart guide you.

Sensual Connection: Take a bath or shower together. Explore and play as you soap up. Open your senses fully to the pleasure of the warm water and the profound comfort of being lovingly washed and groomed. When you emerge, stay close. Brush each other's hair; perfume one another. Allow the whole process be sensuous, fun, and caring. Put on music that suits your mood. Play Touch Hands—naked!—for a few moments. Tune into your lover's energy, adapt to it, flow with it, and show your own energy openly, generously, and joyfully. Have fun!

And Into Bed...

Establish your soul connection by sitting across from each other on the bed and soulgazing. Use pillows under you for comfort. Gaze into each other's eyes and begin to harmonize your breath. Breathe in and out together slowly and deeply. After a while, change to reciprocal breathing: One partner holds the breath and then, as the second partner inhales, the first partner exhales. Continue breathing this way, giving and taking breath from one another. Sink into the rhythm. Visualize a current of energy circulating between and through you. Use whatever image you like—color, a magic fluid, a stream of light—and imagine it flowing out your right hand and into you lover's heart on your outbreath, in through your left hand and into your heart on your inbreath. Continue to gaze steadily into your lover's eyes until you feel that you are ready to move on. Sit quietly for a moment, attending to how you feel.

Awakening Shakti

After a suitable interval, the goddess reclines, and her adoring warrior begins to pleasure her gently and sensually—as in the first assignment. Touch, stroke, and massage all over her body at first, gradually increasing the attention to her outer yoni lips and clitoris. Men: Be teasing and light, and wait for an invitation to enter the yoni with your fingers.

Here is your opportunity to use your knowledge of your goddess and of what awakens her shakti—and to expand your knowledge of this most important of all subjects. (This is, of course, a lifelong study.) Be open and receptive to her suggestions, both verbal and non-verbal. Don't forget all the different kinds of touch and stroking that are possible, and provide plenty of variation. Take your time! Remember the two poles of her sexual center and their different qualities—yang at the clitoris and yin at the sacred spot.

Goddess, receive his attention and touch, concentrating on remaining in your heart and yoni, on staying in the moment, and on remaining connected with him. He could place one hand on your heart to help you connect heart to yoni, and together you can again visualize a flow of energy, this time from his heart out through his hand into your yoni, up to your heart, back through his other hand and into his heart.

Feel free to move, make noise, talk to him—whatever helps you build sexual energy. Orgasm, should it occur now, should be enjoyed and welcomed, but it is not required!

Pleasuring Him

At some point you will want to exchange roles—goddess now pleasures god. All the advice above applies. Men: You are building your energy, but remember to stay relaxed and spread it out through your body. Women: You can help him with this by staying tuned in to his level of arousal through verbal and non-verbal communication. Use both poles of his genital center—yang at the tip of lingam, yin at the perineum—to help increase and balance his energy. You can also help him manage his arousal by using one hand to touch his genitals while moving the growing energy in the pelvic region out toward his extremities and up toward his head with the other hand. Stay connected through eye and heart contact, remember to breathe deeply and slowly, and visualize the flow of radiance between and through you. Be radiant, and witness your lover's radiance! (Note: You and your partner will probably wish to defer orgasm at this point unless he already knows how to do it without ejaculating.)

Connection

By now you are probably ready for the lingam to enter the yoni. This is a very special and powerful moment. Honor it with full eye contact to acknowledge your trust in one another, your full heart openness, and soulful intention. Take your time and savor the moment, perhaps by simply remaining still at first. Then you can begin to play with your energies together, in much the same spirit as Touch Hands. Try different rhythms, different depths and directions of thrust. (One pattern to try is for him to use a very light, shallow stroke four or five times, then thrust deeply once, then go back to light and shallow, and so on.) Try some different positions, especially Yab Yum if you can do it comfortably.

If the goddess needs more yang stimulation of the clitoris, find a way to accomplish this. (A favorite position for this is for her to lie face down while he enters from behind. The tip of the lingam directly stimulates the sacred spot, while she can easily reach underneath herself to add some clitoral stimulation. A pillow or two under the hips may be welcome.)

If he needs more yin energy, he should find a way to communicate this so that she can help him spread his energy and relax. All previous comments about connectedness, breathing, and visualization apply, except that here there is no "leader." Be sure to have fun—try to avoid approaching this as a tense, solemn occasion. Laughter both heals and liberates.

Peak Experience

Climax may take place separately or simultaneously. (As we've said, we think that simultaneous orgasm is overrated. If it happens that way, great, but trying for it introduces an inhibiting goal.) Either way, see if you can approach it slowly and deliberately, and remember to stay relaxed and in touch with your breath, your heart, and your radiance—and with the breath, heart, and radiance of your lover.

Some well-timed words of love, lust, or appreciation as your lover approaches orgasm can increase the depth and intensity of his (or her) experience enormously. Sounding (intentionally "singing" a prolonged tone), especially together, also produces interesting effects. We highly recommend it.

Relaxing

After he ejaculates (or chooses not to), lie together for a while as the lingam softens in the yoni. Remain consciously connected, continuing to circulate your energies with your breath. You might want to imagine reversing the flow—visualizing the lingam absorbing energy from the yoni. Imagine that her breath is sending energy from her heart down to her yoni, where he inhales it into his lingam and up to his heart, then pours it back into her heart on an outbreath.

The moment of separation is also special, and should be attended to. This is an opportunity to acknowledge each other with a Namaste or another heartfelt gesture.

THE COUPLES DO THEIR HOMEWORK

Steve and Kate

After a long, sensuous bath together, Steve and Kate soulgaze for ten minutes. The time passes quickly. They become lost in their feelings for one another as they breathe in and out in unison. (They always get distracted when they try to breathe reciprocally, so they decide not to attempt it today.) Both become more moved and more aroused as the minutes pass, and when Kate lies back on the pillows, they share the feeling that they inhabit a dreamlike space far from the world.

Steve pleasures her slowly and fervently, and she has two knee-trembling orgasms before she makes him lie back on the pillows. She tenderly touches his whole body, and every time she briefly strokes his lingam or takes it in her mouth, she trails her fingers down toward his feet, or up towards his heart and out to his fingertips. He's able to feel his energy rise, disperse out from his genitals, then rise again, each time a bit higher, and she can sense his level of excitement more clearly than before.

When she invites him inside, the vulnerability and openness he senses in her seem ravishingly beautiful to him, and he lies still, looking into her eyes for a while before beginning to move. He's hoping to achieve orgasm without ejaculation, but the passion he feels, and her answering intensity, is too overwhelming for experiments. She comes once again, crying out, and he reaches a profoundly satisfying orgasm while she is still quivering.

Charlie and Nicole

Charlie has decided to try something new, and so, after massaging Nicole all over, he kisses his way down to her clitoris and begins flicking it with his tongue. At the same time, he gently slips a finger into her yoni. Nicole is surprised, but rapidly sinks into the delicious sensations she's experiencing. Once, his touch becomes a little too rough for her sacred spot and she gently pushes his hand. He understands and changes his approach, watching her carefully. A few moments later, she comes while he thoroughly enjoys her surrender to pleasure, not to mention the feel of her yoni pulsing around his fingers.

After pleasuring him, Nicole climbs on top, guides him in and leans back. He helps her reach another orgasm by stimulating her clitoris with his thumb. He finds bringing her off deeply arousing—and he loves the view. After changing positions, he starts to move inside her, but she has other plans. Having diligently practiced her postpartum Kegel exercises, Nicole has terrific control of her strong PC muscle. He supports his weight with his arms so they can maintain eye contact. Both feel that their souls are connected as she brings him to a shattering climax.

They lie still and silent for a long time, idly touching each other as they absorb what has just happened. Nicole is filled with satisfaction about having taken control with such spectacular success; Charlie is processing the revelation that soul sex with his beautiful woman has given him. Both find deep contentment in knowing that, from now on, this bliss is always possible.

Martin and Linda

After a long, luxurious preparation, Martin and Linda begin kissing and touching before they remember to awaken the goddess and god. Martin massages Linda all over, slipping now and then between her legs. He brings her almost to orgasm when she stops him, saying, "I think I'll store some of that energy up, too."

Then it's his turn. She has him help her oil her body, asks him to roll over, and then begins to slide her torso from his buttocks to his shoulders in long, powerful strokes. Next, she has him turn back over and begins the same treatment on his front. Soon, neither of them can wait any longer for the main event.

They make inventive, elegant love, changing positions many times and using some they hadn't tried for years. It's magical, transporting, ecstatic. Linda experiences several long, full-body orgasms—once with amrita—while gracefully helping Martin control his response. He's more relaxed and confident than yesterday, and comes once without ejaculating and is as awestruck by the experience as he was the day before. Finally, though, he decides he wants to ejaculate, which he does at the top of a steep, cresting wave of pure energy.

Curled up together afterwards, they agree that this was better than their very best times back in the old days. "Know why?" Martin murmurs.

"Because of Soul Sex, and because we built up to it for three days?"

"All that helped. But what I was thinking is that it's better because now we really, really know each other. I know every little fold and crease of you. I can't tell you how erotic that is for me."

"Yes," Linda says, "and then there's all the love that we've shared over the years. It's like this big pool under us—always there. And now we know how to tap into it any time we want."

Bob and Paulette

After pleasuring each other at length using plenty of lubricant, Bob asks Paulette if he may enter, and does so with only slight, vestigial worries about maintaining his erection. (He silences these and concentrates on what he is feeling, and on circulating heart energy with Paulette.) For her part, Paulette surrenders fully to his penetration, reaching orgasm almost immediately.

It feels so much like the old days with her that he nearly cries. She's so soft and feminine again, so passionate and yet yielding. Freed at last from uncertainty about how things will go, Paulette sinks more and more deeply into a realm of pure pleasure. Bob's masculine power overwhelms her. Eventually, the waves of energy pulsing through him seem to be moving him toward release, and he finds that he wants very much to ejaculate. He tells Paulette, who focuses her attention on his energy. As he comes powerfully, she is right there with him.

⌒

BELIEFS: HOW WE LIMIT OURSELVES

We hope with all our hearts that you, the reader, have had as joyful a sexual reunion as our couples!

Now that you have a sophisticated understanding of the Seven Dimensions of love and some practice in the really very straightforward techniques and practices that can transform your lovemaking, we need to emphasize once again that dependable, forever-after great sex depends more on the mind and heart than the body.

Magnificent sex results when the flow of energy moves smoothly between body, heart and mind. And what is it that blocks the flow of energy? Quite simply, our beliefs about sexuality, about our lover, and about ourselves. Here are some sex-wrecking beliefs that we frequently encounter in people who come to us for help:

- I am too (choose one: fat, skinny, old, hairy, bald, out of shape, disfigured by surgery, etc.) to deserve good sex.
- I am so beleaguered at work (or by the kids, or by family responsibilities, or by volunteer work, etc.) that I don't have the time (or energy) to have sex.
- I am a mother (or nice woman); mothers (nice women) don't have hot sex; therefore, I do not have hot sex. Alternative version: My wife is a nice woman; nice women don't have hot sex, etc.
- I am a masculine guy and masculine guys are able to please their women without fancy stuff (or sharing, or opening their hearts, or finding out what she wants, etc.).
- I need to stay angry at my partner about X, because if I don't I lose something valuable (or I concede that the offense didn't matter, or I forfeit a weapon I can use in future battles, etc.)
- I need to resist closeness because if I open my heart I will be hurt.

You've seen how some of these beliefs limited our couples' joy in their connection, even their ability to connect at all. And you saw how becoming aware of their destructive thought patterns freed them up to feel pleasure—and love. Kate and Paulette felt that their bodies were too imperfect for good sex; Kate also feared that if she opened her heart again it would be broken. Steve felt that he disappointed Kate as a lover but would not talk about it. Nicole had built a virtual fortress of isolation and loneliness around a basic belief that men just want one thing—to screw—and that sex does not have anything to do with love. She had to overcome some abuse as a young girl that set her up for this belief. Also, she strongly felt that she had to resist Charlie's sexual desire in order not to be a wanton woman. And so on.

In addition, one partner in every couple except for Bob and Paulette—for whom it could not be plausible—were deeply committed to the extremely pervasive "I'm always too tired/busy for sex" routine. This is an easy trap to fall into these days, one that is almost a form of bragging—a busy, exhausted person is an important member of society. How much time we'd save if we would just stop telling one another—and ourselves—that we don't have any time!

In doing the self-evaluations and other exercises in this book, you've identified beliefs you have that have held your energy back. Be sure that you're clear about them. Your challenge from now on is to keep them out of your way.

The most important thing you can do for your sexual happiness is this:

Be aware of the beliefs that have constricted your sexuality and work assiduously at keeping them out of the way of your joy. Remember that they are the ultimate reason for the rut you were in. Watch for them, because dropping into a habitual thought pattern is as easy as falling off a log. So when you find yourself beginning to slide back into an old, destructive line of thought, tell yourself (out loud if necessary), "*I am not going there.*"

Refuse to make yourself unhappy. It works.

EVENING

CELEBRATING YOUR EROTIC WEEKEND

We celebrate the significant and joyful moments in life for many reasons: To show that we recognize their importance, to create a memorable occasion that will stay in the memory, and, of course, to have fun. We all love parties, and, we all love presents. Presenting a gift to your beloved is important to the commemoration of this experience. The token itself is only one part of the gift; the words and emotions that accompany your present will be equally important. Before you hand over your treasure ponder a bit about what you really want to express about your relationship, the last few days, and your future, sexual and otherwise, together. These words will be remembered.

Now, at the end of your weekend, it's time for the two of you to create a celebration of your accomplishments, both as individuals and as a couple. To start a program like this and stick with it takes courage, and optimism, and openness to change—not everyone has those qualities. Whether the program has been a life-changing, soul-stirring experience for you, or a lusciously indulgent voyage into new and deeper realms of sexual and emotional connection, you deserve credit for setting forth on this journey with us. Examining the most private and fundamental aspects of our lives requires focus and an enormous expenditure of energy. Congratulations on having had the guts and good faith to do it!

In our workshops, we finish the course with a gift-giving circle, and then enjoy champagne, chocolate-covered strawberries, and hugs and chatter all around. Your celebration will be more private, just for the two of you, and can be anything special that you both love to do. Food and drink will almost certainly be a part of it—a feast is the most traditional celebration of all. You'll probably want to review your discoveries over the last four days, and discuss your plans for the future. But those discussions won't need to keep you from a sensual and festive occasion. There is no reason to stop building erotic castles in the air. Your life together lies open before you. Become the change you want to experience.

Here's how our four couples celebrated *their* Long Erotic Weekends:

⌒

Steve and Kate

It's been snowing all morning, and by mid-afternoon, there's a thick blanket on the ground. Steve and Kate decide to go out walking in it together. They bundle up and walk over to their neighborhood park, which is empty except for them. They throw snowballs, make snow angels and then decide to build a fort together. Once it's up, snugged in against a big tree trunk, they settle down in their private shelter and kiss.

After a few minutes, in spite of the kissing, they realize how cold it is, and make their way home. There, after a long, warming shower together, they get dressed up a bit and have dinner at the romantic little neighborhood restaurant where they've celebrated both their "anniversaries." Steve has brought something in a bag, and by the time they're ready for dessert and champagne, Kate cannot wait a minute longer to see what it is.

He brings out a clumsily wrapped shoebox and sets it in front of her. "Maybe this is really dumb, but I thought you'd understand it."

Kate tears into the wrapping and opens the box, only to find it filled with shredded paper. She looks up, amused and puzzled.

"I shredded a contract 'in effigy,'" he explains and her eyes light up. "But keep looking."

Hidden under the legal confetti is a heart cut from wrapping paper. Kate begins to feel a lump in her throat as soon as she sees it, and Steve takes her hand.

"Look what's on the back," he says.

She reads aloud, as a tear begins to roll down her cheek: *"Love triumphs over Law—you are the light, the love, the goddess in my life—now and forever."*

Kate continues to cry for a few moments—fortunately, the restaurant is dark and their table—as they requested—is back in a corner. Then she pulls herself together and asks Steve if he's ready for his gift. He sits wet-eyed and smiling as she pulls down the v-neck of her velvet dress to reveal a dainty bow from a box of chocolates stuck between her breasts.

"I give my heart to you again, and again, and again," she whispers in a voice choked with emotion.

Now Steve loses it. Through the tears he keeps smiling and gazing at her as she carefully repacks his gift to her. When dessert arrives, Kate glances down at her bow, and asks him, "Do you want to keep this?"

"I like it right where it is," he replies. "I plan to take it off later myself."

Charlie and Nicole

Charlie orders a special dinner delivered to their room, and arranges candles all around while Nicole is down in the salon getting a manicure. He's become a big fan of candlelight over the weekend. "Maybe I do have some Aesthetic instinct after all," he tells himself as he steps back to check his arrangement. "A hidden artistic side." The thought amuses him. He finds some cool jazz on the radio and has begun lighting the candles when Nicole arrives.

Both are showered, scented and dressed in the hotel's elegant bathrobes by the time a sumptuous spread—with champagne—is delivered to their flickering lair by an amused-looking waiter. Charlie's generous tip instantly changes his expression from knowing to respectful. After happily stuffing themselves, it's presentation time.

Nicole lounges on the sofa as Charlie stands up, faces her and bows in the Namaste pose and then totally surprises Nicole by kneeling before her.

He pulls a piece of paper out of his pocket and reads:

> *I loved you when we met,*
> *I loved you when we wed,*
> *I love you even yet,*
> *And, I'll always love you*
> *Until all our suns have set.*

He looks to be about eight-years-old as he hands it to her. She takes it reverently, holding his gaze and presses it to her heart. "Oh, honey."

She then gets up and makes him take her place on the sofa as she kneels before him. Out of her pocket comes a narrow, stapled-together sheaf of paper. On the front she's written in colored marker, "Coupon Book," plus lots of comic fine print: "One per customer," "Certain restrictions apply," "Must be 21 or over," and so on. "Look inside!" she urges him, giggling with anticipation.

His eyes widen and he begins to laugh as he looks through it. "'One free blow-job (void where prohibited)!' 'Good for one head, neck, and shoulder rub during Monday Night Football!' Ah, honey, how did you *know*? No free rounds of miniature golf, or dry cleaning discounts; just things I can really *use*!" They're both laughing now as he goes through the coupons one by one. Nicole is pleased that she surprised him and pleased by her own cleverness, while Charlie is thrilled by Nicole's high spirits and invention. The last few days he's been seeing flashes of the sharp, fun-loving girl who'd suggested a carnival for their first date. Here she is again.

He gets up and tucks the book of favors carefully in his wallet. "One copy to a customer, too, I bet. Got to take care of this thing."

Martin and Linda

Martin and Linda decide that, rather than go to a restaurant, they'll cook up a big meal at home. They've always enjoyed shopping and cooking together—when they've had time—and they work well together in the kitchen.

They go out to a gourmet market and spend a long time picking out favorite foods, with an eye to the luxurious and sensual. They finally decide on a menu of raw oysters to start, homemade fettuccine with clam sauce, asparagus, a simple chocolate mousse that's a specialty of Linda's, and, of course, carefully chosen wine to go with each course. They even lay in a small bottle of clear fruit brandy for the finish.

Linda puts on a stack of favorite CDs that carry them through the preparation and the meal, over which they linger. Martin is enchanted when he spoons into his mousse, to find that Linda has sunk a whole strawberry in it. Licking it off he says, "I feel like I am in that scene in *Tom Jones*!"

"Why fight the feeling?" Linda murmurs, tending to her own strawberry.

After dinner, they dance in the living room for a while before deciding that it really is time to open their gifts.

Martin pulls out something he's hidden behind a picture on the mantel. It's a clock with a beautifully finished wooden case in the shape of heart that he's made in odd half-hours out in his shop,

"It's meant to say that I will give all the time I can to my incredible wife and our incredible relationship," he explains, drawing her close. "Oh, yeah, and the batteries in the back? I let them show because they symbolize the energy that I promise to devote to making our connection as beautiful as it can be. See?" He pulls out one battery and the clock stops. "Connection broken! Very bad! Quick!" He fits the battery back in. "Magic. Magic!"

Linda agrees, charmed by his clowning. "I love it! What is that wood you used? It's so dark and rich," she asks, setting it down lovingly on the mantle.

"Purple heart, from Brazil." he announces triumphantly.

Then she produces a small appliance box from under an end table. Inside is an enchanting diorama portraying their idyllic, sacred sexual connection. She's used a doll-house bed and two little figures she found at the bottom of an old toy box (she's drawn big smiles on their faces with a red pen), a tiny plastic Buddha, a photograph of a rainbow and another of exploding fireworks, feathers, a bouquet that once belonged to a Barbie and arranged it all inside a space lined with pieces of exotic fabrics from her scrap basket. She's also cut out and colored letters to frame the scene. The sign reads: *M&L's Bower O' Bliss*.

"I give you my wish that we could stay in our bower forever," she says, her voice trembling.

"Oh baby," Martin says, setting down the delightful, fragile scene and pulling her close. "As long as we're together, we can get back here any time."

Bob and Paulette

Bob arranges for an evening at a favorite Caribbean restaurant on the lake. This is nostalgic—they'd spent their honeymoon in a Jamaican beach house. The owner is a friend, so Bob is able to order a special feast ahead of time. Both feel relaxed and contented, and they have a great time. After dessert, they even dance to a couple of numbers from the steel-drum band.

After they sit back down, laughing and slightly breathless, Paulette suggests that they exchange gifts.

She hands Bob a heavy, exquisitely wrapped box. Inside is a smooth, palm-sized stone that she's painted elaborately with shimmering icons. She explains all the symbols to Bob: linked glyphs for male and female, a figure eight for infinity and eternity, Yang and Yin, and several other figures from Native American traditions including (because of Bob's resurrected humor) Kokopeli, the mischievous flute player.

"But," she says, pausing. "The main thing is the stone. It's like our love—the bedrock of my life. Something that's real, unbreakable, immovable, always there." She's becoming tearier as she goes along. "I want this to be the first token on our altar. Oh sweetie," she says, breaking down completely, "I love you so much."

"Oh boy. I'm already choked up," he says, drawing her close and giving her a long, delicious hug. Then, he pulls a small box of matches out of his pants pocket. "How am I gonna do this?" He blinks several times and takes a deep breath while Paulette discretely blows her nose.

"I'm ready. I think," says Paulette, smiling.

"Okay, me too" he says, looking into Paulette's eyes. "You know I'm not creative or talented like you. What I have is this box of matches."

He opens the box and takes out one small wooden match, which he strikes. "This is the radiance we once had that went out." He blows the match out, then lights another. "And this is the light I see in you now and that I want never to lose sight of again." He blows it out, too. Both of their faces are wet with tears, and Bob is actually crying as he recites the last part, but he continues holding her gaze.

"There are 28 matches left in this box. I will light one every year on this day to remind me that you are the light in my life and to look for your radiance every day."

He's not quite through. "And when the box is empty, I'll get another one."

~

These gift exchanges are all ones that we have witnessed in our workshops; we are by no means exaggerating the emotional flow that takes place at these moments. We often have to grab for a Kleenex or two as the gifts are presented. And, somehow, the fact that they cannot be purchased makes them even more special. So if you draw one moral from these scenes, it might be this: If you go out to dinner for your celebration, get a table in the corner. There are almost always tears.

Whatever you present, if the gift comes from the heart, it will be treasured by your beloved, so be certain that you carry through with this assignment. Do not be tempted to bypass this final task; celebrations seal the commitment to the future and honor the past. Enjoy yours!

THE GREATEST GIFT

The tokens and words you have given one another at the conclusion of this Long Erotic Weekend are, of course, mere symbols of the greatest gift of all: the gift your glorious Self. This is, in essence, exactly what you have been practicing all weekend—how to make yourself a gift to your lover, and how to receive your lover as a gift. There are seven dimensions, seven distinct qualities of loving energy you can bestow upon your beloved, and likewise seven your beloved can bestow upon you. Your mission is to open all seven channels to send and receive love. *Now* would be an excellent time to begin the practice that will make this mission succeed.

EPILOGUE: THE BOARD MEETING

It's been a month since you signed your contract, so now it's time to sit down and review your performance, rethink your strategy and re-examine your goals at your first Board Meeting. Be sure to allow at least a half hour, and don't let yourselves wander off into other subjects. You will want to be honest but not punitive, clear but not disparaging, and ready to change what is not working. This is business.

We knew that you would want to check in on the four couples one more time, if only to see how your experience in taking ecstasy home compares with theirs.

Steve and Kate

Kate sits down at the kitchen table with her PDA and the contract in front of her. Steve, naturally, is "just wrapping up" some work in the other room. She sighs, gets up, and makes herself a cup of tea while she waits.

He comes in with *his* electronic organizer and asks if she will make another cup, since she's at it. After bringing him his tea and sitting down, she coolly asks, "You're five minutes late for meetings with clients? Or with the partners? You expect beverage service from your female colleagues?"

He's embarrassed. "Guilty as charged. I'm sorry I was late."

She smiles, relenting, but gets in the last word anyway. "Not terribly businesslike, if you ask me."

"You are right about meeting etiquette, but let's get on to the agenda. Things are a lot better. Don't you think?" Her criticism has put him on the defensive. "That practice session we did for me on ejaculatory control—wow. And we've gotten really good at Touch Hands."

"They *are* better. Definitely. But let's go through it line by line." Kate clearly has no intention of letting Steve off the hook for his "breaches of contract." They agree that their mission and goal statements are still fine, but once they get to the Time/Budget section, she adopts a stern tone.

Consulting her electronic calendar, she states flatly, "You agreed to not work on weekends, plus two weeknights every week. First week, fine. Week two, you brought work home four times, and promised to make up the other day the next week, which you did. But then you worked all day the following Sunday. And last week you missed a night and promised to make it up, which you have not done."

Steve has no choice but to agree. "Penalty time, right? But you know, that Sunday was about that Alterdorfer nightmare—it really was an emergency."

"No doubt. However, you're still busted. You're probably liable for two or three penalties, if I were to get technical." She gives him a speculative look. "Fortunately, I am a kindly goddess." She turns the contract so she can read it. "Shopping trip with no whining. How about this Saturday? I want to look for a beautiful lamp for our bedroom."

"Oh, man! I told Mike we could play racquetball… Oh well, a deal's a deal. I'll do it," he says, glumly recording the appointment in his PDA.

Kate notices Steve's defeated look, and has second thoughts about her feeling of triumph in this moment. The phrase "stingy heart" pops into her head, and she shifts to a less hard-edged tone. "Do we need to renegotiate your time commitment, honey? Is two nights a week too much? Should we back off and make it one night? I know how important it is for you to impress those guys."

Steve looks up at her in surprise, and pauses to think for a moment. "No. I want to make that promise to you—to us—happen. Let's leave it at two along with the weekend for now and see if I can do better."

Kate smiles and kisses him. She feels really pleased at being able to transform a battle by letting go and remembering to love. They go through the rest of the clauses and renew the contract by the end of the half hour. Both feel good about it.

(Kate surprises Steve the following Saturday by taking him not to the lighting store but to a sex boutique, where they browse for a long time, side by side. Finally, they agree on a couple of toys and some new sensual oils, and go on home to try out their purchases.)

Charlie and Nicole

Charlie and Nicole get together at the end of a hectic evening. They've finally got the baby down, and the two older ones engrossed in a cut-throat game of Crazy Eights, which Charlie has just taught them. He's been making a real effort to help with the kids in the evening, and is finding that he honestly enjoys playing kid games with them.

Nicole wipes off a clean place where they can work.

"Okeedoke," Charlie says. "I think we've had a bang-up month. You have been making me a very happy man, and I hope I'm making you a happy woman."

"Happier, for sure, though some days I still feel like my brains are leaking out my ears. But I feel *better* about going bananas, now. It's amazing what orgasms do for your mood."

"Now see? This is what I've been telling you for years!"

She smiles wryly. "But we have had a couple of fights."

He picks up the contract. "I don't think we signed anything about not fighting. But maybe we could do better. What was that thing about sitting down for fifteen minutes and taking turns talking? You think that might help?"

Nicole is nodding and making a note. "I think it's worth a try. And we... No it's really me. *I* have to remember to not take things so personally, 'It's not about me' and 'tell me more' should be etched on the inside of my forehead. Shall we put the talking time in the weekly section?"

"Yeah, let's." Charlie is reading along. "Initiating, check. Soulgazing every morning, check." He looks up. "I *really* like that. And Yab Yum. I feel connected to you for the rest of the day."

"Yeah, me too. At least, I've liked it since we told the kids that Mommy and Daddy need five minutes together before breakfast. Giving them the timer and asking them to call us when time is up was *brilliant*."

"Management 101, sweets—make the guy on the floor feel as if he has some control, even if he doesn't. So. No penalties. That's good."

"But maybe a bonus..."

"Hunh?" Charlie lights up.

"Well, I was thinking. I could get Laurie to come in overnight—she does a lot of that and the kids love her—and we could get a motel room! That do anything for you?"

"You know it does. When?"

"This Saturday night, actually. I already booked Laurie," Nicole says, blushing a little.

"Wife of my heart. Are we ready to sign the renewal of this thing?"

"I think we are." They seal the contract with a kiss.

Then Nicole mentions a bit hesitantly, "One thing I've noticed. You aren't watching that porn stuff any more. I appreciate that."

Charlie is thoughtful. "I've got light in my life now. That's how I feel. It was like I was thirsty and now I'm swimming in a great big lake. You know that knucklehead, Mike? Just today he called me over to look at some chick he'd found on the Internet. I walked away. The poor guy's pathetic, looking at that crap."

"Oh, honey," says Nicole, and can't say any more.

Martin and Linda

"My God," Linda says, plopping into a chair. "What a day."

"Yeah." They'd gotten a stern call from their 15-year-old's English teacher—only a week into the school year. And the dishwasher had backed up during the dinner dishes, leaking dirty water out onto the floor.

"So now for something completely different, okay?" says Martin.

"Right. So how have we done?"

Along with the contract, Martin has brought the wall calendar from their room down with him. All their commitments and actual doings are marked on it. They both study it for a minute.

"Well, we were more than meeting quota before the kids got back from camp," he says.

"That ten days between then and school starting, we just fell apart," Linda sighs. "And that's the reality of our life."

"Noooo," Martin argues, "Now, with them back in school, this is more the reality. The last week has been a lot better. We're using all our tools again and feeding the stream. I know I feel the difference."

"The sparkle really goes when we skip the exercises, doesn't it?" Linda says. "So maybe this month, that's what we should concentrate on. I mean, if we have to let one thing go, let it be the massage or the big session, not the daily connections."

"That, I think, is exactly what we should do. And I think it's important, too, that we try not to be hard on ourselves when things just go nuts around here. All we need is one more worry—about not having enough great sex!"

Linda smiles. "Maybe we were a little over-ambitious."

"I'm not sure I'd say that. I think we should set our goals high—we don't want to get in a rut again. But we should also cut ourselves some slack. We *have* got a lot happening."

"Yeah!" Linda exclaims. "Like a 17-year-old who finds your sex book and wants to know what's going on!"

"You handled that great, sweetie. Telling her that there are lots of aspects to sex, that it's a lifelong thing—that was honest and it seemed to satisfy her," Martin says. "Her real concern was that there's something going wrong with us, like with me and her mom."

"But there isn't." She takes his free hand under the table and squeezes. "You know how I see us sometimes? Like we're soldiers for sex, marching on and not giving up."

"Yep," Martin chuckles, "and we're gonna keep at it no matter what."

They renew for another month and go up to bed.

Bob and Paulette

They decide to meet on their back patio on a sunny Sunday afternoon, steaming coffee mugs between them.

"This should be short and sweet, hunh?" Bob says. "What's there to say except we're doing great, and, hey, let's keep doing it?"

"Not so fast," Paulette says, adjusting her reading glasses. "You know how I like checking things off. I want to go through it and gloat."

"Let's see then. Here's something in the Goal section you can pat yourself on the back for—you saw the doctor and got that hormone thing treated."

"True."

"And, of course, I built the fireplace..."

"And did a beautiful job! You know I love it—and the lovemaking we've done in front of the fire," she says. "And you're going to town with ejaculation control."

"I just can't believe I didn't find out about it until now. I feel like I should start telling other guys—maybe I will. The men on the site would flip their lids. Because you know, I really do feel different—bouncier, like I have more energy. Like I'm... bigger." Paulette can't keep from grinning. "No, not that. Just out on the job, walking around, I feel taller, looser. Like I take up more space. I'm sure that's the reason."

"Maybe it's being in love," Paulette suggests, flirting.

"I've been in love for more than thirty years, hon. No, this is different. I'm serious: I want us to do some more with that Tantra."

"Well, we put that workshop in Hawaii down as a bonus. And we certainly have a bonus coming," Paulette says.

"Let's do it, then. And let's re-up on the whole contract, but maybe add another session a week? We've been pretty much doing that, anyway."

"You hear me arguing?"

⇛

THE FINAL WORD

Whatever has happened in the month or months since you first picked up this book and completed the course, you have been exposed to a new way of thinking about sex. You now know the seven essential dimensions of sexuality; the positive, the negative, and the traps of each; and the outer, inner, and deep aspects of the forceful, positive energy of sex in all the dimensions. And you have had a chance to experience how this new way of thinking can transform your sexual connection with your intimate partner.

Sex is an undeniably powerful force in our lives, and wonderful sex can absolutely transform a relationship. Great sex can sustain a marriage through many a hard time and operate as a healing balm when the winds of fate blow bad news our way. Sex is the physical vehicle for love; it is the exquisite vessel for the interplay of the masculine and feminine; it is the refuge for our tired souls when we have been out in the world too long. And it is the place for joy, laughter, teasing, and a bit of silliness that we all need as a break from the serious business of daily life. Sex is physical, emotional, and spiritual; it makes babies, satisfies urges, communicates abiding commitment, reveals our authentic selves, and overwhelms us with beauty and awe.

There is a sexual birthright that many of us never claim: the privilege to explore sexuality in all its facets as part of our life on this planet. Now that you know what is possible; now that you have tools to both enlarge and deepen your experience of sex, there is no turning back. Shakti and Shiva are out of the box and you are free to consider all of the prisms in your sexual kaleidoscope. Enjoy yourself, enjoy your beloved, and enjoy sex!

⇛

References

General

Haffner, Debra, *From Diapers to Dating*. New York: Newmarket Press, 1999. A book on sexuality for parents.

Holstein, Lana, MD. *How to Have Magnificent Sex: The 7 Dimensions of a Vital Sexual Connection*. New York: Harmony Books, 2001. Clearly describes the traps individuals and couples find themselves in as they look to create wonderful sexual energy. An excellent source for revitalizing your sexual essence.

Zilbergeld, B. *The New Male Sexuality*. New York: Bantam, 1992. A great book on men's sexuality.

Biologic

Barbach, Lonnie. *For Yourself*. New York: Doubleday/Signet, 1975. Written thirty years ago, but still an excellent book on how to achieve orgasm.

Butler, Robert N., MD, and Myrna L. Lewis, MSW. *Love and Sex After 60*. New York: Ballantine Books, 1976, revised 1993. Examines all sexual issues of relevance to seniors.

Cattrall, Kim, and Mark Levinson. *Satisfaction: The Art of the Female Orgasm*. New York: Warner Books, 2002. A very detailed presentation of techniques.

Heiman, Julia, PhD, and Joseph Lopiccolo, PhD. *Becoming Orgasmic*. New York: Prentice Hall, 1988. Another detailed book on orgasmic response.

Judson, Olivia, PhD. *Dr. Tatiana's Sex Advice to All Creation*. New York: Metropolitan Books, 2002. An evolutionary biologist becomes "Dear Abby" for the sexual problems of creatures great and small, and the reader learns about the vast variety of sexual behavior in the animal kingdom.

Masters, William, Virginia Johnson, and Robert Kolodny. *Masters and Johnson on Sex & Human Loving*. Boston: Little Brown, 1986. From A to Z, human sexuality from the experts.

Rako, Susan, MD. *The Hormones of Desire: The Truth About Sexuality, Menopause, and Testosterone*. New York: Harmony Books, 1996. A book about testosterone and all of its implications.

Sensual

Corn, Laura. *101 Nights of Grrreat Sex*. Garden City, NY: Park Avenue Publishing, 1995. Great scenarios in a clever format—a bestseller.

Paget, Lou. *How to Be a Great Lover: Girlfriend-to-Girlfriend Totally Explicit Techniques That Will Blow His Mind*. New York: Broadway Books, 1999. Just what it says. She also has a book for men.

Shelburne, Walter A., PhD. *For Play: 150 Sex Games for Couples*. Oakland, CA: Waterfall Press, 1993. Self-explanatory, great ideas.

Stubbs, Kenneth Ray, PhD. *Secret Sexual Positions: Ancient Techniques for Modern Lovers*. Los Angeles: Jeremy P. Tarcher, 1998. Interesting with male and female comments.

Desire

Barbach, Lonnie. *Erotic Interludes, Pleasures: Women Write Erotica*. New York: Doubleday, 1986. Erotica written by women authors.

Leiblum, Sanda R., and Raymond C. Rosen. *Sexual Desire Disorders*. New York: Guilford Press, 1988. Comprehensive approach to theories regarding causes of decreased desire.

Wolfe, Janet, L., PhD. *What to Do When He Has a Headache*. New York: Penguin Books, 1992. A common problem in midlife sexuality when she wants it more than he does.

Heart

Neruda, Pablo. *100 Love Sonnets*. Austin: University of Texas Press, 1986. A beautiful book of poetry both in English and sensual Spanish.

Pearsall, Paul, PhD. *Sexual Healing*. New York: Crown Publishing, 1994. Using the power of an intimate, loving relationship to heal your body and soul.

Intimacy

Barbach, Lonnie. *For Each Other: Sharing Sexuality and Intimacy*. New York: Doubleday/Signet, 1984. Extensive information on sexuality and couples' issues.

Deida, David. *The War of the Superior Man*. Austin, TX: Plexus, 1997. A provocative book on the need for men to move into the "third stage" of masculinity with sex.

Rosenberg, Marshall. *Nonviolent Communication: A Language of Compassion*. Encinitas, CA: Puddle Dancer Press, 1999. A guide to learning a new style of communication that helps us identify shared values and needs, increase goodwill, and resolve differences peacefully. A must for couples whose energy is sapped by repeated arguments.

Aesthetics

Aldred, Caroline. *Divine Sex*. London: Carroll & Brown Limited, 1996. A complete sexuality book on the Eastern approaches to loving.

Mann, A. T., and Jane Lyle. *Sacred Sexuality*. New York: Barnes & Noble, 1995. A thorough discussion of the origins of sacred sex in a beautifully illustrated book.

Moore, Thomas. *The Soul of Sex*. New York: HarperCollins, 1998. Profound, thoughtful book on sexuality and soul.

Ecstasy

Anand, Margo. *The Art of Ecstasy*. Los Angeles: Jeremy P. Tarcher, 1989. A beautiful, complete, and authoritative book about the practice of spiritual sex.

Deida, David. *Finding God Through Sex*. Austin, TX: Plexus, 1999. A tremendous book about the power of taking your partner to the ultimate sacred experience through powerful sex.

Muir, Charles, and Carolyn Muir. *Tantra, the Art of Conscious Loving*. San Francisco: Mercury House, 1989. A good presentation of Tantra and its application to Western love relationships.

Riley, Kerry, and Diane Riley. *Tantric Secrets for Men*. Rochester, VT: Destiny Books, 2002. Practical information about Tantra that men and women will appreciate.

Videos

Anand, Margo. *Multi Orgasmic Response Ecstasy Training for Women and Their Lovers* and *Multi Orgasmic Response Ecstasy Training for Men and Their Lovers*. Detailed demonstration and explanation of a training regimen for ecstatic lovemaking.

Anand, Margo, et al. *Tantra: Ancient Secrets of Sexual Ecstasy for Modern Lovers*. 800-9TANTRA. Comprehensive guide to the erotic arts of the East.

Connop, Cynthia, and Christine Carter. *The Secrets of Sacred Sex*. Healing Arts. 800-2LIVING. A video guide to intimacy and loving.

Holstein, Lana, MD. *Magnificent Lovemaking*. KERA Television, Dallas, 2001. A spirited and informative lecture on the seven dimensions of sexual connection, produced and broadcast as a public television pledge special. Available at www.LanaHolsteinMD.com

Muir, Charles, and Carolyn Muir. *Secrets of Female Sexual Fantasy*. 808-572-8364. Now you can create heaven on earth in your love life.

Stubbs, Kenneth Ray. *Tantric Massage Video*. 800-9TANTRA. A comprehensive guide to the erotic arts of the East.

Acknowledgments

It is hard to thank all the people who have contributed to our understanding of human sexuality, but we need to acknowledge the most important ones. Dr. Phillip Sarrel gave us an excellent start in medical school, not only with his basic course for all students, but also with his willingness to form an advanced seminar and to train Lana in co-therapy. The late Dr. Peter Attarian continued to support us in this way during our residency training; we miss him greatly. Our close friends Alinda and Richard Page need to be thanked for giving us a shove in the direction of sacred sexuality, and introducing us to the work of Charles and Carolyn Muir, to whom we owe a great deal in the structure of our workshops. Dr. Marty Rossman and the other teachers at the Academy of Guided Imagery taught us how to work with the mind-body connection, and this has informed much of our style. Most recently, the teaching of David Deida has been influential in our understanding of the spiritual aspects of sexuality and of the fundamental nature of the deep masculine and feminine.

In writing and preparing the manuscript, we could not have done without the skillful and timely collaboration of Renee Downing, who became a good friend in the process. Paula Munier and the staff at Fair Winds Press are also thanked for their support of our ideas and approach for the book.

Finally, we would like to thank each other for making this adventure a great deal more pleasurable than we anticipated. We knew we could collaborate effectively in the workshop setting, and now we know we can write together, too. We've learned a lot about our unique gifts and skills, and it has brought us even closer to one another than before.

Lana Holstein
David Taylor

YOUR LONG EROTIC WEEKEND COMPANION CD

Although it is certainly possible to do the exercises in this book by reading and referring to the written text, it is much easier to do them the way the participants in our workshops do—by listening to us give the instructions out loud while you do each exercise. We have therefore created a CD with a track for each exercise, so that you can immerse yourself in the experience and not be interrupted and distracted by having to refer back to written instructions, and we've indicated in the book (with the symbol ⊙) where an exercise has a corresponding track. We highly recommend this as the optimal way to go through the program.

To obtain your copy of the CD, simply go to our website, www.LanaHolsteinMD.com, and click on the "Companion CD" link, where you will find simple and secure instructions for ordering. Readers of this book will receive a discount of 25% off the full retail price of the CD. Simply type in the code word "EROTIC" when prompted for your discount code. You will receive your CD within a few days of your order.